Architecture and Politics in Germany

*for Mary and Dick
from Barbara*

Architecture and Politics

in Germany, 1918-1945

by Barbara Miller Lane

Harvard University Press: Cambridge, Massachusetts: 1968

Acknowledgments

My interest in the subject of this book was first aroused by Professor Fritz Stern, and his continuing interest and advice have encouraged me to bring the work to its conclusion. Professor Franklin L. Ford has seen the manuscript through many drafts and offered invaluable criticism at every stage. To both of them I owe an immense debt of gratitude.

I wish also to acknowledge my great indebtedness to Walter Gropius, without whose help and generosity the book probably could not have been written. He made his remarkable archive freely available to me and on many occasions gave me the benefit of his reminiscences. In his cooperation with scholars, Mr. Gropius has invariably been motivated by a passion for historical accuracy; to work with the papers of such a man is an unusual privilege for a historian.

Ernst May in Hamburg and Hans Eckstein in Munich were also extremely generous with their time and their documents, and Hans-Maria Wingler made helpful comments on the methods of research and very kindly lent me many of the materials which he has used in preparing his documentary history of the Bauhaus. I am grateful to the many other German architects and scholars with whom I discussed the book and regret that their numbers prevent me from thanking them in greater detail here.

Radcliffe College, the Samuel S. Fels Foundation, and the American Association of University Women provided the means to pursue the research; its progress was facilitated by the courtesy of the Institut für Zeitgeschichte, the Bayrische Staatsbibliothek, the U. S. Documents Center in Berlin, Avery Library, the Busch-Reisinger Museum, and above all, Widener Library. My husband furnished a great deal of technical information, advised me in every aspect of the selection and placing of the illustrations, and in general made the work possible by his encouragement, criticism, and patience.

Contents

Illustrations and Sources

Architecture and Politics in Germany

List of Abbreviations

BDA	Bund Deutscher Architekten
DAF	Deutsche Arbeitsfront
DAZ	*Deutsche Allgemeine Zeitung*
DNVP	Deutschnationale Volkspartei
DVP	Deutsche Volkspartei
DWB	Deutscher Werkbund
Gagfah	Gemeinnützige Aktiengesellschaft für Angestellten-Heimstätten
Gehag	Gemeinnützige Heimstätten-Aktiengesellschaft
KDAI	Kampfbund deutscher Architekten und Ingenieure
KDK	Kampfbund für deutsche Kultur
KPD	Kommunistische Partei Deutschlands
NSFP	Nationalsozialistische Freiheits-Partei
NSDAP	Nationalsozialistische Deutsche Arbeiterpartei
RDBK	Reichskammer der bildenden Künste
RFG	Reichsforschungsgesellschaft für Wirtschaftlichkeit im Bau- und Wohnungswesen
RKK	Reichskulturkammer
SPD	Sozialistische Partei Deutschlands
VB	*Völkischer Beobachter*

Introduction

Only three weeks after the passage of the Enabling Act, on April 12, 1933, the Nazi regime shut down the Bauhaus in Berlin. The closing of the by then internationally famous center of avant-garde art and architecture was one of the first steps in a campaign to eliminate many "modern" tendencies in German art and to impose more traditional artistic canons in the name of German national-ism and German history. The Nazi government compelled Walter Gropius, Erich Mendelsohn, Paul Klee, Wassily Kandinsky, and other leading modern architects and painters to leave the country, removed from public view the paintings and sculptures of these men and their followers, and forced into retirement many of the modern artists and architects who remained in Germany. At the same time the new regime sought to establish general control over all the arts through the Reichskulturkammer, a government-spon-sored professional organization to which all artists and architects were forced to belong. By expelling some modern artists and con-trolling the work of the men who remained in Germany, the Nazi government was able to influence profoundly the character of artistic production during the years in which it held power.

The Nazi government's violent attack upon leading modern artists, and its attempt to extend its political control to the visual arts, quickly attracted the attention of historians and political scientists. The best study of Nazi artistic policy was written as early as 1936, when Emil Wernert published his *L'art dans le IIIe Reich*, a comprehensive analysis of the mechanisms of Nazi artistic control. In the decade after the war, Paul Ortwin Rave and Hellmut Lehmann-Haupt carried Wernert's account further, Rave in a dis-cussion of Nazi opposition to modern painting, Lehmann-Haupt in a comparative study of artistic control under Stalin, Hitler, and Mussolini.[1] The wide variety of books on Nazi government which have been written since that time have depended heavily on these works for their discussion of the artistic side of Nazi cultural policy. But none of these books, which concentrate upon the meth-

1

ods of artistic control, has shown why the Nazi regime repudiated some types of art and endorsed others. Nor do they help us to understand the reasons for the great significance of the visual arts in the cultural program of the new government.

Lehmann-Haupt's argument is typical of most of these studies. He claimed that Nazi control of the arts could be sufficiently explained by the need of "totalitarian" regimes to regulate every channel of individual self-expression, even those, like the arts, which are normally least relevant to politics. The role of the arts in Nazi cultural propaganda is explained in a similar manner: "totalitarian" regimes necessarily seek to express their ideology through every medium of communication. But these views, though they may help to explain the setting up of the Reichskulturkammer, clearly leave many questions unanswered. Even if artistic regulation is a necessary concomitant of modern dictatorships, why did the Nazi regime select for violent opposition modern art and architecture, while giving great encouragement to other styles? And even if the Nazi regime sought to express its ideology through all types of communications, why should the arts, and particularly the visual arts, have played such a positive and prominent role in the propaganda of the Nazi state?

This book is an attempt to answer these questions with regard to architecture. Previous studies of the visual arts in Nazi Germany have placed their major emphasis upon painting and sculpture.[2] Yet architecture was far more important in the Nazi artistic program than any of the other arts. The attack upon modern art began with the attack upon the Bauhaus as a school of architecture, and when the regime initiated a positive artistic policy after 1933, it poured enormous sums into its building program and its architectural propaganda. This concern with architecture was not merely a result of Hitler's personal interest. Hitler did supervise the designs of a number of official buildings, but the largest proportion of Nazi construction was commissioned by other Nazi leaders. All these official buildings were ceaselessly photographed and commented upon by Goebbels' propaganda machine, which described them to the public as the "expression" of the Nazi ideology and the epitome of its cultural program. A discussion of the way in which architecture, traditionally the least political of all the arts, became political under the Nazis should help to explain the policy of the regime toward the other arts as well.

It is the contention of the following chapters that the Nazis exercised control over architectural style not simply because it was the habit of the new regime to regulate public opinion. They did so because they saw architectural styles as symbols of specific political views, and they believed this to be more true of architecture than of the other arts. This belief was not, however, the product of the "totalitarian" structure of the Nazi state. The Nazis inherited a political view of architecture from the Weimar Republic, and any discussion of Nazi architectural policy must trace the sources of this inheritance in the republican period.

The political symbolism which architecture acquired in Nazi propaganda had its origins in the circumstances surrounding the development of "modern" architecture during the Weimar period. In the twenties, modern architecture was extraordinarily successful in Germany. Buildings in radical new styles were commissioned in far greater numbers than in any other country. But this brilliant success quickly produced a bitter public controversy about the political significance of architecture, and this controversy was carried on for a decade before the Nazi party began to participate in it. After 1930, the Nazis took the lead in the debate and devised an architectural policy tailored to the views of the opponents of modern architecture. It was thus this earlier controversy which gave political importance to architecture in Germany. To explain the architectural policy of the Nazi regime, we must understand both the development of modern architecture in Germany and the character of the opposition it aroused in the years between 1918 and 1930.

The involvement of German architecture in politics grew initially out of the special character of one type of modern architecture, and out of the special conditions under which the development of this new style began in Germany. At the very beginning of the Weimar Republic, a few German architects created a revolutionary new style, which appeared to be wholly without roots in the past. This style, described in Germany as the "Bauhaus style" or the "new architecture," was developed in France, Switzerland, and Holland at the same time. In these countries, as in Germany, its radical rejection of past architectural tradition represented a response to the cataclysm of war. Throughout Europe, "radical" architects came to share with other intellectuals the belief that the Great War spelled the end of an outworn system of values; and the style which they created was consciously intended to express their violent rejection of the past. Where buildings were erected in this style, its startling appearance was often greeted with dismay by the public. But outside Germany, the proponents of the new architecture received few commissions, and their work did not attract general public interest until the thirties. In Germany, on the other hand, architects like Walter Gropius and Erich Medelsohn executed a great many important commissions during the twenties; and their work, and that of their colleagues, received extensive publicity and wide critical acclaim. But the very success of the new style produced strong opposition, which rapidly became political in character.

The development of political opposition to the new architecture was in part the product of the way in which the German creators of the new style thought about their work. Late in 1918, three years before they had decided upon what form the new style should take, a group of radical architects under the leadership of Walter Gropius began to claim that they were preparing a new, socially conscious architecture which would play a part in the political revolution then occurring in Germany. This new style would "express" the new culture and the new society which they believed the revolution would produce, and they demanded that the newly founded Republic support their work. Their writings and exhibitions made these claims known to a considerable public at the very beginning of the republican era.

These ideas in themselves helped to give the new style revolutionary associations which it lacked in other countries, and the way in which the new architecture developed heightened its appearance of political purpose. The new architecture achieved its success in Germany primarily through government patronage. The Bauhaus, the architectural school which Gropius set up in Weimar in 1919, was the first product of this patronage; a few years later the radical architects received as their largest commissions the great new mass-housing projects built in many major German cities. The new style therefore came to be identified with the liberal and left-wing municipal governments which constructed these housing developments and, because the federal government bore part of the cost of public housing, with the housing program of the republican government. These housing projects were given extensive publicity in popular journals and in the press, which identified the new architecture as part of a "new era" in German society. The association of the new style with a new society and with some type of political sponsorship thus became increasingly common throughout the twenties, not only among its opponents, but also among its admirers.

The public controversy over the new architecture began in Weimar, almost as soon as the Bauhaus was founded, and continued throughout the life of the Weimar Republic. During the period 1919–1924, the citizens of Weimar and Thuringia debated the political and social implications of Gropius' ideas and his school's curriculum; and right-wing newspapers and politicians began to charge the school with fostering "bolshevist architecture" and "art bolshevism." This phase of the controversy over the new architecture ended in 1924, when local opposition forced Gropius to move his school to the more hospitable city of Dessau. From 1924 (when the end of the inflation permitted the resumption of building activity on a large scale) to 1930, the controversy continued on the national level and centered primarily around the character of the housing developments designed by radical architects. During this period, the opponents of the "Bauhaus style," chiefly architects and government officials, described this type of modern architecture as the product of large-scale urbanization and a mass society dominated by machine technology. In opposition to this "bolshevist" style they called for a "German" architecture which would help to retain the values of an older, more rural type of society. By 1929, popular right-wing newspapers had taken up these arguments and had begun to give them wide publicity. As the Nazi party attempted to expand its national appeal after 1928, the breadth of public interest in the association of architecture and politics forced the Nazi leaders to take a stand in the controversy over the new style.

The involvement of German architecture in politics thus had its origins in the specific events of the postwar era. The creation of a radically new architectural style by architects who consciously sought to express a wholly new era in German society, the rapid rise of these men to a leading position in German architecture under the auspices of a "revolutionary" new government; all this grew out of the experience of war and revolution in Germany. But if these events created the conditions for political controversy over architecture, the political involvement of architecture in Germany after 1918 had its ultimate source, not in any single chain of circumstance, but in the characteristic atmosphere of Weimar Germany. This atmosphere, which inescapably, almost palpably, confronts every student of the period, was compounded of extravagant artistic creativity and extreme political instability. Out of the fourteen years of the Weimar Republic, only six, from 1924 to 1930, were years of even relative political stability. Five years of violent revolutionary agitation by both Right and Left preceded this brief period; three more followed it. Both periods of political chaos were accompanied by economic disaster. Politically the Republic was characterized by revolutionary experimentation and utopian hopes; it was stable enough to prolong these hopes for fourteen years, not strong enough to substitute for them a viable new system.

But under this precarious political regime, Germany became, for a brief period, the most active cultural center of Europe. Klee, Feininger, Kandinsky, the Russian constructivists, and many others migrated to Germany; Kafka published his works there; the

Dadaists exhibited there; Josephine Baker and Paul Robeson performed there. Every type of artistic experiment flourished in Weimar Germany, and every new "ism" found an audience. The spirit of innovation extended to every aspect of cultural life: to the stage, in the musical drama of Brecht and Weill and the productions of Reinhardt and Piscator; to the film with the production of *Caligari* and its successors; and, under the leadership of the Bauhaus, to all the applied arts. Like the political system which gave them its protection, the arts were characterized by feverish experiment and utopian hopes for a "new style"; in their brevity, brilliance, and disorder they seemed to share in the essence of the Republic's political life. For citizens of the Weimar Republic, the experience of artistic, political, social, and economic change was a total one; and they therefore easily believed that the new architecture expressed a radically new era.

The way in which political controversy over architecture developed in Germany was thus primarily the result of the Weimar experience and the special factors which conditioned it. But the development of German intellectual history before 1918 also contributed to the political involvement of architecture, by helping to create a political view of art.

For a century before 1870, German nationalism had to remain cultural rather than political in its focus; during that time the quest for "Germanness" in the arts begun by Herder and the Sturm und Drang group was intimately bound up with aspirations toward political unity. After the unification of Germany, many nationalists found a political outlet for their sentiments, but German intellectuals retained the habit of looking for links between culture and politics. Thus, in the eighties and nineties, when opposition to Bismarck's Empire began to develop, and the politics, social structure and economic policies of the new state encountered increasing criticism, a number of German intellectuals translated this criticism into cultural terms. Men like Lagarde, Langbehn, and Moeller van den Bruck, whom Fritz Stern has described as the authors of a "politics of cultural despair,"[3] saw in the politics of the second empire signs of the decay of the national culture in all its aspects and dreamed of a mystical national regeneration. But whereas the German nationalists of the era before unification had looked back to the poetry and drama of Goethe, Schiller, and the "classical age" for symbols of national unity, these latter day prophets turned to the visual arts. In his widely popular *Rembrandt as Educator*, Julius Langbehn attributed to the Dutchman's painting the "Germanic" qualities of irrationalism, individuality, and spontaneity which alone could reverse the decadence of contemporary society. Arthur

Moeller van den Bruck expanded these ideas in a variety of publications from 1902 onward and then, just after the beginning of the first World War, turned to architectural symbolism to express his condemnation of Wilhelmine society. In *The Prussian Style*, he described the architecture of Gilly and Schinkel as expressions of the combination of heroism and obedience necessary to win the war. For Moeller, the process of war itself would fuse these qualities with the romantic and creative spirit of a greater Germany and result in a mystical regeneration of the creative power of the nation. Under the great influence of these two men, these ideas about the political implications of painting and architecture passed into the mainstream of neoconservative thought in Germany. They also helped to condition the thinking of German artists about the significance of their work.

But even before the war, this intellectual tradition had led many German artists to think of their work as having broad implications for the life of the nation as a whole. Among these artists, the most important in their influence upon the development of the architectural controversies of the twenties were Wagner and the German expressionists. Wagner's "music-drama" was to be a "total work of art," in which the most "abstract" of all the arts, music, comes to embrace the whole of life by being joined to drama and poetry. Wagner's prolific writings often predicted that the "art work of the future" would usher in a "spiritual revolution," in, to be sure, some very distant time. Taken in combination with his racism and his German nationalism, Wagner's theories came very close to those of Langbehn and Lagarde. Apart from his Germanicism, however, Wagner's view of the role of music in society resembles the radical architects' definition of the new architecture and may very well have influenced it.

The artistic tendencies of the last few years before the war gave added impetus to this kind of thinking. The multifaceted literary and artistic movement which is usually described as German expressionism produced not only an extraordinary variety of new forms, but also a new philosophy of art. Expressionist dramatists and poets described the arts as the exclusive key to knowledge. Neither science nor conventional religion could explain reality; only the symbolic language of the creative artist offered a bridge between mind and matter. This inclusive view of art had been implicit in much of German aesthetic philosophy for a century, but the writings of the German expressionists gave it new political overtones. Many of the German expressionists were motivated by a social conscience and hoped for a "new society" in which art could be "brought back to the people." They shared in the cultural pessimism of Lagarde and Moeller and like them hoped for some kind of mystical regeneration in the body politic. But insofar as their prophesies had conventional political direction, they tended toward the left, rather than the right. They were therefore the most immediate intellectual ancestors of the radical architects of the twenties. Together with the works of the prophets of cultural despair and the members of the Wagner cult, their writings accelerated a long-standing tendency in Germany to regard the arts as a focus of political concern and provided the background against which the architectural controversies of the twenties and thirties took place.

The intellectual atmosphere of the Weimar Republic gave to these older views a new urgency and a wider public, while the development of architectural style and writing focused these beliefs upon architecture. Thus by 1930 the new style had come to symbolize for a broad public most of the political, social, and cultural changes of the Weimar Republic. Its friends and opponents alike thought of the new architecture as an expression of rapid industrialization and as a symbol of the vast modern metropolis. Moreover, because of its origins and patronage, they identified it with the Weimar Republic itself and the revolution which had created the Republic. When the Nazi party at last entered the controversy over the new style, it was therefore able to discover among the issues in this debate a set of propaganda symbols of immense utility. By opposing the new architecture and supporting its opponents, the Nazi party could proclaim its opposition to the political and economic failures of the Republic without committing itself to a concrete political and economic program. This was the role which the party assigned to architectural propaganda from 1930 on, and the Nazi propaganda specialists exploited these themes with extraordinary skill.

But this opposition to the new architecture as the symbol of the weakness of Weimar society compelled the Nazis to accept the idea that architecture was of central importance to the national life. Hitler's speeches had indeed reflected this view as early as 1920, but the party as a whole was not committed to it until the propaganda campaign against "architectural bolshevism" began. After 1930, the position taken by party propaganda forced the Nazis to promise to launch a building program which would express their own ideology.

The party began to fulfill this promise as soon as it came to power, and an analysis of the Nazi building program therefore affords considerable insight into the character of Nazi ideology. The cultural policy of the new regime as reflected in its building program was, like Nazi ideology itself, confused and contradictory. Among the makers of official architectural policy, at least four different factions developed. Some of the new leaders of government and party sought to recall the traditions of the German middle ages by encouraging neo-Romanesque styles in architecture, while others favored the neoclassical manner in order to suggest that Nazism incorporated "eternal" values. Some were primarily concerned to assert the rural character of Nazi society and therefore encouraged primitive "folk" styles derived from the countryside; others were outspoken in their support of a revolutionary "modern" style which would express the newness of the new regime.

Thus despite the party's claim to have substituted for the new architecture a uniform new "national socialist" style, the rivalries of these factions permitted almost every type of architecture to be constructed, including buildings which closely resembled the work of the radical architects whom the Nazis had opposed. The regime did, to be sure, establish the legal mechanisms with which to exert centralized control over architecture; but this control was far less effective than has usually been supposed. Behind a facade of intensive architectural propaganda, the new state permitted German architecture to develop in relative freedom, under the personal patronage of high party and government officials. Nazi architectural policy was not the product of a monolithic totalitarian system, but of feuds and power struggles. The Nazi building program reflected not a new totalitarian ideology, but a series of conflicting ideas which were themselves rooted in and conditioned by the architectural controversies of the Weimar period.

This history of three decades of the involvement of German architecture in politics touches on many problems which cannot be solved in a book which cuts across so many topics. In the discussion of housing during the twenties, it becomes clear that the Republic's housing program was one of its more significant accomplishments, and one which was hotly debated among Weimar politicians. The political history of this program, largely neglected here, thus offers an important key to the social aims of the major republican parties. The architectural patronage of a few municipalities is described in Chapter IV, but the larger question of the renaissance in municipal patronage of all the arts during the Weimar Republic is of necessity ignored, and this subject is of central importance in understanding the cultural history of Weimar Germany. The description of the opposition of conservative architects to the new architecture in Chapter V shows that, whatever their differences, they all shared a passionate hatred of the metropolis. It would be useful to know to what extent other German conservatives also held this view of the modern city, since the period was one of particularly rapid urban growth. Chapter VI analyzes the development of Nazi architectural propaganda between 1928 and 1933 and shows that this propaganda was heavily dependent upon the ideas of the conservative architects. It is important to know whether this relationship with Weimar conservatism holds true for Nazi cultural propaganda as a whole; if so, then the commitments which party propaganda made before 1933 helped to determine the development of Nazi ideology in ways which are not yet clearly understood. Rosenberg's role in Nazi ideology takes on some new dimensions in this account. He was more influential before and less influential after 1933 than has usually been supposed, and this suggests a need for re-evaluation of his position in the Nazi party. Finally, Chapter VII shows that the architectural control exerted by the Reichskulturkammer was slight indeed and concludes that the regime exerted influence on architectural style primarily through the personal patronage of high Nazi officials. If these observations could be applied to the whole of Nazi cultural policy, we would know a great deal more about the workings of Nazi government. In order to describe the common theme of these subjects it has been necessary to neglect many of their implications. Because the political involvement of German architecture was such a complex phenomenon, conditioned by such diverse political, economic, and intellectual factors, any history of this subject must sometimes play the part of interlocutor, asking questions rather than answering them.

I / The Revolution in Style

When, toward the end of the Weimar period, Nazi writers and speakers attacked what they called the "Bauhaus style" in architecture, they did not attack modern architecture as a whole. Although the "new architecture" formed part of a much broader modern movement in Germany, the Nazis drew a sharp distinction between it and the rest of this modern movement. The party opposed as "architectural bolshevism" Walter Gropius' Bauhaus buildings and the designs which resembled them; it tolerated and often admired other types of modern design. The Nazis drew this distinction because the new architecture appeared to have a separate identity within the broader modern movement. It alone was accompanied by an ideological program; it alone, it seemed, was favored by political patronage under the Weimar Republic. Moreover, while the rest of modern architecture appeared to have developed out of the traditions of prewar styles and thus seemed to have firm roots in the past, the new architecture looked strikingly different. First set before the public in 1922, it appeared to contemporaries to be radically new, the product, not of a further development of the older traditions of German culture, but of war, revolution, and economic disaster.

Despite the fact that the new architecture looked very different from the rest of postwar modern design in Germany, the two wings of the modern movement had a common origin in a vigorous and highly experimental progressive movement which existed before the war, and both drew many of their stylistic features from this prewar work. The new architecture, however, carried the traditions of prewar architecture further and in a different direction from other postwar styles, so that their common sources were at the time obscured. There were in fact two "revolutions" in German architectural style — the broader one, which around 1900 gave rise to the modern movement as a whole, and the narrower one, led by Gropius and his followers after 1918. A definition of both is essential to the

1. New Town Hall, Munich, c. 1879–90.

proper understanding of contemporary opposition to the "Bauhaus style." For only to the extent that the new architecture was really "new" after 1918 could it be condemned as the product of the political revolution, and only insofar as it formed a style distinct from the rest of postwar architecture in Germany could it be identified for attack at all.[1]

During the latter half of the nineteenth century, German building design, like that of the rest of Europe and America, deteriorated into the cluttered, overdecorated eclecticism known in England and the United States as the Victorian style. The pseudo-Gothic town hall built in Munich from 1870 to 1890 (fig. 1), its surfaces crowded with carved ornament, was typical of the taste of these times, which also expressed itself in the disorderly outlines of residences constructed with a profusion of turrets, gables, and "gingerbread" moldings. But toward 1900 a number of architects, under the leadership of such men as Alfred Messel, Peter Behrens, and Paul Bonatz, began to reject this type of chaotic design and to search for simpler new forms. They arrived at the most varied and contradictory solutions. Some stripped the ornament off their buildings, while others invented new types of decoration. Some made use of new building materials like steel and reinforced concrete to achieve new effects — thin walls, great spans, large glass areas — while others worked in heavy masonry. A few rejected all imitation of past styles, although the majority participated actively in a series of historical revivals. The first architectural revolution produced no single, readily identifiable architectural style; but by 1914 it had established a variety of new traditions, upon which postwar architecture drew.

But almost all of these new traditions represented in one way or another a radical transformation of nineteenth century historicism, rather than a rejection of it. Using the vocabularies of the older styles, chiefly Gothic and baroque, in new, more orderly, and more vigorous combinations, the progressive architects gradually derived from them a set of forms which were at once novel in appearance and visually related to the past. One of the finest examples of the early stages of this transformation was Alfred Messel's Wertheim store of 1904 (fig. 2), one of the first of the great Berlin department stores. Messel subdued the Gothic detailing which he employed on the facade into a regular pattern of marching vertical mullions, a

2. Alfred Messel, Wertheim Department Store, Berlin, 1904.

vigorous and uncluttered composition wholly unlike the designs of the seventies and eighties. In this design, Gothic detailing was merely a means, congenial to the structure of the building, toward an orderly formal composition. This cavalier attitude toward historical accuracy allowed Messel to terminate the Gothic mullions in a powerful mansard roof and to lend weight and impressiveness to the entryway with Roman arches.

During the following decade this process of abstraction from historicism was carried further. Typical of much commercial and industrial architecture of this period is Peter Behrens' administration building for the Mannesmann works in Düsseldorf (fig. 3). Although its rusticated masonry base and rudimentary classical pilasters gave it a traditional air, Behrens' design achieved a new vigor through its powerful, uncompromising cubic mass. And although Behrens employed conventional vertical windows, he narrowed them to slits, which, in the oblique view, appeared as continuous horizontal bands, breaking up the facade in a manner prophetic of the ribbon window of later decades.

The transformation of historicism into modern design reached its climax in Paul Bonatz's famous and influential Stuttgart railroad station (figs. 4 and 5), begun in 1913. Bonatz employed the baroque motif of vertical strips of windows separated by ornamental panels, and he stretched a free-standing classical colonnade across the cen-

3. Peter Behrens, Administration Building of the Mannesmann Works, Düsseldorf, 1912.

4. Paul Bonatz, Railroad Station, Stuttgart, 1913–1927.

5. Railroad Station, Stuttgart.

tral block of the building; but these echoes of traditional styles remained mere accents in an essentially new type of design. Without a base and with only a rudimentary cornice line, the building was reduced to a series of simplified cubic masses, whose weight and bulk Bonatz emphasized by using an exaggeratedly rusticated masonry. The most striking feature of the building was the asymmetrical arrangement of these masses, from the vertical administration tower to the massive entry to the horizontally oriented waiting-hall wing at the left. This asymmetrical organization of angular, relatively unadorned forms had no source in the historic styles.

Although this development toward the reduction of buildings into cubic masses and historicist ornament into stylized orderly pattern had its clearest formulation in large public and commercial buildings, a similar process was taking place in residential architecture at the same time. The revolt against the Gothic and baroque gingerbread of the Victorian mansion was led by Paul Schultze-Naumburg, who two decades later became one of the most active opponents of the new style. Schultze-Naumburg employed two methods in his attempt to reform residential design. Most of his houses revived some historical style which was relatively simple in appearance — imitating the half-timbered dwellings of the later middle ages, or, more often, the kind of neoclassical design illustrated in figure 6. The major part of his work was thus progressive, not in transforming historical styles by abstracting from them, but in rejecting all eclecticism and faithfully reproducing a style which

6. Paul Schultze-Naumburg, House in Cologne, c. 1910.

7. Paul Schultze-Naumburg, Steinhorst Estate (near Ratzeburg), c. 1910, garden side.

was orderly to begin with. In some of his houses, however, Schultze-Naumburg discarded nearly all historicist references in favor of a bare, white, stucco architecture. The garden façade of his Steinhorst house (fig. 7), for example, was completely free of surface ornament of any type, and the building was thus reduced to a bare-surfaced cubic mass, tied to tradition only through the use of casement windows and a hip roof.

Simplified forms such as Schultze-Naumburg employed in the Steinhorst estate were also used by Heinrich Tessenow and Bruno Taut in the new low-rent housing developments known as "Siedlungen" which began to become an important feature of German urban development at about this time.[2] In the row houses Tessenow designed for workers at the "garden city" of Dresden-Hellerau in 1910 (fig. 8), the stucco surfaces were left entirely free of ornament and only the simplest frames were employed in the doors and windows.[3] Taut's row houses in Falkenberg (fig. 9), a suburb of Berlin, were more formal and slightly more traditional in appearance, but shared Tessenow's emphasis on smooth surfaces and simplicity of design, without either much explicit historical reference or striving for novelty.

8. Heinrich Tessenow, Row Houses, Dresden-Hellerau, 1910–1912.

9. Bruno Taut, Siedlung Falkenberg, Berlin, 1911–1914.

Although the development of a new simplicity through historicism constituted the mainstream of progressive architecture in Germany between 1900 and 1915, there were a few dissenters who departed from the historicist manner to indulge in bizarre architectural experiments. Peter Behrens and Josef Maria Olbrich, for example, attempted to introduce new types of ornamentation in the houses they built for the Darmstädter Künstler Kolonie (figs. 10 and 11), a project initiated by Grand Duke Ernst Ludwig of Hesse in 1901 to encourage new tendencies in the arts and crafts. Although these buildings have often been described as part of the so-called "Jugendstil," Behrens' curved gables and contrasting bands of masonry and Olbrich's adaptation of Tyrolean ornament had little in common but a self-conscious striving for novelty. Olbrich, however, imposed his geometric ornament upon simplified cubic massing, a combination more fruitful for the future than was most of the experimental work of this period. A similar desire for novelty prompted Hans Poelzig to employ strained and unusual window patterns in his Luban chemical factory in 1912 (fig. 12), an abortive attempt to endow industrial architecture with a new aesthetic. Buildings like Poelzig's and Behrens' remained mere exercises in the development of surface pattern and had little influence except insofar as they expressed a desire for innovation.

10. Peter Behrens, House at Künstler Kolonie, Darmstadt, 1901.

11. Josef Maria Olbrich, House at Künstler Kolonie, Darmstadt, 1901.

12. Hans Poelzig, Chemical Factory, Luban, 1912.

Shortly before the war, however, this desire for radical innovation began to give rise to a few influential experiments with architectural forms themselves. The most important of these were constructed in 1914 for the Cologne exhibition of the Deutscher Werkbund, an organization of architects, craftsmen, and businessmen formed to improve industrial design. The undulating forms of the theater designed for this exhibition by the Belgian Henri van de Velde (fig. 13) introduced a new dynamism into the vocabulary of German architecture which reappeared in the work of "radical" architects after the war. Of the other exhibition buildings, those by Gropius (fig. 17) and Taut (fig. 18) were most significant for the later development of the new architecture.

The buildings by Gropius and Taut had their sources not merely in formal innovation but also in the new structures and materials developed by industrial architecture. A great number of industrial and other practical structures — bridges, factories, exhibition halls — in which the new building materials such as iron, steel, and reinforced concrete determined the forms of the buildings, had been built all over Europe and America from the time of the Crystal Palace, and Germany possessed many examples of the type of wide-

13. Henri van de Velde, Theater at the Deutscher Werkbund Exhibition, 1914.

span structure with large glass areas shown in figure 14. Yet these novel building techniques which were employed so often in Germany before the war were used for the most part in response to the practical problems of admitting light or of spanning large areas; rarely were structural trusses or large glass walls regarded as pleasing in themselves. It was only at a very late stage that a few architects began to experiment with the aesthetic potentialities of the structural materials produced by modern technology.

The most celebrated example of this type of work was Walter Gropius' Fagus factory of 1911–1914 (figs. 15 and 16). Glass and metal panels such as those between the brick piers of the workshop wing (fig. 15) had occasionally been employed by other progressive architects to emphasize a vertical facade pattern. But Gropius' design employed fine detailing and proportions in order to demonstrate uncompromisingly the intrinsic beauty of glass and metal as building materials. And by projecting the panels and joining the glass at the corners, Gropius looked ahead to the lightness and transparency of the continuous glass curtain wall. The rest of the factory as it was finally executed was an assemblage of wings only loosely related to one another,[4] but, by reducing the warehouse buildings (fig. 16) to unadorned cubic masses, Gropius created a forceful visual contrast between their solidity and the transparency of the workshops. His design thus went beyond the practical requirements of the factory and endowed its "functions" with a formal, and highly artistic, formulation.

Gropius experimented with this type of contrast again in 1914,

14. Friedrich von Thiersch, Exhibition Hall, Frankfurt am Main.

15. Walter Gropius, Fagus Shoe Last Factory, Alfeld an der Leine, 1911–1914, Workshops.

in the factory administration building which he built for the Werkbund exhibition (fig. 17). Here the juxtaposition of glass towers and
solid masonry was clearly not "functional" at all, but was employed
entirely for its aesthetic effect. This aestheticism was carried even
further in the "house of glass" designed by Bruno Taut for the same
exhibition (fig. 18). With its faceted dome of colored glass panels,
Taut's building was something of a tour de force, but, together with
Gropius' work, it marked the beginning of a tendency to romanti-
cize industrial materials.

Different as was Gropius' work from Bonatz's and Bonatz's from
Behrens', a common thread ran through most progressive prewar
architecture. Gropius, Bonatz, Olbrich, Behrens, and even Schultze-
Naumburg shared a fondness for simple, cubic architectural forms.
It could be said of most of these architects that they had begun to
think of their buildings not only as the heirs of specific historical
styles, or as practical structures designed to fulfill some specific
purpose, but also as new types of forms in space — almost as abstract sculpture. Despite this common attitude, progressive architects emphasized different forms and materials and held different
views of the value of architectural tradition, so that they produced
many different stylistic vocabularies. A sense of their common
aims, however, brought about a spirit of mutual toleration among

16. Fagus Factory, Warehouses.

17. Walter Gropius, Factory Administration Building, Deutscher Werkbund Exhibition, 1914.

18. Bruno Taut, "Glashaus," Deutscher Werkbund Exhibition, 1914.

architects; each of them regarded his competitors' buildings as progressive. That their various methods did not seem incompatible to them is indicated by the active participation of nearly all progressive architects in the Deutscher Werkbund.

The Werkbund was founded in 1907 to promote modern design, ostensibly in mass-produced goods, but in fact in all other branches of the arts and crafts as well.[5] Friedrich Naumann, politician and political theorist; Ferdinand Avenarius, editor of the influential periodical *Der Kunstwart*; Eugen Diederichs, the conservative publisher; and Hermann Muthesius, architect and popularizer of English period architecture, set up the organization with the idea of improving the position of German goods on the international market by introducing in their design a higher standard of taste. The Werkbund was, before the war, an exceedingly catholic organization and included among its members not only industrial designers and engineers, but also the leaders of what might be called the German "arts and crafts movement" — a movement among small craftsmen and interior decorators who employed period and "folk" motifs in their work.[6] The architects within the Werkbund thought of themselves as working together to improve the nation's industrial culture, and this outweighed their differences. The organization fostered this sense of common purpose and, through permanent exhibitions like that at Cologne and through a series of publications, did a great deal to popularize the varied work of all its members.[7]

After the war, this consensus among progressive architects disappeared, and the common features of progressive design were obscured. One style departed strikingly from both prewar work and the progressive postwar architecture which was based upon prewar traditions. From about 1922 on, Walter Gropius and his followers carried the view of architecture as sculptural form much farther than any other group of architects in Germany, by employing radically simplified cubic masses, assembled asymmetrically and wholly unadorned. This "new architecture" was of course by no means a purely German phenomenon. Its earliest origins were in Holland, where the "De Stijl" group began the development of a cubic architecture during the war, partly under the influence of Mondriaan's painting, partly under the influence of Frank Lloyd Wright. In addition to the Dutch and German groups, the third center of the development of this new style was Paris, where Corbusier worked along similar lines during the interwar period.

But the new architecture was far more influential in Germany than in any other country. Never did this style dominate all or even the majority of German buildings in the twenties, but it early received the sponsorship of various federal agencies, municipalities,

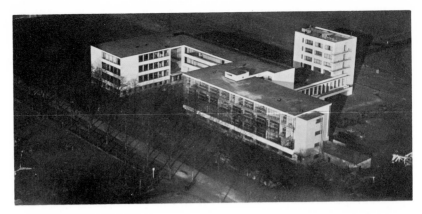

19. Walter Gropius, Bauhaus Buildings, Dessau, 1925–1926, aerial view.

and public housing authorities, which together commissioned a very large number of buildings. The architectural journals devoted many issues to publicizing the new style's newest accomplishments, and in its exhibitions and publications the Werkbund began to give the new architecture its entire support. As a result the architectural profession, and soon the public at large, came to think of the new style as, for good or ill, the most "modern" formulation of "modern architecture."

The extraordinarily rapid development of the new architecture in Germany within a brief period is best illustrated by the Bauhaus buildings themselves. These were the complex of buildings which

20. Bauhaus Buildings.

Gropius built for his school of art and architecture at Dessau in 1926 (figs. 19, 20, and 21). Of all the buildings erected in Germany during the twenties, the Bauhaus complex represents the most highly developed example of architecture conceived as a sculptural arrangement of masses and planes in space. Linked together by a low one-story wing and a high two-story bridge, the three main wings of the building (trades school, studios, and workshops, clockwise from left in fig. 19) have the appearance of a set of abstract forms radiating in space and tied together on a principle of balanced asymmetry. The complex relationship of vertical atelier wing and horizontal bridges shown in figure 21 establishes the central theme of the composition: radiating from one another rather than from a static center, the masses of the building seem visually to be in a state of perpetual motion. This theme was repeated in the wall treatment as well, for the horizontal bands of windows radiate in every case from a square or vertical blank white surface. Considered as surface pattern they produce a continuous movement which carries the eye around the corners of the buildings; considered as openings in the wall, they create an effect of unsupported planes hovering in space (fig. 21). The formal contrast between

21. Bauhaus Buildings.

22. Karl Schneider, Römer House, Hamburg-Othmarschen, 1927–1928, entry side.

transparency and closure with which Gropius had been experimenting before the war was also carried much further in the contrast between the workshop wing, with its famous all-glass curtain wall, and the relatively solid studio wing. But while the Fagus factory and the Werkbund exhibition building were masonry and therefore relatively heavy in appearance, the flat white surfaces and wide glass areas of the Bauhaus buildings transformed the individual wings into light-weight volumes, appearing to float above the ground, not needing its support. Although Gropius could have derived his interest in asymmetry from Bonatz, and although a simplification of buildings into geometric shapes had begun before the war, this remarkable work had, as a whole, little parallel within the tradition of Western architecture.

The new style was employed in Germany in almost every type of building; in schools, factories, movie theaters, stores, office buildings, and above all, housing projects. But not all architectural subjects allowed the kind of manipulation of forms in space which Gropius accomplished at the Bauhaus. The new vocabulary found some of its most creative adaptations in residential buildings: Karl Schneider's Römer house in Hamburg (figs. 22 and 23) displays a

23. Römer House, garden side.

24. Erich Mendelsohn, Schocken Department Store, Chemnitz, 1928–1929.

movement and tension in its composition similar to that achieved by Gropius. But in many cases the new forms were restricted to facade treatment alone. Erich Mendelsohn, for example, used alternating horizontal strips of glass and marble and a smoothly curving surface to give the massive bulk of his department stores an appearance of horizontal motion similar to parts of the Bauhaus buildings (fig. 24). A very different type of facade treatment was characteristic of many of the buildings executed in the new style in Frankfurt am Main, where, as in the municipal trolley park office shown in figure 25, small window openings, asymmetrically arranged in the bare white wall, produced a stark and strained design.

The long, continuous surfaces of mass housing projects offered particularly difficult problems in facade manipulation. To avoid monotony in such buildings, radical architects frequently used such devices as projecting balconies or stairwells, asymmetrical window arrangements, and vivid patterns in bright, primary colors (fig. 26). But many long apartment buildings were constructed in which the new style appeared as an essentially negative attitude, a stripping away of ornament, moldings, and all the characteristic features of traditional buildings (including, of course, the sloped roof), without replacing them with complex pattern or massing. Bruno Taut's and

25. Municipal Building Administration, City Trolley Park Offices, Frankfurt am Main, 1926.

26. Bruno Taut, Apartment House, Berlin, 1927.

Martin Wagner's enormous housing development in Berlin-Britz (fig. 27) has no visible roofs, no base, and only the slightest of window frames; it appears to be simply a continuously curved white surface broken by a regular pattern of openings. The revolutionary appearance of such buildings consisted in their total lack of reference to the past rather than in their introduction of striking new forms.

While the new vernacular was employed increasingly in many types of building between 1924 and the early thirties, the new style, even at the peak of its popularity around 1930, never made up the bulk of new building in Germany. The largest part of new construction during the Weimar period was carried out in other modern

27. Bruno Taut and Martin Wagner, Hufeisen Siedlung, Berlin-Britz, 1926–1927.

styles, which were very clearly related to the progressive work of the prewar period, although they had developed far beyond it. The most popular of these styles employed a vertical masonry grid derived from Messel's buildings, but now turned into a wholly abstract element, entirely dominating the outer surfaces of the building. This design was used with great frequency in tall office buildings where a vertical orientation was particularly appropriate, like the ones by Bonatz and Fritz Höger shown in figures 28 and 29; but it appeared in many other types of building as well (fig. 30). Developing out of the prewar fondness for simple cubic form were, on the other hand, a number of buildings of masonry with uncompromisingly flat surfaces and regular window patterns, like Emil

28. Paul Bonatz, Office Building, Düsseldorf, 1922–1925.

29. Fritz Höger, "Chilehaus," Hamburg, 1922–1923.

30. Adolf Abel, Exhibition Hall, Cologne, 1927–1928.

Fahrenkamp's Berlin office building, shown in figure 31. Such buildings made no overt reference to the historical styles, but their vertical windows and symmetrical entries gave them a more traditional appearance than the designs executed in the new style.

Many other architects whose work was also clearly "progressive" or "modern" chose to retain even more of the earlier manner. Werner March's indoor-sports buildings (fig. 32) each had a group of centrally located pilasters and piers, which gave the buildings a distinctly neoclassical air; but the placing of these elements, which were set as independent elements into a great blank wall of brick, clearly shows the influence of more modern work. Such compromises, of all types, were very numerous. Every kind of modern design in Weimar Germany thus had certain points of contact with the "new architecture," and it is therefore possible to regard the entire development of modern architecture in the twenties as a single, if many-faceted movement. Yet such a view requires the wisdom of hindsight, for to contemporaries the differences were more apparent than the similarities. Only the new architecture rejected every visual link with the work of the prewar era, which had drawn so heavily upon Gothic and baroque sources. Only the new architecture therefore appeared to be wholly without relation to the great traditions of the German past.

In commercial and many other types of building the wide variety of modern styles bridged the gap and softened the contrast between

31. Emil Fahrenkamp, Office Building, Berlin, Fehrbelliner Platz, c. 1930.

32. Werner March, Indoor-Sports Buildings, Berlin, begun 1930.

33. Row Housing, Nürnberg, 1925.

the new architecture and prewar work. But in residential construction, the largest single branch of building, this variety did not exist. Of the housing developments which began to be built in large numbers after the war, a high proportion were heavily ornamented and ponderous in appearance (fig. 33). Many dwellings were constructed in the simpler but still traditional manner of Taut's and Tessenow's prewar work (fig. 34), but beyond this point none but the radical architects ventured in the postwar years. Their buildings, with their flat roofs, white walls, large glass areas, and asymmetrical window patterns, formed a striking contrast to their conservative neighbors.

The distinction between the new architecture and other modern buildings was thus most clearly apparent in dwelling design. And although many of the most famous buildings executed in the new style were institutional structures like the Bauhaus or commercial buildings like Mendelsohn's department stores, the radical architects received the largest proportion of their commissions in public housing. The public controversy over the revolutionary character of the new architecture, outlined in the following chapters, therefore centered around radical architects' housing designs. When, at the end of the twenties, the Nazi party incorporated opposition to the new style into its political program, the distinction between conservative and "revolutionary" housing design played a prominent part in its propaganda.

34. Paul Mebes and Paul Emmerich, "Siedlung Heidehof," Berlin-Zehlendorf, 1924.

II / The New Architecture and the Vision of a New Society

For the first few years after the war, the economic situation prevented any large-scale building construction in Germany, and the men who were to become the leaders of the modern movement were forced to express themselves principally in writing. The new bare cubic architecture did not begin to take definite shape until 1922, when the first experimental work of the Bauhaus appeared; and it was not until 1924, with the dramatic revival of the economy which followed the end of the inflation, that radical architects began to receive the important commissions upon which was based their fame in Germany and abroad. But from 1918 on, these men publicized the idea that the new society created by war and revolution required an entirely new architecture, devoid of all association with the past. They called for a "new community," spiritual and social, in which architecture, supported by the revolutionary government, would act as a powerful educational force among the citizens of the new state. Thus, several years before the new style actually appeared, its prophets had identified it as not merely a new development in "style," but also as a movement with broad social and cultural purposes, closely linked to the left-wing republican government.

These ideas grew out of an atmosphere of ferment in the arts produced by the closing phases of the war. In nearly every European country at that time, modern artists founded revolutionary societies and issued revolutionary "manifestos." In Paris and Zurich the Dadaists proclaimed the need for a total break with all previous art forms, a break which they described as part of a more general cataclysm in culture, society, and politics. In Russia, where the political revolution had already occurred, modern artists such as Kandinsky, Tatlin, and Gabo enrolled in the service of the new government in the hope of providing workingmen and peasants with a new artistic understanding.[1] Until 1921 it looked to most contemporaries as though the Bolsheviks had wholly endorsed the aims of modern art and modern artists.[2]

The spirit of revolt among the arts was strongest, however, not in Russia or in France, but in Germany, where the impact of expressionism gave it added impetus. Even before the war, such writers as Heinrich Mann, Franz Werfel, and Reinhard Sorge had satirized the structure of authority under the Empire and called for a new brotherhood in society which the artist could help to bring about.[3] Under the influence of Kandinsky's writings, expressionist painters also had begun to think of themselves as leaders of a "spiritual revolution," and thus as having an important role to play in culture and society.[4] The two principal expressionist journals, *Der Sturm* and *Aktion,* had begun, by 1913, to sponsor these ideas. Between 1914 and 1918, the widespread disillusionment of German intellectuals with the war helped to spread these views to a larger community of artists and writers. This disillusionment led the dramatists Hasenclever and Kaiser to write against war, and former nationalists like Unruh and Toller to call for revolution against the Empire and its militarism.[5] The same kind of thinking inspired the pacifist paintings of Kollwitz, Grosz, and Dix, so that historians have begun to speak of a politically "activist" phase in German expressionism, beginning during the last years of the war.[6]

Against this background, the revolution of 1918 raised — particularly among the practitioners of the visual arts — exaggerated hopes for the immediate beginning of a "spiritual revolution." In nearly every city in Germany, artists, architects, and sculptors set up "revolutionary" societies which were intended to gain popular support for radical tendencies within the arts and to claim for modern art a social and cultural role within the new state. In Berlin for example, the group of artists affiliated with the Sturm gallery founded the Novembergruppe, and Walter Gropius and his followers formed the Arbeitsrat für Kunst. Munich had its Arbeitsausschuss der bildenden Künstler; Frankfurt, the Freier Bund zur Einbürgerung der bildenden Künste; Bielefeld, Der Wurf; Düsseldorf, Das junge Rheinland. The names of these organizations, with their reference to "youth" and their calculated resemblance to the revolutionary "workers' soviets (Arbeiterräte)," were intended to express their radical purpose.[7] The immediate postwar period also saw a proliferation of art and architectural periodicals with cultural and social aims. Some of these, like *Frühlicht, Das neue Rheinland*, or *Feuer,* were new and ephemeral. Others, like *Der Cicerone, Aktion,* or *Der Sturm,* had been founded before the war but now entered a more radical phase. All of them provided a forum for the many writers who wanted to discuss the role of the arts in the revolution.[8]

The programs of these organizations and periodicals were various and often vague. Most, however, involved some notion of bringing art into greater contact with "the people," the belief that only modern art could perform this function, and the demand that the new state devote its patronage to this end. These hopes received a great deal of encouragement during the first few years of the Republic. In their new platforms, most of the major political parties referred to the importance of the arts for the new state,[9] and, particularly in 1918 and 1919, the left-wing parties gave evidence that they supported "revolutionary" artistic movements. Kurt Eisner, for example, during his brief ministry in Bavaria at the end of 1918, pledged his Independent Socialists to raise the public standard of taste and to guarantee subsistence to struggling artists.[10] Konrad Haenisch, the Majority Socialists' new Minister of Culture in Prussia, promised government support to new tendencies in the arts; and the governments of both Prussia and Bavaria endorsed various schemes for new kinds of art education.[11] Most of these promises of support came to nothing during the inflation years; but the new federal government did create a new office, that of "Reichskunstwart," to take charge of government-sponsored museums and exhibitions, and appointed to it Edwin Redslob, a friend of the modern movement.

Radical architects were thus only one group among the many artistic disciplines concerned with social and political questions during the first postwar years, but they were particularly influential. Just before the war the work of the leading progressive architects had begun to become widely known through the publications and exhibitions of the Deutscher Werkbund, and especially through the Cologne exhibition of 1914. But after 1918 these men assumed leadership in the debate among artists over the role of the arts in the new society, and, in addition, succeeded in molding the public view of the status of the arts in the new state. Their influence on the public was due in part to a general realization of the importance of architecture in postwar reconstruction. The practical question of relieving the housing shortage which had developed during the war was extremely pressing and excited great interest in new and more economical methods of design. Thus, in 1919 and 1920 such questions as the use of cheaper building materials and prefabricated parts for housing received wide publicity and attracted considerable government support.[12]

But architecture had, as well, a powerful symbolic importance in the period of German reconstruction. Indicative of this fact was the brief but impressive popularity of Hans Kampffmeyer's plan for a "Peace City."[13] Kampffmeyer, a state housing official in Baden, suggested in 1918 that a new city be erected as a monument to the constructive forces in German society and as a substitute for war memorials. The plan received warm support from leading industrialists, businessmen, architects, and Social Democratic politicians, although it was not, of course, carried out.

Against this background of great public awareness of the social importance of architecture, it was possible for architects to claim primacy for their art in the cultural work of the revolution. They devised a theory of architecture which embraced all the other visual arts and explained the relevance of these arts to a new society in terms of their relationship to architecture. This view of architecture, which became very common among artists, architects, and writers about the arts during the first few years of the Republic, was mainly the work of Walter Gropius and Bruno Taut. During the years between the armistice and the end of the inflation, these two architects produced an extraordinary volume of publications in support of a wholly new style. Their writings had far more influence upon architects and artists than those of any other individuals, and they therefore played the principal role in shaping the theory of architecture which helped to involve the new style in politics.

Although relatively young men, both Gropius and Taut had achieved prominence among progressive architects before the outbreak of the war. Taut, who was born in Königsberg in 1880, was best known before the war for his beehive-shaped "Glashaus" at the Cologne Werkbund exhibition (fig. 18). In the period immediately after the war his only executed work was a small extension of the Falkenberg Siedlung; but in 1921 he was hired as director of municipal construction in Magdeburg, which gave him the opportunity for architectural planning on a large scale. He left Magdeburg in 1923 and became, shortly thereafter, chief designer for Gehag, the great Berlin housing cooperative. Under his supervision the Gehag built immense housing developments in the later twenties, and Taut's innovations in planning and modular design made these projects among the most important executed in Germany during the Weimar Republic. But it was above all Taut's publications which made him the gadfly of the modern movement. His publications were of exceptional influence and significance, not so much because of the originality of his ideas, but because of the extremes to which he pushed his arguments, the frequency with which he raised issues of common concern to other radical architects, and the very volume of his writings.

Walter Gropius' career was very different from Taut's; if Taut became a leading figure in German architecture, Gropius emerged in the twenties as an architect of international stature. Born in 1883, Gropius was the son of a Prussian architect. At the age of 25, he entered the office of Peter Behrens, chief designer for the AEG (Emil Rathenau's Allgemeine Elektrizitäts-Gesellschaft), where Mies van der Rohe and Corbusier were also trained. Gropius' work for the AEG directed his interests at first toward industrial build-

ing, and he gained his initial reputation through factory design —
through the immediately famous Fagus factory (figs. 15 and 16) and
through the factory administration building he built for the Werkbund exhibition in 1914 (fig. 17). After the war, the Bauhaus buildings in Dessau (figs. 19–21) and the apartment buildings for the
Siemens works in Berlin (figs. 70 and 71) established Gropius as
one of the giants of the modern movement. But perhaps the most
remarkable aspect of Gropius' long career is the fact that he also
had extraordinary abilities as an organizer and a teacher. While
Taut was a flamboyant individualist, Gropius always preferred to
work with a group, either in architectural partnership, or, as at the
Bauhaus, with other teachers and in close cooperation with his
students. This fact has multiplied his remarkably fruitful influence
but has sometimes served to obscure the extent of his individual
creative contributions. These abilities were of particular significance in the development of the controversy over the new architecture in Germany, for it was as organizer and leader of fellow architects that Gropius, neither a contentious man nor one who was
ever in any way involved in party politics, became the chief object
of attack by the opponents of the new style.

Despite the fact that both Gropius and Taut had begun to do
unusually creative work before the war, their prewar buildings still
maintained ties with the architectural tradition of preceding decades, and neither man showed much interest in publicizing the
idea of a revolutionary architecture. But revulsion against the war
brought about a radical change in outlook for both men. By 1918
both Gropius and Taut had learned to distrust militarism. Both
were convinced, moreover, that the outcome of the war signified
not merely a military defeat for Germany, but the defeat of an
outworn system of values, and of an entire era in German culture.[14]
Taut later described his feelings as follows: "It was not possible
for anyone to make use of any pre-war traditions, for that period
was perforce regarded as the cause of the misfortunes of the past,
and because every achievement of those days seemed more or less
to hang together with the origins of the war. . . ."[15]

To both men, war and revolution seemed to be not merely political matters, but events which set in flux every aspect of human
existence and which opened up every possibility to artistic en-
deavor. "Today's artist," wrote Gropius in 1919, "lives in an era
of dissolution, without guidance. He stands alone. The old forms
are in ruins, the benumbed world is shaken up, the old human spirit
is invalidated and in flux toward a new form. We float in space and
cannot yet perceive the new order."[16] The birth of the "new order,"
they believed, would therefore be accompanied by radically new
art forms, without any ties to past traditions. They saw a particu-

larly intimate connection between a revolution in architectural forms and the broader cultural revolution. In Gropius' words: "[Architecture] is the crystalline expression of the noblest thoughts of men, of their ardor, their humanity, and their religion."[17] And they began to think of themselves as leaders, not only of the architectural revolution, but also of the broader cultural one of which they believed it to be a part. Taut described the work of the architect to be that of society's "priest," who, immersed in the "soul of the community" knows the spiritual needs of the people before they do.[18]

In attempting to explain the role of architecture in the new society, both men turned to metaphor. Taut in particular used an exaggerated and visionary style which reflected the excitement and enthusiasm of the first postwar years. The following selection from the first issue of his short-lived periodical *Dawn* illustrates the mood of his writings and the way in which he associated a new architecture with intellectual and political change:

> Oh, our concepts: "space," "homeland," "style"! To hell with them, odious concepts! Destroy them, break them up! Nothing shall remain! Break up your academies, spew out the old fogies, we'll play catch with their wigs! Blast! Blast! Let our north wind blow through this musty, threadbare, tattered old world of concepts, ideologies, systems! Death to the ideologues. Death to the stuffed shirts! Death to titles, dignities, authority! Down with everything serious! . . . Our dawn glows on the horizon. Hail, thrice hail to our Empire of powerlessness! Hail to transparency, clarity! Hail purity! Hail the crystalline, and hail and hail again the flowing, graceful, faceted, sparkling, flashing, airy — hail to eternal building![19]

All of Taut's writings were filled with similar references to light and crystal which were clearly derived from his prewar "house of glass." But in his early postwar writings Taut charged these images with a new fantasy and a new cultural symbolism. He developed the metaphor of a crystalline architecture into a series of fantastic architectural projects intended to act as symbols of hope for a Europe emerging from war and revolution. In a large folio of colored drawings made in 1918 and published the following year as *Alpine Architecture*, he showed the highest of the Alpine peaks sculptured in faceted shapes and joined them by bridges, buildings, and abstract decorative forms constructed out of colored glass (fig. 35). The whole was to be illuminated at night by colored searchlights.[20] The buildings and sculptures would turn men's minds from the war-torn past to the contemplation of beauty, and

SCHNEE
GLETSCHER
GLAS

Firnen
im ewigen Eise
und Schnee ~
überbaut und ge-
schmückt mit
Umbauungen Flä-
chen und Blöcken
von farbigem Glase
~ Bergblüten ~

Die Ausführung ist gewiss ungeheuer schwer und opfervoll, aber nicht unmöglich. „Man verlangt so selten von den Menschen das Unmögliche" (Goethe)

35. Bruno Taut, *Alpine Architektur*, p. 10.

their construction would be a task for the constructive forces of all Europe.[21]

The following year Taut published another set of colored drawings which he called *The Dissolution of Cities: The Path toward Alpine Architecture.*[22] This fantasy, which began with a drawing of a city of skyscrapers toppling to the ground, pictured a new Europe of small and middle-sized communities planned in the shape of stars and containing houses shaped like crystals. The larger communities were to have great glass "Volkshäuser" and temples, and the complex of cities spread out on the plains was to be crowned by faceted shapes and temples carved into a mountain range according to the designs in *Alpine Architecture.* Taut suggested that this reorganization of European community life was to be based on a new era in technology in which airplane travel and solar heat, among other innovations, would free men from their dependence on the old cities. And he believed that this new era would involve new social relations, since there would be no state boundaries and no institution of private property. Typically Taut expressed these ideas in an intentionally shocking form: "Ancient wisdom is reborn. Complete openness in sexual things. The idea of property is conquered. Thus also that of marriage."[23] But the main emphasis of the book was that if society were given a beautiful architectural form, it could again become the object of "faith and love."[24]

Taut's other major book of this period was *Die Stadtkrone*, a discussion of the planning of the "new cities," which contains the clearest explanation of what Taut thought to be the social and cultural meaning of the new architecture.[25] The beautiful cities of the past, Taut argued, those of Egypt, Greece, and medieval Europe, had had at their center a monument which expressed the religious ideals of their society. If the "spiritual revolution" was to have a meaning the new city too must have such a monument, and for it Taut proposed a group of community buildings with a "house of crystal" at their center. The beliefs which these buildings were to express could not be those of old Europe, for "the old religion is gone." But: "It is unthinkable that millions of men will fall prey to materialism, will live on, without knowing the reason of their existence. . . There must live something in each human breast which lifts man above the temporal and makes him feel a part of his community, his surroundings, his nation, and all mankind."[26]

Taut called this new belief upon which his proposed city planning was to be based the "soziale Gedanke": the social ideal, or, perhaps, the faith in human society. It was not, he hastened to add, political Socialism, but "socialism in an unpolitical sense, above politics . . . [it is] the simple straight-forward relationship of men to one another which bridges over the gap between warring classes and nations and binds man to man.''

To Taut, then, the goal of the revolution in which the new architecture was to take part was the creation of a human brotherhood, with organic community ties, and more than material aims. In designing buildings for this new society, Taut said, it must be the aim of the architect to make people conscious that they are "organic members [Glieder] of a great architectural structure," and he demanded of the public buildings that they be "organisms . . . expressing the human community."[27] Among these buildings the crystal palace would symbolize the spiritual aspect of the community. Characteristically, he described building as a joint work of painters, sculptors, metal workers, and the like, under the direction of the architect, thus expressing what he believed to be the proper relationship among the arts while at the same time pointing to their important social role as spiritual interpreters of the new society. Thus in *Stadtkrone* Taut endowed the new architecture with a dual function: the expression of new community relations in city planning and in the design of public buildings, and the bringing of the other arts into the service of the spiritual needs of society. This was the main message of the book; it rarely paused to give consideration to the practical problems of planning the future city and was clearly intended, like Taut's other writings of the period, as a parable.

Gropius' writings during this period were much less elaborate than Taut's, but they were probably more influential because of Gropius' position of leadership among modern artists and architects. Characteristically, most of his writings took the form of contributions to such joint publications as the Arbeitsrat für Kunst pamphlets, the catalog of the "exhibition for unknown architects" sponsored by the Arbeitsrat in April of 1919, or the programs issued by the Bauhaus. In these essays, Gropius, like Taut, wrote about the role of architecture and the arts in a "spiritual revolution" which he believed must follow upon the political one. But for Taut's "crystalline" architecture, Gropius usually substituted the metaphor of the medieval cathedral and the artisans' guild which constructed it. "Not until the political revolution is perfected in the spiritual revolution can we become free," Gropius wrote in 1919, and he described this event as "the rebirth of that spiritual unity which [once before] found expression in the miracle of the Gothic cathedrals."[28] By "spiritual unity" he meant, he said, the "creative spirit of reconstruction" among the people at large. Extending the metaphor to society as a whole, he predicted that only after the spiritual revolution "will the people again join together in building the great art work of their time . . . the freedom cathedral of the future."[29]

In these phrases Gropius was attempting to suggest something like Taut's rebirth of human brotherhood, for he sought a model for the society to be produced by the spiritual revolution in the medieval building guild. Each of Gropius' writings of 1919 summoned contemporary artists to join in the "cooperative work" of "new craftsmen's guilds, without the class divisions which attempt to erect a barrier between artists and craftsmen." These new guilds, he said, would "prepare the way" for the "cathedral of the future," for: "Our time will throw aside respect for the dead mask of organization which blinds us and leads us into error. The relationship of man to man, the spirit of small communities must conquer again. Small fruitful communities, secret societies, brotherhoods . . . building guilds as in the golden age of cathedrals!"[30]

This type of cooperation between artists and architects and between the arts and the "crafts" symbolized to both men cohesion and unity in society. In these terms both men attempted to suggest two separate goals for the "spiritual revolution": a cooperative spirit among the members of the new society, and the endowment of their association with spiritual significance through art. Gropius, however, extended the metaphors of "unity" and "cooperation" to the education of the modern artist and his role in the new society.

"Architects, sculptors, painters, we must all return to the crafts!" was the well-known slogan around which Gropius structured his writings for the Arbeitsrat für Kunst and his program for the Bauhaus.[31] As he used it, the phrase had many implications, but it was not, as many contemporaries thought, a repetition of the older repudiation of industrial production by Ruskin and Morris. Rather, Gropius meant that to achieve a wholly new type of artistic expression artists must return to the fundamentals of their training, for "architects, painters, and sculptors are craftsmen in the original sense of the word."[32] Gropius was therefore critical of the "professional artists" turned out by the academies, who seemed to him to be socially useless and formed what was frequently described during the revolutionary years as the "art proletariat." The academies, he believed, attempted to cultivate a talent which necessarily could belong only to a very few — the ability to become self-sufficient painters and sculptors and architects. They therefore produced great numbers of half-trained men who could have been made socially useful by training in a craft which could be used in the service of architecture.

Gropius' plea had, in addition, its own proletarian overtones, for the German "Handwerk" means literally, "hand-labor"; and Gropius spoke of the various types of artists, including independent painters and sculptors, as "Werkkünstler," "artist-workmen," or simply as "Werkleute," "working people."[33] Finally, the slogan was intended as a general statement about the creative personality and its importance to society. Just as the new artist was to develop his creative ability out of a training in manual skills, so the creative member of society could profit by a similar "reintegration" of thinking and doing. Gropius' program for the Arbeitsrat für Kunst urged that each of the nation's primary schools provide manual training.[34]

In their writings of 1918–1921, Gropius and Taut gave a kind of poetic unity to ideas so popular in the writings of the time that it is now virtually impossible to determine their original sources. Taut's discussion of the symbolic importance of community buildings in the new city may have drawn upon the work of the "Society for People's Assembly Halls," which grew out of another of Hans Kampffmeyer's plans for commemorating the peace.[35] Taut himself acknowledged the debt of his *Stadtkrone* to Kampffmeyer's *Friedenstadt*.[36] But the painter Karl Schmidt-Rottluff, who had no contact with Kampffmeyer, also drew up a project in 1919 for a new type of city, constructed on a mountain, which would serve as a symbol of a new art and a new society; and the idea appears in the writings of other architects not closely associated with Taut.[37] The necessity for finding an architectural expression for new "organic" social bonds was also elaborated upon by the well-known art historian, Fritz Hoeber, early in 1919[38] and given a new formulation by Paul Klopfer, a teacher in Weimar's Building Trades School, in 1920.[39] Gropius' belief in the importance of craft training to art education and hence to a revolution in the arts was shared during the same period by prominent architects and teachers like Peter Behrens, Otto Bartning, Bruno Paul, and Fritz Wichert, and it also appeared in the programs of art and architectural students in Berlin and Munich.[40] Even the idea of the "building guild" had a separate formulation in the efforts of Martin Wagner to reorganize the building trades into profit-sharing cooperatives.[41] Wagner, who after 1925 was one of the principal planners of the great Berlin housing projects in which these cooperative trades associations were often employed, called them "soziale Bauhütten." He and many trade union officials thought of them as models for a new type of social organization.[42]

The extent to which radical artists and their supporters subscribed to these general ideas is indicated by the membership of the Arbeitsrat für Kunst, the organization inspired and led by Gropius. Among the 114 signers of the organization's first program which appeared early in 1919 were painters like Heckel, Hoetger, Meidner, Nolde, Pechstein, Rohlfs, Schmidt-Rottluff, and Feininger; the sculptors Marcks and Kolbe; Paul Cassirer, publisher and owner of an important Berlin art gallery; Karl Ernst Osthaus, director of Germany's most influential museum of modern art at Hagen; Adolf Behne, the architectural critic; and many of the architects who would lead the modern movement later in the twenties including Gropius, Taut, Bartning, Hilberseimer, Hans and Wassili Luckhardt, and Mendelsohn.[43] The program which they signed closely resembled the writings of Gropius and Taut outlined above and was probably written by them.

The Arbeitsrat für Kunst was founded late in 1918 by Gropius, probably together with Taut, Cesar Klein, and Adolf Behne, as an attempt to "reunite art and the people" since "art must no longer be the privilege of the few, but the pleasure and life of the masses. The joining of the arts under the wings of a great architecture is the goal."[44] During its short life the organization published at least two pamphlets on architecture and a collection of essays on the role of the arts in the revolution entitled *Ja! Stimmen des Arbeitsrates für Kunst*. It also held several widely reviewed exhibitions in 1919 and 1920.[45] These activities were intended at least in part to call its ideas to the attention of the political authorities, and gain their support for its program. The demands which the Arbeitsrat put forward in its April program included the following: the provision of funds and land for new "utopian" building projects (such as housing developments and "people's assembly halls") to be constructed jointly by artists, sculptors, and architects; the dissolution of the old state-supported art and architectural schools and the encouragement of new types of art education based upon training in the crafts; the destruction of "aesthetically worthless monuments" and buildings, and the building of war monuments "only after careful consideration."[46] The first of these items reflects Taut's thinking, the second Gropius', while the rejection of war monuments clearly indicates the strongly antimilitarist sentiment which the members of the organization shared with its founders.

Although modern artists and architects, led by Gropius and Taut, succeeded in provoking widespread discussion of a "new architecture" during the first four years following the revolution, the number of buildings actually constructed by the radical architects during these years was very small. There were, of course, no public funds available for "utopian" building projects; and the principal modern buildings of the period — a few churches, houses, factories, and isolated larger buildings — were privately financed. Moreover, despite, or perhaps because of, the atmosphere of feverish prophesy and exaggerated hopes in which they worked, the radical architects did not agree among themselves about the actual character of the new style, and they outdid one another in bizarre experiments which had comparatively little influence upon the future development of German architecture. Around 1922 the Bauhaus, founded in 1919, began to make its first important contributions to the development of the new architecture. At the same time, as the prophetic mood began to ebb and as more commissions became available, the new style began to take shape in Germany. But prior to 1922 the "new architecture" appeared to the German public primarily as a new interpretation of art and architecture which had grown out of the revolution. The fact that this view of architecture was essentially nonpolitical was obscured by the enthusiasm with which the radical architects had greeted the revolution and by the apparent sympathy of the state toward their claims.

Among the most bizarre early attempts at a new style were Erich Mendelsohn's Einstein Observatory in Potsdam, and Hans Poelzig's Grosses Schauspielhaus in Berlin (figs. 36 and 37), both built in 1919. The design of the Einstein tower, which grew out of a series of fantastic drawings Mendelsohn had made during the war, re-

36. Hans Poelzig, Grosses Schauspielhaus, Berlin, reconstruction.

37. Erich Mendelsohn, Einstein Observatory, Potsdam.

38. Erich Mendelsohn, Hat Factory, Luckenwalde.

ceived enormous publicity, partly because of its extraordinary appearance, but also because the observatory was constructed for the purpose of helping to prove Einstein's very controversial theory of relativity.[47] The way in which Mendelsohn carried the windows around the corners of the building was prophetic of his later work, but as serious architecture both the Einstein tower and the Schauspielhaus remained almost wholly without influence in the history of style. Equally bizarre and somewhat more fruitful for later design were Gropius' Sommerfeld house of 1921, which reflects the influence of Frank Lloyd Wright, and the "Dombauhütte," which Behrens designed for the Munich trades exhibition in 1922.[48] Mendelsohn's Luckenwalde factory (fig. 38), begun in 1921 but not completed until 1923, began to suggest that combination of horizontal surface pattern and asymmetrically arranged geometric forms which would dominate the new style in Germany; but its jagged roof lines had more in common with the Einstein Tower than with Mendelsohn's definitive later work. These early buildings, often inappropriately lumped together as "expressionist" architecture,* had only two qualities in common. Each represented a radical break

* See for example, Banham, "Expressionism: Amsterdam and Berlin," *Theory and Design*, 163–184; Nikolaus Pevsner, "Finsterlin and Some Others," *Architectural Review*, CXXXII (1962), 353–356, and "Taut Reprinted," CXXXVI (1964), 319. It is convenient, certainly, to have a term for the bizarre character of the buildings and projects of 1919–1921. But in view of their diversity, "utopian" or "fantastic" architecture describes them better than "expressionist." The latter term should be restricted to its original and most meaningful usage: the description of a specific tendency in literature and painting between 1905 and the middle twenties. Here some unity of style exists.

with the past, and each incorporated in its design a sense of motion. This sense of motion may also, in a sense, be said to reappear in the "dynamic balance" of the Dessau Bauhaus buildings or the "perpetual," though horizontal, motion of Mendelsohn's department stores, but in every other respect the end of 1921 brought a sharp break in the development of architectural style in Germany.

Beginning with such buildings as Mendelsohn's Weichmann department store of 1922 and the project for mass housing exhibited at the Bauhaus early in the same year, a few architects began to develop the additive geometric structures and the bare flat surfaces which were to become characteristic of the new architecture in Germany after 1924, when building activity revived on a large scale. Although Mendelsohn's works were among the earliest to be executed in the new vernacular, the Bauhaus came to be the most influential center for the development of the new style. Its influence derived not only from the buildings exhibited and executed at the school but also from the publicity it received as a new type of state-supported educational institution based upon many of the architectural theories of 1919.

In April of 1919 Gropius obtained the permission of the new Social-Democratic government of Saxe-Weimar to combine Weimar's old art academy and its applied arts school into a new institution, the "Bauhaus," or "House of Building."[49] The curriculum of the new school carried out Gropius' ideas about a return to the crafts in a modernized version of the medieval building guild. The "fine" arts had no special prerogative within the school; painting and sculpture were not taught at all, but classes in weaving, carpentry, and other crafts involved in constructing, decorating, and furnishing buildings were accompanied by instruction in "form." Much of this training followed a relatively traditional pattern at first and was carried on by craftsmen drawn from existing crafts shops; but for the "Formlehre" Gropius recruited men like Klee, Kandinsky, Schlemmer, and Gerhardt Marcks, who as "masters" led their apprentices. Gropius also instituted a type of instruction in the basic principles of design which he believed underlay both the arts and the crafts. This was the famous "Vorkurs," in which, under the direction of Johannes Itten and later of Albers and Moholy-Nagy, students were encouraged to unlearn all the traditions of European art and to make a new beginning through experimentation with natural materials and abstract forms. After completing both Vorkurs and crafts instruction, students were expected to be able to support themselves as professional craftsmen; but they were encouraged to remain in the school for a third stage of training in which they could practice applying the skills which they had learned to architectural design.

These courses represented the basic curriculum of the school, but

39. Walter Gropius,
Municipal Theater,
Jena,
reconstruction.

Gropius constantly enlarged the range of its studies and activities. To the projects of the early workshops, which included pottery, weaving, metalwork, carpentry, and architectural design, were added, in 1921, informal work in typography; in 1922, Schlemmer's teaching of stage design and choreography; and in 1923, the study of photography under Laszlo Moholy-Nagy. Visiting lecturers kept the school in touch with artists of other countries and with practitioners of the other arts: J.J.P. Oud and Theo van Doesburg introduced the school to the ideas of the De Stijl movement; Stravinsky and Bartok lectured on music. Other extracurricular activities included performances of modern music, experimental films, and lectures on modern physics and biology. Many of these additional activities had little to do with architectural training, the alleged goal of the school; but the fact that they centered in an institution devoted to "building" supported Gropius' contention that the new architecture would lead a broad revolution in culture and gained further publicity for his ideas.

Gropius was not very successful at first in winning the architectural commissions which he needed to complete his educational program. The state government promised to give the school a tract of land on which experimental buildings could be constructed, but negotiations over the gift were not completed until 1923.[50] Meanwhile, Gropius and his students designed a set of models for a housing development to be built on the tract, and these were displayed at the school's 1922 exhibitions in Weimar and Berlin. In 1923, the first, and only, house in the proposed housing development was completed and exhibited during the summer. Designed by the painter Georg Muche, with furnishings and fixtures by the students, it was shown to the public as the joint effort of all the arts and crafts at the Bauhaus. Gropius himself was engaged by the city of Jena to rebuild its municipal theater in 1922 (fig. 39); he produced a forceful design, but it did not become as well known as the projects which were publicized as the work of the Bauhaus as a whole.

Although the housing designs of 1922 never progressed beyond the project stage, they were extraordinarily important and influential (fig. 40). The exhibition models consisted of a series of cubes which could be assembled in different combinations to form different types of houses. Precisely because they were models, devoid of any architectural detailing, they showed the new, bare, cubic architecture in its most dramatic form. The choice of a housing development was also prophetic, because after 1924 mass housing was to provide radical architects with their most important commissions. The models appealed both to the architects who sought architectural forms divested of all traditional associations, and to architects and planners who cared little about style but believed that the modular construction would lend itself to prefabrication, providing an inexpensive solution to the housing shortage.

The exhibition house of 1923 had a less elegant exterior and was most important as a precedent for a new type of interior design. Its

40. Walter Gropius and Bauhaus Students, Models of Houses Designed in Standardized Units.

41. Georg Muche, Bauhaus Students and Faculty, Exhibition House, Interior.

42. Bauhaus Exhibition House, interior.

bare wall surfaces, large window areas, geometric fixtures and furniture, together with the brightly colored textiles in abstract patterns which were used as upholstery and decorations, came to be characteristic of the interiors of buildings executed in the new style (figs. 41 and 42). The exhibition house was probably more widely publicized than any other building in Germany before 1927, for the 1923 exhibition attracted representatives of nearly all Germany's leading newspapers, and most of them devoted long articles to what the exhibition prospectus had called the "dwelling-machine."*

There has been a great deal of speculation about the origins of the new forms of housing design exhibited at the Bauhaus in 1922 and 1923. Some writers stress the importance of Itten's replacement as director of the Vorkurs by Moholy-Nagy, advocate of Russian constructivism.[51] Certainly the development of the new architecture at the Bauhaus was part of a broader shift in emphasis in the school's curriculum, but because Moholy arrived only in 1923 his employment may be regarded as a result, rather than a cause, of the movement toward cubic, constructivist forms. More convincing is the argument that Theo van Doesburg's lectures at the school in 1921 introduced a wave of enthusiasm among German architects for the ideas of the Dutch De Stijl movement.[52] But it is hard to find

* Wohnmaschine. Thus named because of the open plan, which was supposed to promote efficient circulation.

43. Erich Mendelsohn, Weichmann Department Store, Gleiwitz.

44. Erich Mendelsohn, Villa Sternefeld, Berlin.

any direct connection between particular German buildings and the buildings and paintings of the Dutchmen. If any foreign source influenced the new design in Germany, it was probably Corbusier's "Maison Citrohan," a sketch of a standardized design for low-cost housing far more advanced than the Bauhaus projects, which was executed in 1920 and known in Germany by 1921.[53] But there are also precedents for buildings like the housing projects of 1922 and the Jena theater in Gropius' Fagus factory; and ever since the Werkbund debate between Van de Velde and Muthesius in 1914 over standardization, there had been a considerable number of German architects, Gropius being one of the most prominent, who favored the idea of standardized building types to which the new style was so well suited. If the Bauhaus, and German architects in general, received the ideas of Corbusier, De Stijl, or constructivism with enthusiasm, it was because they were ready for them.

Whatever the immediate sources of the new forms, the transition to the new style began to appear in the work of several other architects at the same time. In 1922 Mendelsohn employed flat surfaces and rigidly geometric forms in his Weichmann department store in Gleiwitz, Silesia (fig. 43), while in his Villa Sternefeld of 1923 (fig. 44) he balanced these forms and planes in the "constructivist" manner which was to be so prominent in the larger modern buildings of the later twenties. In 1923 Otto Haesler built a small

45. Otto Haesler, Siedlung Italienischer Garten, Celle.

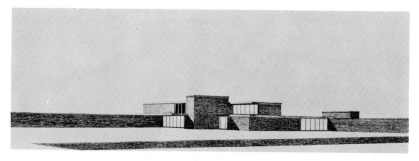

46. Ludwig Mies van der Rohe, Project for a Brick Villa.

housing development for Celle, near Hannover, in which the housing units were composed of cubic shapes put together in the additive fashion of the Bauhaus models (fig. 45). In Haesler's designs, the new style in all its starkness was employed for the first time in mass housing in Germany. In the same year, Mies van der Rohe initiated his personal version of the new style in his project for a brick villa (fig. 46). Taut was less original than these men in his few executed works of these years; but in 1924 he began to advocate a type of interior design similar to that exhibited at the Bauhaus (fig. 47), and the official position which he held in Magdeburg gave him greater influence than Haesler, Mendelsohn, or Mies.

When Magdeburg's Social Democratic City Council made Taut director of municipal construction in 1921, he hoped for the kind of grandiose building projects which would express the "dawn" of a new era in Magdeburg. During his first two years in office, Taut set up a new authority to oversee the expansion of the city and projected a general plan for Magdeburg's growth, which included rings of parks and gardens and a series of sports fields. He planned, in addition, a huge set of housing developments for workers; a set of

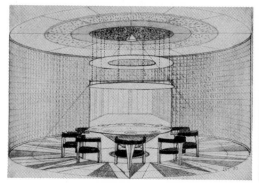
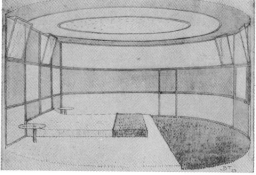

47. Bruno Taut, Design for Dining Room and Bedroom, from *Die Neue Wohnung*.

48. Oskar Fischer, Decoration of the Facade of the Barasch Store, Magdeburg, executed under the administration of Bruno Taut as Stadtbaurat.

community buildings including a forum for the exhibitions, festivals, and fairs of state and city; and an urban assembly hall. Of all these projects, however, only the "Halle Stadt-und-Land," a reinforced concrete exhibition hall of daring design, was begun during Taut's term of office.[54] When he found that the city government was not yet able to finance the sweeping plans which he drew up on paper, Taut turned to a less expensive alternative — the repainting of the city's buildings in bright colors, which, he said, was the best substitute for a "glass architecture."[55] Part of this general plan was completed: Taut had a number of the streets in the city's housing developments repainted, refurbished the old city hall, and persuaded some of the city's businessmen to have the facades of their office buildings decorated with abstract patterns by modern artists (fig. 48). These painting projects received considerable publicity, and the practice of giving abstract pattern to buildings and groups of buildings by means of contrasting colors was adopted by Otto Haesler in 1923 and was thereafter very popular among designers of housing developments in the new style.[56] Taut also received a few major commissions from private sources in Magdeburg including an important market hall for the city's slaughter yards;

but he retired to private practice in Berlin at the end of 1923, disgusted at the lack of opportunity for carrying out his larger plans. After the city's financial recovery, however, Magdeburg became one of the major centers of the new architecture under Taut's assistant and successor, Johannes Göderitz; and between 1924 and 1930 Taut's programs were used as a basis for the planning of housing developments and urban expansion.

Although architectural practice was absorbing more of their time from 1922 onward, both Gropius and Taut continued their intensive efforts to publicize the new architecture. In 1922 and 1923 Gropius gave a series of lectures which were intended at least in part to publicize the two Bauhaus exhibitions of those years, and in 1923 he published the well-known and widely read "Idee und Aufbau des Staatlichen Bauhauses in Weimar" as an introduction to the exhibition of 1923. Taut wrote only one book between 1922 and 1925, a popularly written discussion of the new style in housing, but it reached a comparatively wide public.[57] The writings and speeches of this period were very different from those of 1918–1921, and reflected the change which had taken place in design. Taut and Gropius no longer referred to the political revolution, which was by then an accomplished fact, nor did they continue to employ the prophetic tone of their earlier writings. They began instead to see the "new era" as primarily a machine age, and to explore the relationship between the machine and the new architecture. At the same time, they continued to employ much of the same imagery which they had used before and attempted to show that the new style then being developed "expressed" a social and cultural revolution, which they now tried to define more clearly.

In *The New Dwelling: The Woman as Creator,* published in 1924, Taut discussed in detail the social and cultural implications of the new type of housing which he and other radical architects proposed to construct. The book was influential from the first and became increasingly important as the new style came to play a greater and greater part in the public housing programs of the later twenties. The social and cultural effects of the new housing emerged, Taut said, partly from the use of compact "functional" planning and partly from the new aesthetic of the design, which together provided a symbolic language expressive of the new age.* The new type of

---

* Art and "function," said Taut, could not be separated: "selbstverständlich, dass es ein bloss Praktisches oder ein bloss Schönes eigentlich nicht gibt; man spricht nur getrennt von jedem, um sich eines sprachtechnischen Hilfsmittels zu bedienen. Im Grunde genommen gibt es nur eine Sache, die nicht verschiedene Seiten hat, sondern deren jede Seite wie bei einer Kugel gleichzeitig alles enthält" (*Die neue Wohnung,* 32). This view, which endows practical things with spiritual significance through art, was shared by Gropius and explains why both men were able to transfer their enthusiasm from utopian building projects, which could "spiritualize" society on a large scale, to the microcosm of the dwelling and the technical problems of its construction and design.

planning, using step-saving plans and labor-saving equipment of the type shown in the Weimar exhibition house, would free the housewife from household drudgery and enable her to be "creative" in domestic matters, participating in the creation of the new aesthetic. This aesthetic, Taut said, consisted in a return to the basic principles of architecture: light, color, and cubic space. Taut argued that the new architectural forms would, in addition to encouraging the development of the creative process in the home, provide an appropriate background for a "spiritual revolution" akin to that which he and Gropius had written about in the early twenties. The characteristics of this revolution still remained sweeping and vague; they included a new opportunity for the perfection of the personality of the inhabitants, for "only in freedom from disorder can the personality develop freely," and a new "mental attitude, more flexible, simpler, and more joyful." Taut claimed, finally, that these new attitudes were a part of a new and more rational way of life brought about by the machine and industrial production. Taut thus still believed that the new architecture expressed a revolutionary "new era," but this new age now seemed to him to be dominated by the machine and industrial production. *The New Dwelling* departed strikingly from the visionary tone and political implications of Taut's earlier writings, but it helped to perpetuate the idea that the new style was bound up in social and cultural change.

During the same period Gropius was giving even more emphasis to the role of the machine in the new architecture. This idea was not, of course, new to Gropius in 1922. Before the war he had already submitted to Emil Rathenau a project for prefabricated housing, and as a member of the prewar Werkbund he necessarily subscribed to its program of introducing quality into industrially produced goods. But his writings during the first three postwar years had placed their major emphasis upon the metaphor of a return to the "crafts" in "building the cathedral of the future," terms which to some extent appeared to reflect a Ruskinian romanticism. After 1921, although he continued to regard the Bauhaus as a new version of the old building guild, he constantly emphasized that the purpose of providing crafts training for artists was to bring about a new relationship between the artist and the machine, and he saw the "cathedral of the future" as embodied in a machine aesthetic. "There is no real difference between the crafts and industry," he told students at Jena's Technische Hochschule in May of 1922, "only that the crafts involve the whole [process of production], while industry today has lost this concept."[58] Crafts training at the Bauhaus, he explained, implying the inclusion of the

Vorkurs, enabled artists to design simplified forms — suitable for standardization — which could serve as the basic components of machine-produced goods.[59] It therefore brought about the return of the artist to industrial production where, using the machine as another kind of tool, he could "bring art back to the people" through the mass production of beautiful things.

The final goal of this training was the invention of a new architectural aesthetic which Gropius described in his introduction to the exhibition of 1923: "We want to create a clear organic architecture, whose inner logic will be radiant and naked, unencumbered by lying facades and trickeries; we want an architecture adapted to our world of machines, radios, and fast motor cars, an architecture whose function is clearly recognizable in the relation of its forms,"[60] and in his speech on "the work of the artist in economics and technology" a few months earlier: "Just as the Gothic cathedral was the expression of its age, so must the modern factory or modern dwelling be the expression of our time: precise, practical [sachlich], free of superfluous ornament, effective only through the cubic composition of the masses.[61]

In language reminiscent of 1919, Gropius continued to claim that the educational program of the Bauhaus, which brought the arts and architecture back into the service of society, would produce "a complete spiritual revolution in the individual" and a "new style of life."[62] And as in his earlier writings this "spiritual revolution" had social implications as well, although they remained ill defined. In his Jena speech he argued that the "new unity" for which education at the Bauhaus provided a model would overcome such social ills as "the fragmentation of existence . . . [the fact that] economic life had become an end in itself rather than a means in the service of men . . . [that] competition, rather than mutual help, rules our material life . . . and that personal responsibility is excluded from our political life by controls, commissions, and parliaments."[63] Such statements sounded far less revolutionary than the prophecies of 1919, but they helped to identify the director of the Bauhaus and the designer of the Jena theater with those who continued to call for sweeping social change even after the revolution of 1918 was an accomplished fact.

Although the writings of Gropius and Taut shifted in tone and emphasis between 1918 and 1924, they retained a consistent purpose. During these years both men sought above all to discover a new principle of structure and order in German society with which to oppose the chaos of war and revolution. They wished for a process of reintegration in all spheres of life: in thought, in society, in the education of the "well-rounded man," between everyday life and spiritual things, between culture and industry, between artists and society, and among the arts. They characterized this reintegration as "a new unity" or, as Gropius once called it, "a new totalism." They found its symbol and its midwife in a new, socially conscious architecture. These ideas were in the main nonpolitical. Yet the very inclusiveness of this view of architecture endowed the new style with a broader set of associations. Thus by the time the aseptic forms of the new architecture were introduced to the German public on a large scale, they labored under a heavy load of symbolism which in turn provided substance for those, both friendly and unfriendly, who sought to interpret them in cultural, social, or political terms.

III / The Controversy over the Bauhaus

Opposition to the new style in Germany had its origin in Weimar and Thuringia during the early postwar years. The establishment of the Bauhaus in Weimar in 1919 set off a storm of local controversy over the cultural and political significance of the new school and the ideas it represented. During the years 1922–1925, the controversy became a major political issue in Thuringia, and, in turn, a cause célèbre in the national press as well. These developments were the product of a complex of local cultural traditions, personalities, and political tensions which were in combination peculiar to Weimar and Thuringia. But during the course of the debate, arguments for and against the Bauhaus were developed which influenced the thinking of a broader public and furnished ammunition for the later opponents of the new style. The "battle over the Bauhaus," as it was called, helped to form the pattern for the future course of the controversy.

The Bauhaus met two successive waves of public opposition during its six years in Thuringia. The first, confined primarily to Weimar, centered around Gropius' attempt to incorporate the old art academy into the Bauhaus. It died down in 1920, as soon as the opposition had succeeded in securing the re-establishment of the academy. During the course of this first attack, the charge that the school sheltered left-wing political activities was made for the first time. Opposition revived again in 1922 in response to the Bauhaus exhibition of that year. From then on both the architectural style developing at the school and the ideas of its faculty and students were attacked as leftist and communist; and these charges were taken over by the right-wing political parties of Thuringia as a weapon against the left, which supported the school. By 1925, when a right-wing government succeeded in expelling the Bauhaus from Thuringia, a clear-cut political alignment on artistic issues had taken place, both in Thuringia and in the national press which reported the debate.

The attacks which were made upon the school during both periods of public opposition came from a variety of sources and centered around a variety of themes. But in nearly every case the opponents of the school presented themselves as the defenders of "German" culture against the innovations of the Bauhaus. Because of this point of view the opponents of the school began to attack its work as a symbol of some kind of cultural or social decadence, and they urged a return to older cultural traditions of the German nation or the German "race." This type of argument was taken up by the conservative architects who opposed the new style in the later twenties, and played a very prominent role in Nazi architectural propaganda thereafter. Alongside the political alignment on aesthetic questions produced by the Bauhaus controversy, this development of cultural criticism in terms of architecture was therefore the most important product of the debate over Gropius' school.

Before the war Weimar had been a quiet provincial capital, chiefly notable as Germany's principal literary shrine. But in April of 1919 when the Bauhaus began its classes, Weimar stood at the very center of the tumult of Germany's political revolution. The national constituent assembly, unwilling to meet in Berlin, had turned to the famous home of Goethe and Schiller as the site of its deliberations, which lasted from February to July. The Assembly met under the protection of the provisional Social Democratic government of the state of Saxe-Weimar, which had replaced the ducal government whose capital had also been in Weimar. Negotiations to enlarge the state into the new territory of Thuringia and to move its capital had already begun. In this atmosphere of profound political uncertainty the population of Weimar remained politically conservative. The situation of the Bauhaus was thus complicated from the beginning by the existence of political tension in the town. Set up and financed by the radical state government, the school was inevitably regarded as politically suspect by the strong conservative element in Weimar.[1]

Moreover, Weimar was not likely under any circumstances to welcome either radically new art forms or antiacademic tendencies in art education. In the industrial and cosmopolitan cities of the north and west, where it was easily accepted, the new architecture had little competition from established architectural traditions. But Weimar was physically dominated by the legacy of the ducal past; and its complex of parks, gardens, and palaces made it one of the most charming of Germany's historic towns. Weimar's attachment to traditional art forms, nourished in this way, was powerfully enhanced by the presence of the ducal art academy. The academy, established in 1860, had achieved an impressive national reputation by the beginning of the twentieth century, and was particularly well known for its classes in landscape painting. Alongside the art academy, the last Grand Duke had set up a very progressive applied arts school shortly before the war under the direction of Henri van de Velde. But before the war the applied arts were not culturally respectable in the way they were to become under the aegis of the Bauhaus. Weimar was thus known in Germany for its handsome neoclassical architecture, important school of academic painting, and associations with a sacred literary tradition. Its civic pride depended to a large extent on these associations with the past.

The Bauhaus, dedicated to a new beginning in the arts and the product of state, rather than city initiative, was thus a source of irritation to the town from the start; and the attitudes of the new faculty and students helped to embitter the relations between town and gown. The arrival of the new art students, for whom there was no adequate housing, caused difficulties in itself; but the fact that they came from all over Germany and abroad, dressed in the bohemian manner, and were in a few vocal cases political radicals, annoyed the City Council and led it to deny the school's urgent requests for help in housing and feeding the students.[2] The anti-academic passages in Gropius' writings and his explicit encourage-ment of the most modern artistic tendencies in the new school similarly aroused the suspicions of the city's leading citizens.[3] But the chief source of trouble with the town was the way Gropius virtually did away with the old art school, combining it with the applied arts school and providing the united faculties with a new curriculum. The existing faculty of the academy were not dis-charged; and they were permitted, if they chose, to continue to teach their usual classes, largely composed, of course, of students remaining from the old academy. But the new curriculum was taught jointly by local craftsmen and by the artists and sculptors whom Gropius recruited during the course of the first six months. By the fall of 1919 it had become clear to both academy professors and townsmen that the academy was to have no part in Gropius' long-range plans for the Bauhaus.

A full account of the controversy resulting from these disagree-ments is made difficult today by the fact that Weimar and its local records lie in the Soviet zone of Germany. But the general outline of the debate may be reconstructed from the large collection of newspaper clippings and other published materials which Gropius brought with him from Germany in 1934.[4] As far as can be deter-mined from this record, public discussion of the Bauhaus first occurred on a large scale in mid-December 1919, when the by-elections for the City Council were held. At that time, a group of dissatisfied citizens, artists, and academy professors formed a "Free Union for City Interests" and held a public meeting to consider complaints against the school.[5] During the following months, this group, allied with local journalists, waged active war upon the school, which, although it survived their attacks, was forced into a defensive position for the duration of its stay in Weimar.

Present at the meeting of December 12, in addition to a large number of citizens, were representatives of the City Council and students and staff of both the Bauhaus and the academy. The meeting began with a debate, moderate in tone, between Gropius and Emil Herfurth, a teacher at the Weimar Gymnasium and a leader of the "Free Union." Claiming to represent those "who view the new art with caution," Herfurth explained that the opponents of the school would be satisfied if the art academy could be preserved intact and if the new teachers and students would show more respect for the "traditions and customs" of Weimar. Gropius replied in a conciliatory manner, pleading for "an attitude of patience and trust toward the new movement." He argued that the public assembly had no competence to judge artistic questions and should restrict itself to practical questions. After this exchange, however, the meeting degenerated into a name-calling session which permitted no debate of the real issues involved. Its tone was set by its chairman, a Dr. Kreubel, who compared modern painting to the artistic efforts of the insane, citing the psychologist Prinzhorn as his authority.[6] Kreubel labeled the school a "Spartacist-bolshevist institution" without explaining what he meant, and permitted catcalls of "Jewish art" and "foreigners."[7]

Most of the rest of the meeting was taken up with the confused and agitated speech of an academy student, Hans Gross, on "German art." Gross's address referred to "personality, energy, and will" as the only true sources of art and claimed that they were dying out in a Germany threatened by international domination, "the wolf thirsting for the blood of the German people."[8] It was not at all clear what Gross meant, and he later claimed that the speech had nothing to do with the Bauhaus but was merely an excerpt from a lecture on folk art (Heimatkunst) which he had given in Hamburg several months previously. But such was the temper of the assembly that most of those present supposed Gross to be making a bitter attack upon Gropius' school, and they applauded it as such.[9]

During the next two months the controversy had a tone similar to that of the first meeting, for the opponents of the school continued to express their criticisms in political and chauvinistic terms. Opposition to the school was taken up immediately after the meeting of the twelfth by *Thüringer Landeszeitung "Deutschland,"* a nationalist newspaper published in Weimar with a large circulation throughout Thuringia. Two of the paper's journalists began a long series of articles on "foreign" and "un-German" influences at the Bauhaus. These writers were Leonhard Schrickel, an author of feature articles for many Thuringian newspapers, and Mathilde Freiin von Freytag-Loringhoven, *Deutschland's* art critic, who as a member of the Weimar City Council kept these issues alive there as well.[10] Typical of these articles was Schrickel's treatment of the Gross affair on December 18. He claimed (wrongly) that Gross had been officially censured for his speech by Gropius and by the Bauhaus student council, and he described the action of the latter as follows: "Is it believable that the opinion of foreigners is decisive in the student assembly? That foreigners sit in judgement over German art students? People whose un-German ancestry (Galicia, Slovakia?) is apparent a mile off? Who even give themselves airs over their 'international' (more correctly, a-national, homeless) attitude? Who constitute an anti-German encampment in order to drive out Germans of belief and birth?"[11]

Schrickel also made much of the fact that the painter Sachs, a member of the Spartakusbund in Munich, had visited the school and that the faculty had distributed what he called a "Spartacist" pamphlet on the arts, published by the republican government in Berlin.[12] He elaborated upon these charges in three further articles in January of 1920, and *Deutschland's* editorial staff, together with Freytag-Loringhoven, drew upon his arguments for their comments on the controversy.[13] The repeated attempts of the Bauhaus staff to prove that nearly all the students were German or of German extraction had no effect on Schrickel's argument, which regarded Weimar and its art academy as "German" and all else as foreign."[14]

Toward the end of December, a group of about fifty citizens and local artists joined in a petition to the state government demanding the continuance of the art academy as a separate institution and recording a series of complaints against the Bauhaus.[15] Among the signers were Herfurth, Schrickel, Freytag-Loringhoven, Professor Fleischer (who had recently resigned from the academy staff), and a number of local artists, most of whom were graduates of the school. Chief among the criticisms of the school were its alleged treatment of Gross, the favoritism shown to "foreign" students, and the instances of "Spartacist" activity of which Schrickel had written.

In response to the petition, the state Ministry of Culture initiated an official inquiry, which, after several months, cleared the Bauhaus entirely on every charge of political activity or favoritism toward "foreigners."[16] Meanwhile, however, the events of December, widely reported by the local press[17] and embroidered upon by *Deutschland*, stirred up enough additional local concern to provide a second public assembly with an audience of over a thousand.[18] The meeting of January 22 was called by the successors to the "Free Union," two "citizens' committees" headed by Herfurth and (very probably) by Professor Fleischer. It was not a forum for public discussion, but a formal gathering at which the committees made public their resolutions against the Bauhaus.[19] The resolutions repeated the charges of foreign and left-wing influence at the school, giving the latter the new formulation that "there is an obvious connection between expressionism and Communist ideas." In addition the resolutions contained an implied demand for the dissolution of the Bauhaus: "We cannot afford to support two institutions at once, and Weimar's fate depends upon our art academy. . . . Our future development cannot represent the opposite of what made us great in the past."[20]

A few days later the artists among Herfurth's followers published independently an explanation of their motives in joining the campaign against the Bauhaus. This document differed significantly from the resolutions, for it did not mention charges of left-wing political activities and instead concentrated upon the cultural dangers inherent in modern art: "In courageously taking up the battle against the excesses of extreme expressionism and against the new spirit of impiety, impatience and destruction which is attempting to take root in our dear city, we know that we are in agreement, not only with all true friends of Weimar . . . but also with all those who have recognized the disintegrating effect which this sick and intolerant art movement exerts, particularly upon our youth."[21] This emphasis upon the "spiritual" dangers of modern art was to be characteristic of the artists, architects, and art critics who opposed the Bauhaus in Weimar, while the nonprofessional opponents of the school were the chief source of political attacks. For the first time many of the more moderate academy professors were among the signers of the artists' statement.[22]

But despite this attack upon the "disintegrating" cultural influence of the school and the persistent suspicion that the Bauhaus was harboring political agitators, the main issue in the first "battle over the Bauhaus" in 1919 and 1920 was the fate of the old art academy. When the state government promised at the end of January to consider supporting the academy as a separate institution, local controversy immediately died down.[23] *Deutschland* abruptly ceased its attacks on the school,[24] as did the "citizens' committees," and the academy professors awaited the judgment of the Landtag.

The fate of the academy was finally settled six months later after the administration recommended to the Landtag a dual appropriation which would allow both schools to function independently of one another.[25] In the parliamentary debate which followed, nearly all the participants* appeared to be influenced by Gropius' plea that politicians should not judge artistic matters.[26] The two chief conservative parties, the DVP and the DNVP, joined in opposing the appropriation for the Bauhaus; but their spokesmen claimed that they were doing so on purely financial grounds and expressed their approval of the theoretical aims of the school.[27] The spokesman for the SPD also denied that political motives entered into his party's support of the school and praised the dual appropriation on the ground that "the state must not discriminate between old and new artistic tendencies."[28] Only the speaker for the Independent Socialists indulged in recriminations, accusing the opponents of the appropriation for the Bauhaus of "philistine resentment of the modern world-view."[29] The consensus of the debate was that judgment of the Bauhaus must wait until the school had had time to develop and could display some concrete accomplishments. The double appropriation was passed by a large majority, and the academy resumed its separate functions in March of 1921.[30]

It was not until two years after the original controversy had died down that opposition to the school revived. The occasion was the first major Bauhaus exhibition, in the spring of 1922.[31] This new opposition, which became more vigorous after the second large exhibition in the summer of 1923, did not now center around the fate of the old art academy but instead concentrated upon the work of the school. In contrast to their sympathetic reception in the nation at large, the exhibits were consistently attacked by the bulk of the Thuringian press on aesthetic and philosophical grounds. During 1923 these arguments were taken over by right-wing politicians, and there followed a series of heated debates between right and left in the Landtag over the political and cultural significance of the Bauhaus aesthetic. The artistic accomplishments of the school thus produced a new and even more bitter controversy in

* The parties with a significant representation in the Landtag at this time were as follows: the Unabhängige Sozialistische Partei Deutschlands (USPD), or Independent Socialists; the Socialist Party (SPD); the Deutsche Volkspartei (DVP), or People's Party; and the Deutschnationale Volkspartei (DNVP), or German Nationalist People's Party. The parties of the radical right and left, the Nazis (NSDAP), the National Socialist Freedom Party (NSFP), and the Communist Party (KPD), will be discussed below.

Thuringia, which did not end until the Bauhaus was expelled in 1925.

The Bauhaus exhibitions displayed the mature work of the school for the first time and, in the housing models of 1922 and the exhibition house of 1923, provided the German public with its first view of the much-heralded "new architecture." Both exhibitions were widely advertised in Germany, and the exhibition of 1923 was attended by representatives of most of the major newspapers and periodicals of the country. The exhibits, particularly the crafts and architectural displays, enjoyed great critical success in the national press.[32] Within Thuringia, too, the exhibitions found some support: from Paul Klopfer, who praised the "new spatial conception of the new architecture," and from Bruno Adler, critic for the Socialist paper *Das Volk*.[33] But the reactions of Thuringian observers were predominantly unfavorable. Most of the local criticism of the exhibitions attempted to show that the school was artistically unproductive, thus answering the argument of 1920 that criticism of the school must await a view of its artistic accomplishments. In her reports on the exhibitions, Mathilde von Freytag-Loringhoven derided all the exhibits except those of the crafts workshops; and these, she argued, were inspired not by Gropius, but by Van de Velde's prewar school.[34] A syndicated article entitled "Much Ado about Nothing," which appeared first in the *Jenaische Zeitung* in 1923, alleged that the school's leadership had been forced to display the work of outsiders in order to cover up its failure to educate its students.[35] The exhibition house of 1923 was described as a mere shack thrown up for the occasion, without aesthetic value.[36] These articles were typical of a large body of press reaction which regarded the work shown at the exhibitions as meaningless nonsense.

On the other hand, a few of the school's local critics took seriously the aesthetic qualities of the work displayed but regarded it as symbolic of cultural values which they opposed. Here is to be found, more clearly than in the brief references to "cultural disintegration" and "foreign art" of the 1919–1921 period, the origin of the claim made so frequently by the later opponents of the new architecture, that the modern movement fostered the decay of German culture. One of the more interesting and prophetic of these Thuringian writers was Arthur Buschmann, a Weimar architect, who was probably the first to attempt to explain the new architectural style in racial terms. To Buschmann, the reduced cubic forms of the housing models of 1922 represented "an attempt to return to the primitive art forms of inferior races."[37] Primitive art, he argued, could be beautiful when it was a genuine product of the race; but when sought after by civilized men, it reflected the harmful effects of racial admixture. Buschmann's ideal architecture was neoclassical; its "balance and harmony" represented to him the highest expression of white civilization. In departing from the classical tradition, the Bauhaus buildings were helping to engender cultural "decadence" and racial "disintegration." Thus, Buschmann believed, the work of the Bauhaus represented a symptom of fundamental cultural decline, for "this tendency in art could never occur except in this age of deterioration."

Another important aspect of the attack on the cultural dangers of the new style was the claim that it represented an attempt to mechanize dwelling forms in a way that must end in subjecting men to the machine. This view first appears in the numerous reviews of the 1923 exhibition published by Franz Kaibel, the owner of a small Weimar publishing house, who wrote art criticism for several Thuringian newspapers. Referring to the mechanical equipment installed in the model house and to the nickname of "the dwelling-machine" which had been given it, Kaibel wrote: "when the machine penetrates . . . [the home] it pulverizes the last impulses of the individual personality, my own corner, where I can be 'I'."[38] The results of "mechanized" dwelling, he warned, would be the decline of German culture and the advent of a machine "civilization" without "culture."

There were many influential prewar writers from whom Buschmann could have drawn his racist interpretation of art and Kaibel his warnings about the cultural effects of mechanization. Wagner, his son-in-law Houston Stewart Chamberlain, and Arthur Moeller van den Bruck had popularized the idea that healthy art is rooted in a healthy "race"; Moeller and Julius Langbehn had argued that the prevalence of machine technology would destroy truly creative "culture," supplanting it by a decadent and materialist "civilization." But the phraseology employed by Buschmann and Kaibel and, in Kaibel's case, overt reference to Spengler, suggest that both men derived their terminology from *The Decline of the West*. Spengler published the second volume of his gloomy cultural prophesies in 1922, and his arguments were creating a sensation in the German press just at the time that Thuringian writers were beginning to attack the Bauhaus as an agent of cultural decadence. Thus, although earlier writings such as Moeller's and Langbehn's remained influential, it was probably Spengler's work which did most to color the thinking of those who opposed the new architecture with "cultural" arguments.[39]

The right-wing parties in the Thuringian Landtag began early in 1923 to turn to account the unfavorable press reactions to the

Bauhaus exhibitions. When the government requested in March that the Landtag provide additional funds with which to finance the summer exhibition of the Bauhaus, the right-wing parties — DVP, DNVP, and the agricultural party known as the "Landbund" — opposed the request on the ground that the school had already proved itself "unproductive."[40] Herfurth, now a DNVP deputy, introduced a resolution on behalf of his party requiring the Bauhaus to "enter into a closer relationship with Thuringian culture," which implied that the school must remain an artistic failure unless subordinated to the Weimar art academy.[41] The ensuing debate, during which both Socialists and Communists hurled charges of "philistinism" at the right,[42] ended in a clear-cut political alignment on artistic questions. The school was strongly defended by the SPD, whose spokesman described its work as, potentially at least, a reflection of Socialist ideas. "The Bauhaus is not specifically Socialist," he said, "because there can be no [true] Socialist culture or art until the Socialist economy has been achieved." But in the "period of transition . . . it is the great task of the Bauhaus to give artistic expression to the standardization of production" and to create, "through dwellings or metaphysical building," a community architecture.[43] The DNVP resolution was roundly defeated by a coalition of Socialists, Democrats, and Communists, which at the same time approved the additional appropriation for the next exhibition.

In March the attitude of the right wing in the Landtag was not reflected in any general public outcry against the school in Weimar or Thuringia, but grew out of the specific occasion of the request for supplementary funds. Right-wing political opposition did not begin to present a real threat to the Bauhaus until the fall and winter of 1923, when it had been fortified by critical reactions to the second exhibition, and when the increasing confusion of the political situation in Thuringia encouraged political extremism of all kinds. The summer of 1923, during which the economic distress caused by the inflation reached its height in Germany, had brought increasing political instability to all of southeast and central Germany. In Bavaria the separatist movement gained strength under the encouragement of the right-wing state government and its illegal Freikorps units, which toward the end of the summer began to mass along the northern border between Bavaria and Thuringia. In Saxony the Socialist ministry entered into cooperation with the Communists, and a new ministry formed of both parties encouraged the formation of Communist paramilitary organizations.

Thuringia, sandwiched between the two states, was soon affected by this political polarization.[44] In October Communists entered the Thuringian ministry, and in the following month Thuringia, like Saxony, was occupied by strong Reichswehr units sent by the central government. General Hasse, in charge of the forces in Thuringia, removed the Communists from the ministry and ruled for a time under martial law, keeping his troops in readiness for a possible invasion from the south. The arrival of the Reichswehr was followed by political reaction in Thuringia, which culminated in a decisive right-wing victory in the elections of February 1924. The victors were the so-called "Ordnungsbund" — a coalition of DNVP, DVP, and Landbund — which won a large plurality; and a small group of extreme nationalists and proto-Nazis known as the "völkisch-soziale Block." [45]

In the fall of 1923 the Bauhaus had thus become dependent upon a state government run by Communists as well as Socialists, and during the following months of political tension accusations of revolutionary political activity at the school were renewed in the press for the first time in three years. The *Weimarische Zeitung*, a tabloid which specialized in sensationalism, described the school in December and January as a willing tool of Communist cultural policy. "A seedbed of Communists," the paper's editors called it on one occasion, adding, now that Kandinsky had come to the staff, that these were "in part imported from Russia." [46] At about the same time, an investigation initiated by General Hasse helped to publicize this sort of charge. Acting in response to communications from the school's local opponents, Hasse made a formal search of the Bauhaus premises for revolutionary literature and interrogated Gropius. [47] The investigation, according to a letter of protest by Gropius, made the school suspect before citizens and students. [48]

In the fall, too, the opponents of the school won a new and influential ally in Arno Müller, a Weimar locksmith. Müller held prominent positions in Weimar's Association of Tradesmen, its taxpayers' association, and in Thuringian crafts organizations. The Bauhaus had begun to have some success in selling models of its products to industry, and Müller initiated a series of newspaper attacks on the school which sought to make political capital out of the rather slight competition which the school offered to Thuringian craftsmen. He demanded for Thuringian "Handwerk" the "right of self-determination" in choosing its crafts school and claimed that "everyone in trades and crafts circles desires the dissolution of the Bauhaus." [49] Müller's arguments introduced into the Thuringian debate another basic component of the attack upon the new architecture. When the controversy over the new style developed on a large scale in the national press after 1926, radical architects were often charged with endangering the welfare of the building trades by their "mechanized" architecture.

When the campaign for the Landtag elections began in February of 1924, the local critical reactions to the exhibitions, the attacks of Müller and the *Weimarische Zeitung*, and the political positions taken in the March debate over the supplemental appropriation, led the Ordnungsbund to make opposition to the Bauhaus part of its campaign platform. A political advertisement of February 6 listed the Bauhaus as one of the chief among several instances of "Socialist-Communist" favoritism designed to "crush" local craftsmen and small tradesmen.[50] The advertisement also argued that the government, aided by the Bauhaus, planned to "destroy" the middle classes by attacking individual enterprise and fostering large-scale, "communalized" trades and industry. Thus when the Ordnungsbund won its plurality and a new DVP-DNVP coalition ministry was formed, the public expected that the state government would take immediate action against the Bauhaus.[51]

Herfurth, now a Staatsrat in the government, apparently urged this course, but the political complexion of the Landtag led Richard Leutheusser, the new Minister President, to favor a more cautious attitude toward the school; and most of his party followed him.[52] The general aims of the "völkische" deputies were much more radical than those of the Ordnungsbund, and in order to avoid cooperating with them the government sought the support of the Democrats and moderate Socialists, who, of course, supported the Bauhaus.

By March of 1924 the hesitation of the new government had become clear to the school's local opponents, and they began a further campaign against both the Bauhaus and the government. This campaign, which rapidly gained the backing of the extremists in the Landtag, brought to a climax the "battle over the Bauhaus." The leadership in the final phase of opposition to the school was greatly changed from that of 1920. Many of the earlier academic opponents of the school in Weimar were alarmed at the growing extremism of the attacks on the Bauhaus and cooperated with Gropius in a "Cultural Council," founded in March for the purpose of protecting the arts from political interference.[53] Nor did *Deutschland* any longer play a major part. The sources of the most bitter opposition were instead the writings and activities of Arno Müller and the editorializing of the *Weimarische Zeitung*. Müller wrote a series of protests and petitions against the school, but the most effective of his attacks was the scurrilous pamphlet which came to be known as the Yellow Brochure. The Brochure, published by Müller at the end of March, contained an extraordinary variety of manufactured scandal.[54] It invented speeches by Gropius favoring a Communist government in Thuringia; it listed instances of immoral behavior among students and faculty; it claimed that the faculty kept the number of students small in order to use state funds for their own expenses; and it described cases of insanity among the students caused, it said, by the teaching methods of the school.

The Yellow Brochure furnished Thuringia's less scrupulous journalists with ammunition for the rest of the year. After its publication Schrickel's articles on the Bauhaus consisted almost entirely of paraphrases of its contents, and the attacks of the *Weimarische Zeitung,* often published several times a week, took their tone and much of their information from the pamphlet.[55] The articles in the *Weimarische Zeitung,* of which the following remarks were typical, were composed of lurid generalizations, susceptible of neither disproof nor prosecution:

> The Bauhaus in Weimar has unfortunately taken on a bright political color from the beginning, and in various cases has been a particularly strong supporter of Communism. Yes, certain events and continually reported characteristic manifestations leave no doubt that a Communist center of soviet Russian origin is being built up there. . . . And the consequences of all this which can be seen in the social life of the Bauhaus community!!! . . . We don't need to name individual cases in which [immorality] . . . is publicly celebrated by the students. People must be prevented from sending their sons and daughters there.[56]

While the extremist element in Thuringia concentrated upon this kind of compound of political and moral charges, the claim that the school fostered "cultural" decadence, first developed by Buschmann and Kaibel, reappeared in the writings of a group of somewhat more moderate critics. Significantly this group included a number of writers from outside Thuringia, who began to participate in the spring and summer of 1924 in what had previously been a local debate.

One of the most influential of these outsiders was Konrad Nonn, editor of the Prussian Finance Ministry's architectural journal, the *Zentralblatt der Bauverwaltung.** Nonn became involved in the Thuringian debate by misquoting in the *Zentralblatt* some of Paul Klopfer's more critical remarks about the school. Klopfer protested

---

* Nonn, an engineer rather than an architect, held a government post in the Prussian Building Administration (he was Oberregierungsrat and Baurat). An amateur archaeologist, he also edited *Denkmalpflege und Heimatschutz,* published by the Prussian Ministry of Finance, between 1921 and 1927. He joined the Nazi party in 1930 or 1931 and was reinstated as editor of both the *Zentralblatt* (which he had also left in 1927) and the *Denkmalpflege* in 1934.

in *Deutschland* early in April, and Nonn answered him in the same paper in what proved to be the first of a series of articles against the school. Each of Nonn's articles was in turn answered by members of the Bauhaus staff or by one of the school's supporters; the whole controversy received full coverage in the Thuringian press and influenced the further course of the debate there.[57]

In essence Nonn's arguments combined the claims of the extremists among the school's opponents with those of the more sober critics who had viewed the school's art and architecture as signs of cultural disintegration. Like Buschmann and Kaibel, Nonn called the school culturally destructive: "The cultural importance of the Bauhaus is that there all true constructive culture is perpetually destroyed." Like Dr. Kreubel in 1919, he likened the works of the school to the efforts of Prinzhorn's insane artists and warned that "the members of the school lose contact with the world in a pathological manner ... [and] its art work bears every sign of the deepest spiritual abandon and disintegration." Nonn's writings also recast in a metaphysical vein the Yellow Brochure's slanders about the effects of the school's teaching. "The subjectivism of instruction at the Bauhaus," he wrote, "only releases instincts which lead to chaos.... It cripples the spiritual development of young people and must be prevented from spreading." Nonn did not, in 1924 at least, repeat the extremists' claim that the school was Communist, but pointing to Gropius' work in the Arbeitstrat für Kunst and misquoting one of the Bauhaus publications, he argued that "the Bauhaus was intended from the beginning as a political rather than an artistic force, for it was announced as a gathering place for all those socialists who ... wanted to build the cathedral of socialism."[58]

Nonn's attacks were quoted and paraphrased in *Deutschland*, the *Jenaische Zeitung*, and the *Weimarische Zeitung*, and they influenced the thinking of a new organiaztion formed to combat the Bauhaus.[59] This was the "Union for the Preservation of German Culture in Thuringia," founded in May to counteract the influence of Gropius' Cultural Council and to convince the Ordnungsbund to support the dissolution of the Bauhaus.[60] The group published a series of statements which paraphrased Nonn's denunciations of the educational methods at the Bauhaus, and which returned again and again to the theme of cultural decadence. Typical of the group's views was the formal protest against the continuance of the Bauhaus which it published in July:

The exhibitions and publications of the Bauhaus represent decadent values which the leadership and masters of the Bauhaus inflate theatrically into "art." ... It is presumption to declare that the state sins against culture by withdrawing its support and friendship from this institute. The bloodless and sick art instinct and the empty science . . . which up to now have been supported by the heads of the state and by those of its branches which are responsible for the cultural development of the state, do not maintain and further our culture. They further only decadence.[61]

The renewed attacks upon the school gradually influenced the actions of the Landtag and the government. In the Landtag the "völkische" deputies began to take the initiative against the Bauhaus, adopting the arguments of Müller and the *Weimarische Zeitung*. On the fifteenth of April, the NSFP introduced an interpellation based on the Yellow Brochure and demanded the immediate and complete disestablishment of the school.[62] Herfurth reportedly sided at least in part with the extremists; [63] but the DVP was reluctant to accept evidence from the Yellow Brochure, and Leutheusser, the Minister President, defended the school.[64] Soon after the Landtag reconvened for its summer session, the issue was introduced again by Dinter, the "Nazi" Deputy, who now had the support of the Landbund members as well as the NSFP.[65] Under increasing pressure, Leutheusser referred the question to a budget committee scheduled to meet in October and made the renewal of the contracts of Gropius and his staff, which expired April 1, dependent upon the committee's decision.[66]

When the budget committee met, it was against a background of steadily increasing opposition to the school in the Thuringian press. The committee, sitting during the first two weeks of November, considered petitions received by the government on both sides of the issue, together with the various proposals of its own members.[67] The right-wing members of the committee now agreed on a set of charges against the school, and their accusations represented a catalog of most of the criticisms made against the school since 1919: that it fostered Communist political activity, that it was dominated by "foreigners," that it had failed to carry out its aim of encouraging the crafts, and that it represented tendencies in art which were too extreme to receive state support.[68]

But the right did not yet agree upon what measures should be taken against the Bauhaus. Marschler, representing the NSFP, together with the Landbund deputy, proposed that all funds be immediately withdrawn from the school. The DVP deputy, on the other hand, was willing to accept the proposal of the Socialists and Democrats that the school be maintained at about the same level, with few changes in faculty or curriculum, but he insisted that Gropius be discharged. It was the compromise solution of the DNVP and the government which was finally endorsed by both the committee and the Landtag. As Herfurth described it, state funds for the school would be cut by about sixty percent,[69] and in order to resume a "close connection with Thuringian culture," the Bauhaus would be recombined with the art academy, presumably in a subordinate position. This solution ostensibly left open the question of the continued employment of Gropius and the Bauhaus staff,[70] but did not, obviously, permit the school to function as it had. In December Gropius entered into negotiations with Dessau in Anhalt, and in April of the following year the majority of the Bauhaus' staff and students moved there, taking the name and reputation of the school with them.[71]

The subsequent actions of the Thuringian government showed a moderation which sheds a significant light on the character of the opposition to the Bauhaus in Thuringia. Herfurth's argument that the school should "return to its original objectives" was accepted; the "Bauhaus" which remained in Weimar concentrated on crafts and architectural training, leaving art education, for the most part, to the old academy with which it was now loosely affiliated. But the new director whom the government chose to head both schools was not a local painter or artisan, but the Berlin architect Otto Bartning, who, although older than Gropius, was one of Germany's most radical architects. Bartning, who was later to become a firm adherent of the new style, was known in 1924 for a series of highly original "utopian" projects.[72] He had not, however, been closely associated with the Arbeitsrat für Kunst as Gropius had, nor had his work enjoyed the sponsorship of any political party or government. His reputation in Thuringia was, moreover, one of greater friendliness toward the "crafts" than Gropius had shown. The moderate right in Thuringia was thus satisfied to be rid of Gropius' radical claims to artistic and cultural revolution and to see his emphasis on industrial production moderated; a milder form of architectural innovation was acceptable to them. The minority of extremists were not satisfied, but their views did not prevail until 1930 when a Nazi ministry finally made a much more complete change in the character of the school.

By 1924 the debate over the Bauhaus had made the school and its work known in Germany as nothing else could have done. Nearly every major newspaper in Germany and most of the more popular magazines had carried an account of "the battle over the Bauhaus" and had reprinted the arguments of either the supporters or the critics of the school. For example, Nonn's arguments and the answers of the Bauhaus staff were published not only in professional journals like the *Zentralblatt* and *Deutsche Bauhütte*, but also in the liberal *Kölnische Zeitung* and in *Die Hilfe,* the cultural and political magazine which Friedrich Naumann had founded before the war. The fate of the school became an issue of national importance; to a much greater degree than in 1920, the school received the support of nationally known newspapers, professional organizations, and many of Germany's leading intellectuals. The Werkbund again sent a protest to the Thuringian government,[73] and this time so did the BDA, the national association of German architects.[74] Other petitions in defense of the Bauhaus were signed by men like Gerhart Hauptmann, Albert Einstein, and Theodor Heuss, and by large numbers of German artists and architects; many trade unions and building associations also drew up similar documents.[75]

The great majority of these supporters were chiefly concerned with the fact that artistic questions had been turned into political issues. The *Königsberger Hartungsche Zeitung's* reporter expressed the opinion of most of the liberal and moderate press when he wrote, "Politics must absolutely never be allowed to influence art forms. Artistic values are permanent and must remain independent of changeable politics."[76] The BDA adopted a similar point of view in its petition: "The BDA obviously cannot set itself up as the representative of any particular artistic tendency . . . , but it will always oppose bureaucratic and administrative attacks which hinder the creative process."[77]

But the very extent to which these opinions were reported in the press helped to publicize the fact that the school had become involved in politics. And while many people might deplore this involvement, a significant number of those who took part in the national debate on both sides echoed the local political judgements of the Bauhaus. *Vorwärts,* the national paper of the SPD, called the school "one of the chief accomplishments of Socialist cultural policy in Thuringia."[78] The editors of *Die Rote Fahne,* the organ of the Communist party, after criticizing the school's leadership for being "not political enough," approved the "attempt to build up a new culture" which they felt that the school's exhibitions had shown.[79] They suggested, as the Socialist Landtag Deputy Brill had in 1923, that the school's work would produce a suitable art for proletarian society when that society had been achieved. Few of the nation's politically conservative papers gave much prominence to the debate, but when they did they repeated the political charges of the local extremists. The *Berliner Lokal-Anzeiger,* for example, described the school as "a seedbed of young Communists, recruited from the East."[80]

By 1924, then, a pattern of response to the new architecture had developed in Thuringia which was suggestive for the future. The local opponents of the Bauhaus charged it with Socialist or Communist affiliations because of its dependence on political patronage and its alleged association with large-scale industrial production. They attacked its aesthetic too, as a symptom of cultural decadence, and some of the school's critics linked both types of charges with theories of racial decline. These assertions about the cultural and political symbolism inherent in the work of the Bauhaus very closely foreshadowed the arguments of the Nazis and the conservative architects who supported them. These later arguments developed in a very different context which, however, displayed significant parallels to the Thuringian situation in the early twenties: the existence of a group of disaffected artists and craftsmen; the development of widespread criticism of the political patronage given to modern architecture; and the beginning, at the end of the twenties, of renewed economic discontent and political disorder.

Behind the specific accusations which were made against the new architecture in Weimar there lay a vaguer yet more disquieting sentiment: the fear that iconoclasm in the arts must extend its effects to broader realms of the cultural and social order, disturbing, in the end, all established traditions. A similar but more positive belief in the interrelationship of architecture, society, and culture had formed the basis of Gropius' writings and speeches and was represented in the very structure of the Bauhaus itself. The debate over the Bauhaus brought these issues into national dispute even before the new style in architecture had gained much influence in Germany.

IV / The New Architecture in the Service of Society

Until 1924 the "new society" gave radical architects little opportunity to translate their visions into reality. But after the stabilization of the mark, a phenomenal building boom, paralleled only by that of the early days of the Bismarckian Empire, provided German architects with a great many important commissions. From the beginning of this revival of building the creators of the new style received an extraordinarily large amount of work compared to architects working in a similar vein in other countries. Despite important individual contributions by men like Corbusier in France and Oud in Holland, Weimar Germany became the center of the development of the style which in succeeding decades was to revolutionize architecture in Europe and throughout the world.

During the years 1924–1930, the new architecture gained acceptance in almost every field of building in Germany from private dwellings to factories and churches. But the most important projects executed by the radical architects were almost all part of the public building programs of Weimar Germany's mushrooming cities. Commissions for hospitals, schools, market halls, public baths, stadiums, and above all, public housing projects, were given in some cities exclusively to radical architects, and work of this type everywhere formed the special province of their activity. The unique development of the new style in Germany was thus made possible by public patronage, and its great success was to a considerable extent the product of the new political and social situation which gave rise to the massive public building programs. Gropius and Taut had correctly foreseen the dependence of the revolution in style upon a new political and social policy.

After 1924 nearly every major city in Germany attempted to supply an accumulated demand for schools, hospitals, and other community structures. But the volume of public construction was greatly increased in this period by the building of mass housing developments, often on an enormous scale. This type of project soon came to form the largest proportion of public construction, and it provided radical architects with their most important commissions. Financed by a variety of federal, state, and municipal agencies, the postwar public housing program represented an attempt to relieve the critical housing shortage which the war had created. The migration of rural populations to the industrial cities in response to the expansion of war industries had brought about a new demand for urban housing which could not be satisfied in wartime. In addition a tendency toward early marriages and toward the disintegration of the large family unit had created an increased demand for small dwellings which could not be met at a time when new dwelling construction was at a standstill. Similar problems developed in every major country involved in the war, but they were prolonged and exaggerated in Germany by continued stagnation in building construction during the inflation years. They were aggravated as well by a rigid system of rent controls, enacted between 1917 and 1922, which helped to prevent new construction on private initiative and worked against an equitable distribution of space in already existing dwellings. As a result, the government was forced to assume major responsibility for housing construction; and during the peak years of the building boom, public funds were used in more than seventy per cent of all new dwelling units.[1]

The origins of this housing program may be traced back to March 1918, when the Prussian Landtag, faced with the wartime housing shortage, passed a housing law based on "the right of every citizen to a sound dwelling within his means." The law set up a program of state loans to the cooperative building societies known as "gemeinnützige Baugesellschaften" and required the establishment of regional and municipal supervisory agencies (Wohnungsfürsorgegesellschaften) to oversee the planning and financing of publicly aided dwelling construction. The Prussian machinery for administering state loans was taken over on a federal basis in October of the same year.[2] After the Revolution, the "right to a sound dwelling" was incorporated into the new Constitution and administrative rullings established a set of minimum standards for public housing.[3] The wartime machinery for distributing and administering federal loans was re-established, but the loan funds themselves could not be appropriated during the inflation period.[4]

The housing program of the new Republic therefore did not begin to function until February of 1924, when a controversial new tax of approximately fifteen per cent on rents of previously erected dwellings made large sums available for new dwelling construction. The major part of the tax revenue was lent on very favorable terms to the building societies, whose work in turn was to be guided by the Wohnungsfürsorgegesellschaften or (in municipalities where these were absent) by the municipal building administrations.[5]

The building societies which thus became the major instruments of the new housing policy had originated in the nineties in an effort to alleviate the crowded housing conditions which were the product of hectic industrialization and urban growth in the late nineteenth century. The societies (gemeinnützige Baugenossenschaften and -gesellschaften) were cooperative, limited-profit organizations which attempted to counter the effects of private speculation in land and housing by buying large tracts, often outside the existing urban limits, upon which they built low-cost, high-standard dwellings for sale or rent to their members. The first societies were frequently philanthropic in origin; but before the war, building societies had been formed by nearly every type of professional and laboring group. The building society movement as a whole was not affiliated with any particular party but was rather the property of the small men of every political complexion — white collar workers as well as laborers, minor officials, and even, in a few cases, farm workers.[6] As a result, the federal housing program of the twenties was supported by nearly every major party in Germany, although since it originated under their administration, the Social Democrats claimed it as their own. Only those right-wing parties representing the heavily taxed home owners or frustrated private capital opposed it, and these did so at first only slightly, for the severity of the housing shortage clearly called for a severe antidote.[7]

In fostering the growth of the building society movement, the federal housing program indirectly favored the growth of municipal influence in public housing. Municipal building administrations of course had to work closely with the building soceties on questions of land purchase and general planning, but in addition many cities won almost complete control over their local building societies by buying shares in them or by founding their own.[8] In such cases it was the municipal administrations which took the initiative in matters of design. Faced with the problem of solving the housing shortage through a mass housing program which would avoid the prewar evils of overcrowding, the municipal authorities and the newly strengthened building societies often turned to the men who offered new solutions in housing design and called radical architects into positions of principal responsibility.

Celle, near Hannover, was the first German city to employ a radical architect to design its public housing. Otto Haesler's tiny and bizarre "Siedlung Italienischer Garten," described in Chapter II (fig. 45), represented an important milestone in the development of the new architecture, and his later buildings for the town were nearly as influential. These included a series of larger housing projects, a new school, and a few smaller municipal buildings which, with their austere cubic forms, were extremely novel in appearance. In his housing developments, moreover, Haesler introduced an important new type of site planning. Instead of the old urban apartment block constructed around an interior court, Haesler's "Siedlung Georgsgarten" of 1924 (figs. 49 and 50) contained rows of buildings arranged at right angles to the street.[9] This "finger plan," which provided all rooms with a maximum of light and air, came to predominate in the designs of radical architects after 1924[10] and was a distinctive characteristic of their work.

But the first city to begin a really large-scale public building program was Frankfurt am Main, and it remained the only city in Germany where every type of municipal construction was directed and designed by radical architects. Frankfurt's long tradition of comprehensive city planning and housing reform had already prepared public opinion for such a program before the war. Some of the earliest and most progressive of the building societies were located there,[11] while under the prewar administration of Mayor Adikes the city had enacted sweeping condemnation and eviction laws which permitted it to acquire large tracts of land for parks and housing developments.[12] This prewar program was revived in 1924 when the City Assembly chose as its new mayor Ludwig Landmann,* a former Assemblyman and since 1917 an active advocate of large-scale planning.[13] Landmann in turn hired Ernst May, an architect wholly sympathetic to the new style, as director of all municipal construction; for the next six years he gave May's work his full support, overriding whatever opposition May encountered. Landmann explained his view of May's task in the following words, echoing the thinking of Gropius and Taut: "Our new era must create new forms for both its inner and its outer life . . . and this new style must find its first concrete expression in city planning and in housing."[14]

May's office, that of "Dezernent für Bauwesen," was especially created for him, and it gave him unprecedented powers. He was to have general supervision of all municipal building projects, and he was entrusted with the preparation of a general plan which would control and direct the city's future expansion.[15] He and his staff were to design all new public housing, and May was made head of the city's largest building society, now largely owned by the municipality.[16] His powers also allowed him and his staff to perform a number of important subsidiary functions connected with the

* Landmann, himself a Democrat, was supported in the Assembly by the Socialist, Democratic, and Center parties.

49. Otto Haesler, Siedlung Georgsgarten, Celle.   50. Siedlung Georgsgarten.

housing program. Through May's office, for example, went all applications for municipal and federal building loans; and by approving or rejecting the plans thus submitted, May's staff was able to exert influence upon the character of housing which was only partially financed with public funds. In addition, May had full authority over the building code officials (Baupolizei), who in many cities obstructed structural and even stylistic experimentation.[17] Also under his jurisdiction in this capacity were signs of all sorts — from store signs to bill boards — and his office drew up models for such advertising which merchants were expected to follow.[18]

The recipient of these unique powers was a powerful personality in his own right, who shared and even extended Landmann's view of the comprehensive nature of his task. Between 1919 and 1925 May had done progressive work as a designer and administrator for a government agency which built public housing in Silesia, and before 1919 he had worked with Raymond Unwin in England, becoming, under Unwin's influence, an advocate of the garden city movement.[19] Prior to 1925 he had not employed the forms of the new style in his work; but when he came to Frankfurt he began to take over and develop the work of Haesler, Gropius, and Taut, believing the new style to be more appropriate to the job ahead.[20] He thought of himself as helping to create "the new Frankfurt," and between 1926 and 1930 he published a magazine under that name which sought to demonstrate that the new style in architecture and planning was the appropriate expression of "a new and definitive metropolitan culture."[21] Like Taut, however, May emphasized "the

51. Siedlung Bruchfeldstrasse, Frankfurt, street.

new dwelling" as an expression of the new culture;[22] and, of course, his most significant work in Frankfurt was in the city's public housing.

May's first housing projects in Frankfurt were two relatively small developments: "Bruchfeldstrasse," on the southwestern out- skirts of the city; and "Hohenblick," at its northern extremity. The apartment buildings of the Bruchfeldstrasse (figs. 51 and 52) were begun first, and their appearance announced uncompromisingly the radical nature of May's break with traditional forms. Flat-roofed and bare-surfaced, the buildings were distinguished by the zigzag massing along the street, an unusual abstract window pattern, and horizontal bands of contrasting colors. The overall effect of the Siedlung was as exotic as Haesler's Italienischer Garten, from which May presumably derived the idea of painting a pattern on the stucco. The buildings were unusually low for urban apartment

52. Siedlung Bruchfeldstrasse, court.

buildings and were given something of a suburban setting by the provision of extensive gardens at the back, a practice which was to be typical of May's housing. Unlike Haesler, however, May arranged the buildings along the street, around a large U-shaped court, a plan which he never wholly abandoned. The small project was given a focus by the introduction of a community center at the head of the interior court, again a typical feature of May's work (fig. 53). Siedlung Hohenblick, which was begun a little later (fig. 54), was somewhat less startling in appearance, though it was given a strained and distinctive surface pattern through the irregular placing of its small windows. It consisted mainly of row housing, to which May gave preference from then on.

In locating Hohenblick and Bruchfeldstrasse in the outskirts of the city, May showed from the start a desire to create suburban residential communities. The general plan for the city's expansion which he drew up in 1926 showed a series of rings of such new communities around the old city, separated from it and from each other by broad stretches of parks and cultivated fields.[23] This conception was never realized on the scale in which it was conceived,

53. Community Center, Siedlung Bruchfeldstrasse.

54. Siedlung Hohenblick, Frankfurt.

55. Siedlung Römerstadt, View from the Nidda Valley.

for although most of May's Siedlungen were located in or next to open land owned by the city, many of them were relatively small and cut off from one another by other built-up areas. But one section of the outer ring of May's plan was completed before 1933, along the Nidda valley about five miles to the northwest of the city center. For this area May and his staff designed three large contiguous housing developments — "Praunheim," "Römerstadt," and "Westhausen" — which contained in all nearly 4,000 dwelling units. Together the three Siedlungen formed an independent new community, and they contained much of May's best work.

The three developments were stretched out in a long curve along the northwest bend of the little river; Römerstadt, at the northern end of the arc, looked back toward the city over a broad tract of open land (fig. 55). The planning of the projects was surburban in character with low-density land use. Each project contained a number of apartment buildings built along the main boulevard which connected them, but most of the units were widely spaced row houses, set away from the street and separated at the back by large gardens (figs. 56 and 57). All three developments were provided with shops, and Römerstadt and Praunheim contained schools and restaurants as well (fig. 58).

56. Siedlung Römerstadt, Row Housing.

57. Siedlung Römerstadt, Row Housing.

58. Siedlung Praunheim, Restaurant.

In designing the exteriors of these projects May employed all the varied vernaculars of the new architecture in their most radical forms. The horizontal curves of an apartment house following a sweeping bend in the main boulevard formed one focal point at Römerstadt (fig. 59), while across the street the vertical forms of the projecting stair halls of the four-story apartment buildings formed a marching pattern on otherwise almost blank facades (fig. 60). The apartment buildings at Praunheim, on the other hand, had long horizontal bands of balconies balanced asymmetrically against the vertical terminals formed by the stair towers. At Praunheim the upper third of the facades of many of the row houses had no windows, which gave the buildings a distinctive, top-heavy appearance, and a kind of horizontal unity. The various rows and blocks of buildings were either white or painted in bright colors — rust, bright blue, black, yellow, and green. All had, of course, flat roofs and flat surfaces. The overall effect was gay, bizarre, and radically different from all of Frankfurt's older architecture. The new community looked indeed like a "new Frankfurt."

The dwellings themselves set a new standard in compact planning and the use of mechanical conveniences in mass housing. They were centrally heated, and some of the apartment houses contained public washing machines and other laundry facilities. Each dwelling was equipped with a modern bath, then a very novel feature in low-income apartment housing, and each was provided with a standardized, built-in unit of modern kitchen equipment, which came to be known as the "Frankfurter Küche." The cost of installing these conveniences in low-cost housing and the added expenses incurred by the liberal use of land forced May and his staff to seek economical methods of construction and interior planning. The floor area of the dwelling was kept to a minimum;[24] pullman kitchens, built-in furniture, and even folding beds were therefore employed to save space. This attention to careful planning of interior space led May's office to an important departure from traditional dwelling design. Previously, small apartments had been divided up into a number of cubicles of equal size and more or less indeterminate purpose, including a "Wohnküche" or substantial kitchen which acted as a living room as well, and two or three other rooms which might serve as either bedrooms or parlor. May's new design, employed first at Praunheim, was less adaptable but

59. Siedlung Römerstadt, Apartment Building.

60. Siedlung Römerstadt, Apartment Building.

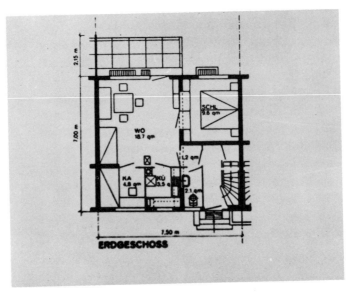

61. Siedlung Westhausen, Frankfurt, plan.

gave an effect of greater spaciousness and openness: it alloted the largest amount of space in the unit to a living-room-dining-room, to which were adjoined the kitchen alcove and minimum-size bedrooms (fig. 61). As a result family activities were necessarily concentrated in the living room, and this feature of housing in the new style gave rise to much criticism among its opponents.[25]

In a further effort at economy, May encouraged the standardization of building parts and the use of new kinds of machinery in building construction. For Hohenblick and Praunheim he and his staff also devised a revolutionary type of pre-cast concrete slab construction which, far in advance of its time, encountered difficulties in execution but received a great deal of favorable publicity and came to be known as the "May system."

The Nidda valley development remained the most impressive of May's housing projects in Frankfurt, but the developments "Bornheimer Hang," "Hellerhof," and "Heimat," with close to 1,000 dwellings each, were also constructed as independent communities located on the outskirts of the city. Twelve smaller projects were also built under May's direction; the entire program, when completed, contained 15,000 dwellings, more than ninety per cent of all new housing built in Frankfurt between 1925 and 1933.[26] All but the smallest of these housing projects contained churches, schools, and other community facilities, and these formed the largest proportion of Frankfurt's municipal building aside from housing.

May's unique building program owed its success not only to the support of Mayor Landmann's administration but also to the enthusiasm with which it was received by the public at large. Frankfurt's liberal press usually greeted his work very favorably and only occasionally treated it with gentle satire, while the right-wing papers criticized him very mildly and intermittently.[27] The residents of his housing developments, when interviewed by local papers, generally indicated satisfaction with the planning and design of their housing.[28] Even among the building trades, where there frequently was resentment at the introduction of new methods of construction, May found substantial support.[29] On only two occasions, when he attempted to extend his influence to such nonarchitectural matters as the design of the city emblem and the design and quality of gravestones and graveyard decorations, was he widely criticized.[30] As a political appointee and a member of the administration May was opposed by the opposition parties, and on one occasion the DNVP even went so far as to describe not only the man but also his work as "Socialist."[31] But this type of criticism did not reflect any significant popular opposition as it had in Weimar. When in 1930 May accepted the Soviet government's invitation to plan new cities in Siberia and left for Moscow with part of his staff, nearly every paper in Frankfurt praised his work and regretted his departure.* The members of his staff who remained carried on his work even in the face of the depression, virtually unhampered by either public or political interference until the national victory of the Nazi party in 1933.

Housing in the new style was also constructed on a massive scale in Berlin, where more than 14,000 dwelling units were built by radical architects between 1924 and 1933.[32] Since 1918 the city had been one of the principal centers of new tendencies in architecture. Most of the constructed works of the early twenties were located there; and there the progressive art galleries of Paul Cassirer, the Graphisches Kabinett, Der Sturm, and the Juryfreie had from the first exhibited the newest projects and acted as centers for discussion. As the new architecture developed after 1922, it found en-

---

* Bruno Taut and a number of other German architects followed May to Russia. Discouraged by the beginning of the depression at home and encouraged by such writings as El Lissitzky's *Russland: Die Rekonstruktion der Architektur in der Sowjetunion* (Vienna, 1930), these men hoped to obtain large-scale planning commissions from the Soviet government. They were, of course, bitterly disappointed. The Soviet government had already begun to discourage modern work among Russian artists and architects, and although willing to commission large planning efforts, lacked the resources to carry them out. When they arrived the German architects met systematic bureaucratic obstructionism and eventually official disapproval of the style of their work (see especially Rudolf Wolters, *Spezialist in Sibirien*, Berlin, 1933). But by the time they decided to return to Germany, the Nazis had taken power, and many were denied re-entry permits. Some of the German architects in Russia became stateless persons as a result.

thusiastic and wealthy private patrons in Berlin, and a number of
the new style's most imposing individual buildings were built
there.[33] But until the late twenties, the conservative views of Prussian officialdom prevailed in the central building administration of
the city. The impetus toward the use of the new style in public
building thus came not from the city officials in Berlin but from the
building societies themselves and particularly from one of the largest of them.[34] This was the "Gehag," or Gemeinnützige Heimstätten-
Aktiengesellschaft, which was responsible for more than seventy
per cent of the housing built in the new style in Berlin.*

The Gehag was founded in 1924 as a merger of several older
building societies, with additional capital from the Berlin trade
unions and the Berlin Wohnungsfürsorgegesellschaft. Its leading
spirit was Martin Wagner, director of one of the subsections of the
municipal building administration in Berlin-Schöneberg and a pio-
neer in the development of economical methods of building construction.[35] Wagner was dissatisfied with Berlin's progress in low-
cost public housing, and he envisioned a union of all Berlin's
building societies in order to construct efficiently very large-scale
housing developments. Although he was himself a member of the
SPD and deeply involved in a movement for a kind of guild socialism in the building trades, Wagner did not intend that the Gehag
should have a political orientation. He was able, however, to enlist
only a few building societies; the majority of the Gehag's capital
came from the Socialist trade unions and Wagner's own socialized
building trades movement, and most of its officials were Socialists.
At Wagner's request, the society hired Bruno Taut in 1924, and its
entire housing program was carried on under his direction until
1933, when he, like May, went to Russia to plan new cities.

Gehag's construction was concentrated in a few very large projects, including Taut's and Wagner's "horseshoe" development in
Berlin-Britz, begun in 1925 (fig. 62), and the "forest" development
in Berlin-Zehlendorf, begun by Taut in 1926 (fig. 63), each of which
contained several thousand units when completed. Like May's,
these projects were located in outlying suburbs of the city; and
although Berlin land prices ruled out any extensive use of row
housing, the developments were conceived as garden suburbs, con-

---

* The best available information on the Gehag is in *Gehag: Gemeinnützige Heim-
Stätten-Aktiengesellschaft 1924–1957* (Berlin, 1957), since most of the organization's
records were confiscated and destroyed after the war by the East German government. One German building society also located in Berlin was as large as the Gehag:
the "Gagfah" or Gemeinnützige Aktiengesellschaft für Angestellten-Heimstätten,
which consistently built in a conservative style and often employed such prominent
prewar housing designers as Schmitthenner and Tessenow. See *16000 Wohnungen
für Angestellte* (Berlin, 1928).

62. Hufeisen Siedlung, Berlin-Britz, aerial view.

63. Waldsiedlung, Berlin-Zehlendorf, aerial view.

64. Waldsiedlung.

taining three-story apartment buildings with lawns and gardens between.[36] Constructed on exceptionally wide streets and boulevards, with carefully arranged major spaces, the developments managed to be both urban and parklike.[37] Many of the individual building designs were among the finest executed by modern architects, who under Taut's direction avoided the blank, strained facades which characterized much of May's work in Frankfurt (figs. 64 and 65). But although every effort was made to achieve variety in de-

65. Waldsiedlung.

66. Hufeisen Siedlung.

67. Hufeisen Siedlung.

sign and site planning, the rows of large apartment blocks produced an impression of massiveness and repetitiveness unavoidable in projects of this size (figs. 66 and 67).

The same novel amenities were provided in the Gehag developments as in May's housing, and there resulted a similar necessity for economy and efficiency in construction and planning. The dwellings were kept small, although they were, for the most part, slightly larger than Frankfurt's.[38] A number of standard apartment plans, such as those shown in figures 68 and 69, were designed for each development by a special planning staff under Taut's direction in order to cut construction costs by constant repetition of the same unit.[39] Like May, Wagner was active in devising more economical methods of construction; and the Gehag usually employed the socialized building guilds, which had adopted his methods.

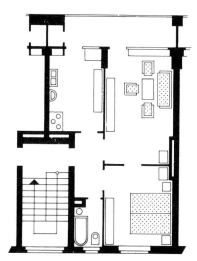

68. Bruno Taut, Hufeisen Siedlung, Standard Plan.

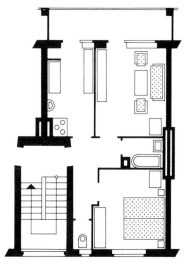

69. Bruno Taut, Waldsiedlung, Standard Plan.

70. Walter Gropius, Siemensstadt, Berlin, Apartment Buildings.

71. Siemensstadt.

Beginning in 1927, others of Berlin's numerous building societies began to follow the example of the Gehag. Between 1928 and 1932, for example, several major societies cooperated in the construction of the Reinickendorf development, located in Wittenau, which contained over 1,000 dwellings. It was designed by hitherto rather conservative architects,[40] who now modeled their housing on the work of Taut and Wagner. The other major Berlin project of this period was the "Siemensstadt," begun in 1929 by the building society which had been set up in 1914 by the Siemens combine to build housing for its workers. Siemens invited some of Germany's most original and best known architects to participate, among them Häring, Scharoun, Bartning, and Gropius. The refined designs they produced summarized the architectural achievement of the decade, and became world famous (figs. 70 and 71).

Through the work of the Gehag, the new style eventually gained some influence in Berlin's municipal architecture as well. Wagner, now well known for his housing, was made director of the central building administration in 1927 and attempted to initiate a program of municipal construction and planning similar to May's, whose work he admired and whose power he envied. He succeeded only in part. Under Wagner's influence, the new style began to be employed in the design of many new schools and hospitals and in some municipal administration buildings (fig. 72).[41] He also exerted an indirect influence on the work of the building societies, although unlike Frankfurt's, Berlin's societies remained financially independent of the municipal administration. Like May, he drew up plans for the expansion of Berlin's suburbs; but although these received a great deal of publicity, they did not have much influence on actual construction.[42] Several of the many new public buildings which he planned were executed, however, including the well-known Wannsee baths, consisting of swimming and recreational facilities stretching for a quarter mile along a bend in the Havel; and two exhibition buildings, part of a large project for a new fair grounds

72. Police Administration Building, Berlin.

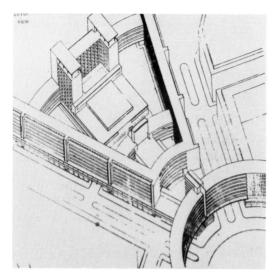

73. Erich Mendelsohn, Project for the Rebuilding the Alexanderplatz, Berlin. Designed under the administration of Martin Wagner.

74. Erich Mendelsohn, Columbus House, Berlin. Part of the planned reconstruction of the Potsdamer Platz.

adjacent to the Funkturm in Witzleben. Wagner also planned the enlargement and reconstruction of a number of Berlin's public squares, and the rebuilding of parts of the Alexanderplatz and the Potsdamerplatz were completed under his administration (figs. 73 and 74). Wagner publicized both the accomplishments and the projects of his administration in a series of pamphlets and public exhibitions, and like May he began to issue a magazine (*The New Berlin*) in which the new architecture was represented as a part of a new era in the city's culture.[43] The architectural contents of *The New Berlin* consisted primarily of unrealized but far-reaching projects, indicative of the character of Wagner's administration.

But if Wagner did not accomplish the kind of unified building program which May achieved, his failure was due to the very size of the city and the complexity of its administration rather than to the presence of organized opposition. Like May, Wagner could count on an enthusiastic reception in the liberal and left-wing press; and although the Hugenberg papers* liked to call him "the red Stadtbaurat," they too frequently applauded his work.[44] His

*Alfred Hugenberg, leader of the Deutschnationale Volkspartei, owned several Berlin newspapers and a chain of movie theaters.

75. Hugo Häring, Project for the Reconstruction of the Ministergarten, Berlin. Designed under the administration of Martin Wagner.

plan to cut a street through the historic "Ministergarten" (fig. 75) foundered on the opposition of leading citizens;[45] but when the residents of Zehlendorf objected to the flat roofs and urban character of the massive forest development, he overruled them with ease, confident of the ultimate support of public opinion.[46] Wagner's party membership and the Socialist character of the Gehag drew personal attacks on him from the national DNVP;[47] but within Berlin itself he encountered no significant political opposition, and he continued in office until 1933.

As centers of the construction of public housing in the new style, Frankfurt and Berlin remained isolated until after 1927. The main goals of May's and Wagner's programs, the construction of small, low-cost dwellings in a suburban setting, were shared equally by almost all the building societies and municipal building administrations of Germany; but until after 1927 the great majority of these organizations preferred to build in a more traditional style. The apartment blocks which they constructed were perhaps less heavily ornamental and simpler in outline than was usual before the war, but their massive hip roofs and vertical casement windows, often with shutters, gave them a thoroughly traditional appearance (fig. 76). These apartment buildings were often constructed around a large, planted interior court, after the manner of the best efforts of the prewar years, but they also often used the finger plan which the modern school employed in most of its projects.

In addition to the large apartment blocks, conservative architects also sought to build row, semidetached, and even fully-detached houses wherever possible. This was done even in very large cities, such as Düsseldorf, and the designers made every effort to give the dwellings a period appearance with high tile roofs,

76. Apartment Block, Münster, 1925–1927.

77. Single-family dwellings, Düsseldorf, 1925–1927.

78. Multi-family Dwellings, Dresden, c. 1925.

shutters, and occasionally even medieval or baroque detailing (figs. 77 and 78). To increase the traditional effect, houses were often grouped around a square or village green (fig. 79), and these designs as a whole represented a strong effort to give a village or small-town appearance to suburban developments in large and medium size cities. Such projects were in most cases relatively small, for they were usually the product of a municipal policy which favored the construction of many small developments rather than a few large ones. As more and more municipalities began to build large-scale mass housing projects, they also began to adopt the planning and design of radical architects.

79. Row Housing, Hannover.

The growing success of the new style in public housing was aided in 1927 and the years following by the publicity which attended a few small experimental projects which, either through the originality of their design or the prominence of their designers, exerted a great deal of influence upon the development of modern architecture in Germany. First among these was the set of buildings designed by Gropius and his staff for Dessau in 1926 and 1927. Dessau's Democratic mayor, Fritz Hesse, and the other liberal and Socialist officials of Dessau and Anhalt gave the school the kind of loyal support which May received from Landmann in Frankfurt, overriding a few scattered attempts at local opposition and providing the school with the architectual commissions it had sought but failed to receive in Thuringia.[48] These included the famous school buildings themselves (figs. 19–21), whose asymmetrically balanced masses and surface patterns profoundly influenced the entire development of the new style after 1926; an employment office (fig. 80); and a small housing project in Törten, a suburb of Dessau, com-

80. Walter Gropius, City Employment Office, Dessau.

81. Walter Gropius, Siedlung Törten, Dessau.

pleted in 1927 (figs. 81 and 82). In the latter, Gropius employed a slab construction similar to that devised by May and experimented with new building materials. Owing to the refinement of the design and the fame already attaching to the school, these innovations received even more notice in the press and professional journals than similar contemporary work in Frankfurt and Berlin.[49]

In 1928, believing the school to be firmly established at Dessau, Gropius left the Bauhaus and returned to private practice in Berlin. He was succeeded by Hannes Meyer, whose brief term of office was politically turbulent and marked by dissention among both faculty and students, and then by Ludwig Mies van der Rohe, who led the school during the first years of the depression. Gropius himself continued to play a leading part in architectural design, particularly in his housing developments at Siemensstadt (figs. 70 and 71), Karlsruhe, and Spandau. But the seminal role of the Bauhaus in German architectural development ended with his departure in 1928.

Perhaps even more important than Gropius' Dessau buildings in popularizing the new syle in housing was the Stuttgart "Weissen-

82. Siedlung Törten, Detail.

83. Weissenhof Siedlung, Stuttgart.

hof Siedlung," a group of single-family residences, row houses, and an apartment building, constructed by the Werkbund in 1927 (fig. 83). The Siedlung, which was open to the public between July and October of 1927, was intended as a public exhibition of the various forms of "the new dwelling." Under the general direction of Mies van der Rohe, the most prominent modern architects of Europe — among them Oud, Corbusier, Gropius, and Taut — produced a set of highly original designs which Mies introduced to the public in his opening speech as "part of the great struggle for a new way of life."[50] Some of the buildings became internationally famous and influenced not merely housing but every type of architecture. Both Corbusier's cubic house (fig. 84), supported off the ground by stilts and almost completely open on the inside, and Mies's apartment

84. Corbusier, House at Weissenhof Siedlung.

85. Ludwig Mies van der Rohe, Apartment Building, Weissenhof
Siedlung.

building (fig. 85), with nearly continuous horizontal bands of windows and capped with floating planes, were among the designs
which exerted a dramatic impact upon the architectural development of other countries. All of the buildings at Weissenhof were
expensively built and furnished and had little direct relevance to
the problems of constructing mass housing, but the exceptional
quality of the designs helped to gain acceptance for the new forms
among both architects and laymen. The exhibition, which also included a separate exhibition hall containing photographs and plans
of modern housing, furniture, and mechanical equipment,[51] was
enormously popular and widely publicized. As many as 20,000
visitors a day came to see what "the new dwelling" looked like,[52]
and the buildings and the claims of their designers were discussed
at length in both the national and the international press.[53] The
great publicity which the exhibition received helped to identify
the new style with housing in the public mind and to create the belief that the new housing had broad cultural significance.

Both the Weissenhof Siedlung and Gropius' project in Dessau
received part of their funds from a new federal agency set up by
the Labor Ministry and the Reichstag in order to support experiments in economical methods of building mass housing. The
"RFG," or Reichsforschungsgesellschaft für Wirtschaftlichkeit im
Bau- und Wohnungswesen, founded in June 1927 with an appropria-

tion of ten million RM, was not intended to support any particular style in housing design; but since radical architects were the chief experimenters in this field, most of the money which the RFG spent between 1927 and 1931 was channeled into their projects.[54] These included, in addition to the Weissenhof and Dessau Siedlungen, May's Praunheim project and a large "satellite city" planned for Spandau, which was begun in 1930 but never completed. The RFG also published and distributed among the profession extensive reports on all these projects, and included in them not only discussions of construction and planning but also extracts from the writings of Gropius, Mies, and others on the social and cultural significance of the new style.[55]

In 1927 the housing designs of radical architects had thus begun to receive very wide publicity; and increasingly after that date the examples of Celle, Frankfurt, and Berlin were followed by other cities. In Magdeburg, Stadtbaurat Johannes Göderitz and his staff completed 2,000 dwelling units in 1927 and 1928 (fig. 86); Cologne

86. Siedlung Gross-Diesdorferstrasse, Magdeburg.

87. Wilhelm Riphahn, Siedlung Kalkerfeld, Cologne.

constructed two large modern developments totaling more than 4,000 units (fig. 87). A number of smaller cities like Altona and Duisburg built nearly all their new housing in the new style after 1927.[56] Finally, several individual large projects bearing a close resemblance to Taut's and May's work were constructed in Breslau, Hamburg, and Düsseldorf before 1930. Many additional projects were constructed even after the onset of the depression, so that by 1932 public housing developments in radical styles had been begun in the majority of Germany's larger cities.[57]

In the secondary centers of its development, the new style encountered even less opposition than in Frankfurt or Berlin. In Magdeburg, Taut had of course experienced some local resistance to his plans for repainting much of the city; but Göderitz, under whose administration most of the municipal construction was actually carried out, was warmly supported by the public.[58] And in those cities like Düsseldorf, Celle, and Cologne where most of the municipal projects in the new style were designed not by members of the municipal building administration but by private architects, the new style encountered no substantial public opposition.[59]

Despite its novel and often bizarre appearance, the new architecture thus gained acceptance in public housing and other municipal architecture in Germany with extraordinary ease. It did not encounter the kind of local political and popular opposition which had forced the Bauhaus out of Weimar and it was increasingly sponsored by public officials of nearly every political persuasion who approved of radical architects' economical building methods and high standards of comfort and convenience or who, like Landmann, supported their broader cultural claims. Yet the very form of its success — in mass housing and through public patronage — laid the basis for the involvement of the new architecture in further debate over its social and political significance.

V / The Debate over the New Architecture

The radical architects owed their success in Germany in the later twenties not only to the patronage of the federal and municipal governments but also to the energy with which they continued to publicize their work and their ideas. Through a constant stream of books, pamphlets, articles, and speeches they impressed their views on the profession and on the public with the result that, although buildings in the new style represented only a minority of total construction in Germany in the twenties, both the general press and the architectural journals soon concentrated an exceptional amount of attention on the new architecture. Public discussion of the work and claims of modern architects thus became fashionable and won the radical architects further popularity. At the same time, the great extent of the publicity which the new style received helped to keep alive the issues raised in the Bauhaus controversy and to gain a public hearing for the opponents of the new architecture. By 1930 public debate between the supporters and the opponents of the new style had reached very considerable proportions. As a result, the Nazi party began to recognize the political value of the controversy and to give architecture a major role in its propaganda.

In their efforts to publicize the new style, the radical architects continued to be led by Gropius and Taut. Each published two profusely illustrated books and a large number of articles between 1924 and 1930, and Gropius also founded and edited the magazine *Bauhaus* in 1926.[1] But these efforts were now supplemented by those of many other architects: by Wagner and May, whose *Wohnungswirtschaft, Das neue Berlin,* and *Das neue Frankfurt* contained articles of general interest and had a wide circulation; by Adolf Behne, Gropius' early associate in the Arbeitsrat für Kunst; and by Ludwig Hilberseimer, teacher of architecture at the Bauhaus from 1928.[2] Mies, Mendelsohn, and Hugo Häring also contributed their share of articles both to professional journals and to the daily press. These attempts to popularize the new style were greatly aided by the Werkbund, which lost the diversified character it had

had before the war and identified itself almost exclusively with the new architecture. In addition to its series of major exhibitions on the new style, the Werkbund also published *Die Form*, an influential periodical devoted to the work of radical architects.[3] Like *Das neue Frankfurt* (fig. 88) and *Das neue Berlin*, *Die Form* employed a lavish and attractive format with the Bauhaus typography and included articles on every aspect of architecture, the arts, and the crafts.

In order to strengthen their position within the profession, Grop-

88. *Das neue Frankfurt*, April/May, 1930, cover.

ius, May, Taut, Wagner, and about twenty more leading modern architects formed their own organization in 1926, calling themselves "Der Ring." The members published joint statements in the professional journals, held their own exhibitions, and voted together in the National Association of German Architects (BDA), tactics which helped to secure Gropius' election to the directorate of that important organization in 1927.[4] In 1928 the members of the Ring joined with their colleagues in England, France, and Italy to form the "International Congresses for Modern Architecture" (CIAM), which helped by exhibitions and publications to gain further influence for the new style among architects both in Germany and abroad (and remains today an extremely influential body).[5] The work of these organizations was aided by the attention and support which radical architects received from the nation's professional journals. *Wasmuths Monatshefte, Moderne Bauformen,* and *Bauwelt,* the most influential architectural periodicals in Germany, began as early as 1926 to devote their issues almost exclusively to the new architecture; and from 1928 even the relatively conservative *Deutsche Bauzeitung* and *Zentralblatt der Bauverwaltung* concentrated upon the new style.

From the time of the Bauhaus controversy and the erection of the first model house in Weimar, the work of Gropius and his school had been widely discussed in the press and popular journals by writers on the arts. But after 1926 the construction of the striking new housing developments and other projects, combined with the writings and exhibitions of the Ring architects and the Werkbund, produced an even greater amount of critical and popular writing on the new style. Thus, despite its recent origin, the new architecture was judged important enough in 1927 to merit a full volume in the "Propyläen Kunstgeschichte," a series of scholarly histories of world art and architecture; and in 1929 the Langewiesche Press issued three of its popular "Blauen Bücher" art handbooks on "Modern German Architecture."[6] The art critics of the daily press commented at length on every new book or exhibition which dealt with the new style; and the columnists of the semi-popular journals, like *Der Cicerone, Die Hilfe,* and *Die Glocke,* discussed the social and cultural significance of the new buildings.[7] The new style was a popular subject in the Sunday supplements and in the women's magazines, which frequently illustrated the Bauhaus buildings and the new housing projects and commented upon the virtues of "the new dwelling."[8] In the later twenties, radical architects were in great demand as speakers for civic organizations and women's clubs, and at the beginning of 1930 they conducted a series of six programs on the national radio network.[9]

Through this publicity, the new style came to be vividly associated with a public image of a "new era" or a "new Germany." The satirical magazine *Uhu*, describing the vocabulary needed by "modern" men, listed "Bauhaus style" among the terms characteristic of the "new era." Under the heading "Only Ten Years — Another World," the *Münchner Illustrierte Presse* published pictures of modern architecture along with motorcyclists and outdoor sports.[10] A collection of essays entitled *The New Germany* included sections on the new style among other descriptions of the work of the new "peace-loving" Republic.[11] By 1930 the new style was widely regarded as a kind of national accomplishment: in its travel guides the national railroad urged foreign tourists to visit the Bauhaus buildings, and when radical architects held exhibitions abroad the German press hailed their work as a national triumph for German culture.[12]

In the face of the remarkable publicity which the work of the Ring architects received, most German architects remained attached to more conservative, if in many cases quite progressive, styles and avoided public debate. But around the middle of the decade a few architects who did not accept the new style responded to the Ring architects' proselytizing with aggressive tactics of their own. Among the most effective of these active opponents of the Ring architects were Konrad Nonn, influential editor of the *Zentralblatt der Bauverwaltung* and the first architect of national repute to attack the work of the Bauhaus; Paul Schultze-Naumburg, the famous designer of elaborate country mansions during the prewar era; and Emil Högg, professor at Dresden's Technische Hochschule. They disputed the claims of radical architects in the professional journals and countered the stream of publicity supporting the new style with a series of books and newspaper articles of their own. These men did not attack the broader development of modern architecture in Germany, which they admired as a creative continuation of the historicist tradition; rather they sought to undermine the Ring architects' claim to predominance within this modern movement. Nonn, Högg, and Schultze-Naumburg gradually recruited to their ranks a considerable number of important conservative architects, and during the years 1925–1930 this group waged ever more bitter war upon the authors of the new style. While they began by criticizing the new buildings on practical grounds, they rapidly progressed to a condemnation of the new style in the language of the Bauhaus controversy and described the new architecture as the product of an "un-German" culture, a proletarian social policy, and a "bolshevist" political program. In response to the popular association of the new style with a "new era," they erected their own architectural symbolism and described their own designs as expressions of a national revival and an ordered rural society. During the second half of the decade, the controversy over the Bauhaus was thus continued, but in a new form, becoming a debate over the cultural and political significance of the new architecture as a whole.

The arguments of the conservative architects against the new style derived in part from older traditions of cultural pessimism in Germany, but they were conditioned as well by the claims which the Ring architects made for their work. These claims had a new emphasis in the later twenties, for as the radical architects became more and more involved in the practical problems of constructing mass housing they tended increasingly to concentrate on the technical aspects of building technology and planning. In much of their writing they adopted Gropius' view that "The time for manifestoes in support of the new building is past. They helped to establish our intellectual presuppositions, [but] it is high time to begin making a calculated and exact evaluation of practical experience."[13] Gropius himself acted on this principle from about 1925 on; after that date the majority of his speeches and articles, particularly those directed to a professional audience, were devoted to such questions as the planning of housing developments for maximum light, air, and garden area, the use of economical building methods and materials, the problems involved in prefabricating housing, and the proper construction of the flat roof.[14] In those of his speeches which were addressed to the general public, he frequently stressed the material benefits to be conferred by a new building technology, prophesying, for example, a day when everyone could own his own prefabricated, "transportable" house.[15]

The same subjects were also, of course, a major concern of Wagner and May, although Wagner usually stressed the sociological benefits of new types of planning and construction at the same time as he sought to demonstrate their economy.[16] May on some occasions went so far as to claim that construction methods determined style itself, arguing that only the standardization of building parts and the use of modular construction could provide the set of consistent forms necessary for a uniform aesthetic.[17] Shortly after he began to design for the Gehag, Taut too began to write articles devoted to discussion of economical building methods and related technical questions; and during this period he gave greater emphasis than he had before to the idea that "the architect must be a sociologist, economist and serious scientist" as well as an artist.[18]

The questions of efficient interior planning and the use of

mechanical equipment in housing which Taut had raised in *Die neue Wohnung* also continued to receive a great deal of attention from all the Ring architects and particularly from May, who devoted three issues of *Das neue Frankfurt* to these subjects.[19] This discussion of technical questions was not confined to a consideration of individual dwellings or apartment buildings, for Gropius, Hilberseimer, Wagner, and May frequently wrote about such subjects as the organization of mass transportation systems and the problem of smoke control in the location of industry.[20] All of these men were deeply concerned with the problems of over-all city planning.

This emphasis on practical matters did not mean that the Ring architects ceased to publicize the idea that they were creating a new aesthetic, expressive of a new society and a new culture. Gropius and Taut continued to argue that the new forms had "spiritual" significance in themselves and that the new architecture, by uniting the work of the arts and industry, could provide a model of cooperation and synthesis for society and culture.[21] Under the influence of these ideas, the Ring issued a public statement at the time of its formation describing its intention "consciously to renounce the empty forms of the past . . . and to prepare an architectural culture for the new era in economic and social organization."[22] The same views inspired the periodicals and organizations which supported the new style: the subject matter of *Das neue Frankfurt* and *Das neue Berlin* emphasized the interrelationship of all aspects of art, culture, and society, and *Die Form* followed their example. In the first issue of *Die Form*, which appeared in 1925, the Werkbund announced its participation in "the attempt . . . to achieve a new aesthetic form [Neugestaltung] and a new order for economic, social, and spiritual life on the basis of new conditions."[23]

But the attention given to practical problems by the radical architects in their public utterances, combined with their interest in the social and cultural role of architecture, helped to influence the interpretations of the new architecture by professional commentators in a way which few of the Ring architects intended. Even friendly writers began to see the new style as merely engineering and planning and the Ring architects as seeking to subordinate art to the machine or to the practical needs of society. Through the writings of a series of influential critics the new style came to be known as "functionalism," *Zweckmässigkeit*, or "the new practicality," *die neue Sachlichkeit*. The wide acceptance of this interpretation allowed conservative writers to argue that the "new society" which the new architecture claimed to express was a mechanistic and materialistic one, devoid of traditional "German" spiritual values.

Probably the first man to identify the new style as "functionalism" was Emil Utitz, a young professor of art history in Halle. Early in 1923, even before radical architects had begun to write extensively about construction and planning problems, Utitz described housing such as Gropius' and Haesler's as zweckmässig and sachlich and claimed that in its planning for efficient circulation and maximum comfort the new architecture derived its inspiration from modern factory design.[24] He had little to say about the aesthetic qualities of the new style except that the simplicity and sobriety of the new forms "express" the qualities of the workaday world, and, although he admired the social utility of radical architects' work, he complained that this "style of labor" was not enough. "Men require warmth and rejoicing, splendor and brilliance . . . elegance . . . the qualities of life appropriate to the hours after work is done." These themes were taken up by Ernst von Niebelschütz, the *Magdeburgische Zeitung*'s prominent art critic, who in 1924 described the first buildings in the new style as "engineering architecture . . . which pays no attention to the requirements of feeling or sentiment." Similarly Paul Westheim, who as editor of *Das Kunstblatt* had done a great deal to promote expressionist art, wrote a disparaging article in *Die Glocke* which described the new style as "a new romanticism of the engineer and the machine."[25]

The popularity of this type of interpretation was greatly increased by the appearance of Adolf Behne's *Der moderne Zweckbau* in 1925. Behne was not only a well-known architectural critic, but had been closely associated with the radical architects from the first and was presumed to speak for them. The book traced the development of "functional" and "practical" architecture from progressive industrial and commercial building of the first two decades of the century through the recent work of Gropius, Mendelsohn, Mies van der Rohe, and similar designers in other countries, and described the German architects' work as the best application of Sullivan's dictum "form follows function."[26] Although Behne warned that "it is an error to see the functionalists as utilitarians,"[27] he too emphasized the role played by efficient planning and machine construction in the new architecture. Indeed, he often spoke of the buildings themselves as similar to machines, calling Mendelsohn's Luckenwalde factory, for example, "a form which follows the functions of the factory and the course of production in the way that the parts of the machine do."[28]

Behne's interpretation was followed rather closely by Gustav

Platz, author of the volume in the Propyläen Kunstgeschichte series, and by many writers after him. Platz praised radical architects' attention to functional planning as a "work beneficial to culture," but he meant that their main service was to help raise the standard of living. He described modern housing as the "mechanization of building," and regarded the new architecture as essentially the product of modern technology.[29] This view was also repeated in 1929 by the Director of the Mannheim art gallery, Gustav Hartlaub. Hartlaub, one of the most influential patrons of modern art in Germany, called the radical architects "the engineers of today," whose highest goal it was "to serve the [mundane] needs of the common man."[30]

The new style thus came to be considered by many of Germany's most influential critics as primarily a set of solutions to technical and sociological questions. Behne and Platz thought of it as glorifying a new era in technology; Utitz and Hartlaub believed it expressed a new concern for the material welfare of the masses. These were the senses in which the term "neue Sachlichkeit" was usually employed.[31]

There were, to be sure, a significant number of critics who believed the new forms to be aesthetically important in themselves and not mere outgrowths of function or construction. Both the prominent young art historian Alexander Dorner and Max Osborn, the *Vossische Zeitung*'s distinguished critic, admired radical architects' "new form language," which to Osborn meant "a wonderful precision in geometric shapes," and to Dorner, "the intensive structure given to space."[32] This view reached a wider public through the work of Walter Müller-Wulckow, author of the Blauen Bücher series on modern architecture, who believed that the new style "is characterized by a passionate desire for pure forms, a desire which penetrates deeper into the idea and essence of reality than the mere love of ornament ever could. Strange as it may sound, these logically planned and constructed buildings embody a metaphysical yearning. These creations of the machine age reflect a new phantasy of the spirit and a new mysticism of the soul."[33]

Müller-Wulckow called this desire for pure forms "our generation's will to Sachlichkeit." He thus employed the term in the auxiliary and almost contradictory sense which the German language gives it: that of concern with essential reality as distinguished from the chaos and relativism of everyday life. In viewing the new architecture primarily as abstract form and only secondarily as a matter of functional planning and machine technology, Müller-Wulckow approached the real thinking of Gropius and Taut more closely than did Platz or Hartlaub; and his view corresponded more accurately to the way the new style had in fact developed in Germany. But, owing to the energetic activity of the Ring architects in publicizing their experimental work in construction and planning in the later twenties, it was the mechanistic interpretation which prevailed in Germany and abroad, and it has continued to do so almost until the present day.[34]

It was thus on practical grounds that many of their opponents began to attack the Ring architects. The first full-scale critique of the new building methods being introduced by radical architects was *ABC des Bauens*, a "manual of the good old tested ways of building," published by Paul Schultze-Naumburg in 1926. Before the war, Schultze-Naumburg had been one of Germany's most highly respected architects, known best for country mansions built in the "Biedermeier" style, and for a series of influential essays on interior design.[35] His prewar buildings set a new standard in simple uncluttered residential design and placed Schultze-Naumburg among the leaders of the progressive movement. But after the war commissions for large residences were scarce and the influence of the radical architects began to discredit historicism. In 1926 Schultze-Naumburg no longer held the same position of prominence among German architects which he had enjoyed before the war, nor was his new work well known to the public. His defense of "good building traditions" initiated a long series of writings in which he attempted to re-establish the prewar prestige of progressive historicist architecture and through which he eventually became the leading opponent of the new style in Germany, gathering around him a number of other influential conservative architects. At the end of the twenties, Schultze-Naumburg moved on to a variety of emotionally charged and extremely vituperative arguments against the new architecture, and these won him the support of the Nazi party. In the early thirties, Schultze-Naumburg became the party's principal spokesman on architectural questions. But after 1933, although Nazi propaganda continued to borrow his arguments, the new regime did not patronize his work. In the end, Schultze-Naumburg forfeited all claim to intellectual respectability and received nothing in return, a fate he shared with many other conservative supporters of National Socialism.

ABC des Bauens was ostensibly a handbook of architectural terms, couched in common sense phraseology for the use of both laymen and professional architects. But in reality nearly every entry discussed one of the new building methods being introduced by radical architects and compared it unfavorably with older methods. Proceeding alphabetically item by item from "flat roofs" to "prefabricated housing" to "economical building methods,"

Schultze-Naumburg stressed the untried nature of these methods, their impermanence, and their shoddiness. Although these ideas had been given enormous publicity, he said, none had been proved to work out in practice. "The people who advocate [these methods]" he wrote, "are almost always men with very little real professional knowledge."[36]

Schultze-Naumburg developed these observations further toward the end of 1926, when he joined in the controversy over the flat roof which took place that year. In May of 1925, the magazine *Bauwelt*, already very sympathetic to the work of the radical architects, had published a series of articles by Gropius and a number of modern architects from other countries, on the subject of the use and construction of the flat roof. In February 1926, the considerably more conservative *Deutsche Bauzeitung* published a lengthy attack on the flat roof written by Dresden's Oberbaurat Kurt Hager; and after Gropius had replied to Hager in its pages, the magazine published Schultze-Naumburg's answer to Gropius.[37] Hager claimed that the flat roof could not provide adequate drainage of rain and melting snow and argued that only the sloped roof was appropriate to the German climate. The flat roof, he said, was practical only in southern countries and was really an "oriental" form. After Gropius pointed out that flat roofs had been used in Germany for over a century, Schultze-Naumburg took up the attack with the argument that the introduction of flat roofs had coincided with "the decline of good building traditions during the nineteenth century." At that time their use had been part of the tendency of an industrial society to build "not as beautifully and well as possible, but merely as cheaply as possible." Flat roofs had been discarded, he said, during the "revival of sound building methods before the war," and their reintroduction was simply a "fad begun in the name of a modern aesthetic." Like Hager, Schultze-Naumburg found the flat roof to be 'inappropriate to the German climate and customs," and, he added, "it is imediately recognizable as the child of other skies and other blood," thus anticipating the racist interpretation of architecture which two years later became his stock-in-trade.

In the later twenties Konrad Nonn also joined the apostles of "sound building methods." During 1927, the last year that he edited the *Zentralblatt der Bauverwaltung*, Nonn published a series of articles on the new Bauhaus buildings which attempted to prove that Gropius' use of the flat roof and large glass areas was "wholly impractical" and "not founded on Handwerk as Gropius claims."[38] While the articles repeated Nonn's earlier claims that the work of the school was "culturally destructive," their main conclusion was similar to Schultze-Naumburg's: "in the Bauhaus buildings . . .

functional purpose is suppressed in the name of a fad in taste, and the result is the opposite of what we usually call 'modern functionalism.' " Nonn followed this series on the Bauhaus with attacks on the "impractical" construction of the housing at Praunheim, Törten, and Weissenhof, which had been financed by the Reichsforschungsgesellschaft as part of its program of developing new building methods.[39]

Nonn's later articles appeared not in the *Zentralblatt*, but in *Deutsche Bauhütte*, an architectural journal edited by Hannoverian building officials, which remained, after the *Zentralblatt* changed its policy, the only professional magazine which consistently and violently opposed the new style. Its attacks had begun as early as 1924, when H.A. Waldner, one of its editors, criticized "the industrialization of building at the Bauhaus," warning that the employment of standardized construction in housing would cause large-scale unemployment among the building trades;[40] toward the end of the decade they became both more numerous and increasingly scurrilous in tone. In 1929 the magazine devoted an entire issue to photographs of cracks in the Törten Siedlung, and in 1930 it published two books of the same sort entitled *Reformed Building Methods for Less Expensive Housing Construction* and *Building Sins and the Wasting of Our Building Funds*.[41] The former contained an expanded discussion of construction failures at Törten; the latter offered photographs of cracks, peeling paint, streaks caused by dampness, and rusted fittings at Törten, Praunheim, and Weissenhof.

These attacks won the support of many members of the building trades and crafts, particularly those for whom the use of flat roofs and steel or concrete construction meant less work or at least the necessity of learning new methods. Nonn's article against the Bauhaus brought responses from the "national guild of building foremen," which called the methods taught at the Bauhaus "a grave injury to the whole of the German trades [Handwerk]," and from the national union of German roofers.[42] The roofers were among the most active opponents of the new style among the building trades; in 1926 their journal published several articles in reply to *Bauwelt's* series on the flat roof and devoted an entire issue to the virtues of the sloped roof, which it called "the German roof."[43] Under the heading "Flat Roofs, Flat Heads," the *Roofers Newsletter* attacked the "swinishness" of using flat roofs in housing developments and accused radical architects of disturbing the German landscape with a "foreign" type of building.[44] Complaints in a similar vein appeared in the journals of the bricklayers and brick manufacturers, who opposed the use of steel frame or concrete construction, and in the carpenters' and stonemasons' trade-union magazines, which criticized the use of artificial building materials in the new housing developments.[45] The threat to these trades was largely illusory, for buildings constructed with steel or concrete frames formed a very small proportion of total building construction in Germany, and although flat roofs were widely used in the new housing, they were laid by members of the roofers' guilds and unions. But the introduction of new building methods offered the building trades a convenient explanation for the existence of unemployment among their members, particularly during the first years of the depression.

Criticism of the building methods of the Ring architects, attractive as it was to disaffected architects and craftsmen, never in itself aroused much interest outside the building trades and the architectural profession. It was only by adopting the terminology of the Weimar controversy that the opponents of the new style found a wider audience. The most popular and notorious arguments of this type were developed by Emil Högg and in Schultze-Naumburg's later writings. In addition to the claim that the new style was impractical, both men began to condemn the radical architects precisely for their emphasis on technical questions. Högg and Schultze-Naumburg incorporated sociological and cultural criticisms of "industrialized" buildings into a nationalist and racist theory of architecture which was intended to serve as a theoretical defense of historicist architecture.

The first important attack of this kind was made in the fall of 1926 by Emil Högg, at that time professor of architecture at Dresden. The occasion was a speech Högg made to the National Congress of German Architects and Engineers, which he intended as a reply to the public statement with which the Ring had shortly before announced its formation.[46] Högg attacked the new methods of building construction, but not merely on the grounds that they represented poor technique. Instead, he declared that the use of standard parts and plans in "mass apartment buildings and warehouses for families" would produce "nomadic architecture," leading to "uprootedness, spiritual impoverishment and proletarianization." Högg strongly emphasized the destructive effects of repudiating past traditions, arguing that "in their love of newness for its own sake" the members of the Ring had introduced a "confusion of artistic goals and an incoherence of execution which suits the spiritual condition of Germany today." And as some of the opponents of the Bauhaus had done earlier, he concluded that the break with the past and the adoption of a totally new aesthetic meant the creation of a "bolshevist" architecture.

After drawing this image of a culturally and socially destructive architecture, Högg offered a description of a genuine "German" architecture. This was the "great unified development of prewar art," the work of Messel, Theodor Fischer, Bonatz, and Fritz Schumacher, who, he said, had used the old traditions of German architecture and developed them further. This "folk architecture" was still being developed, Högg believed, by men like Fritz Höger and Paul Schmitthenner, but it was threatened by "an attempt to impose upon German architecture an attitude essentially foreign to it . . . a dangerous, a death-dealing spirit, for it will murder our finest possession, the German soul." In defending the old traditions of German architecture, which stemmed from the preindustrial period, Högg was also led to include in his speech an attack upon urbanization, which he equated with the massive housing projects of the new architecture. "Let us be rid of skyscrapers and asphalt and return to the green German soil!" The antiurban theme was not given great emphasis in Högg's speech of 1926, but later on it was to become a major element in the attack on the new architecture.

Högg's speech attracted a good deal of attention both inside and outside the profession. The speech was reprinted and quoted in several of the professional journals which had been participating in the attack on the new architecture, and Högg himself repeated the speech in substantially the same form on several later occasions.[47] But the leading role in the attack on the new architecture was assumed by Schultze-Naumburg, who gave to the nationalist argument enunciated by Högg the racist formulation which was generally adopted by the opponents of the new style in the later twenties. Although it had a powerful prewar tradition behind it, the idea that racial characteristics are reflected in art only began to be widely discussed in Germany around 1926. In that year Hans F. K. Günther published his controversial *Race and Style*, and at about the same time and probably independently, both Schultze-Naumburg and Albrecht Haupt, Baurat in the Hannover building administration, began to describe the sloped roof as part of the German "racial physiognomy."[48] Schultze-Naumburg began to concentrate upon this type of argument in 1928 when he published, in quick succession, *Art and Race*, an explanation of how all the arts including architecture expressed racial identity, and *The Face of the German House*, a study of the racial character of the "German house."[49]

In *Art and Race* Schultze-Naumburg attempted to prove that modern art and architecture in Germany reflected a cultural decadence which had its roots in biological causes. The argument was developed first in the section on painting, which derived in part from Günther, and was then applied to architecture. Schultze-Naumburg began with Günther's contention that artists always paint their own self-portraits and that therefore their physical or racial type can be read from their paintings. He illustrated examples of distortion and semiabstract treatment of the human form in cubist and expressionist painting and compared them with photographs of individuals suffering from various physical and mental diseases which he believed the paintings resembled. From the resemblance he concluded not that the authors of the paintings represented any particular "race," but that they were physically and mentally degenerate; he called them "the uncreative men, formless and colorless, the half and quarter men, unbeautiful men who desire no beauty, who set their stamp upon our time."[50] He argued, moreover, that their art was not merely a reflection of degeneracy, but also its cause. The artist, he said, should "make visible a wish-picture, so that the entire folk can strive toward beauty and attempt to resemble it"; he suggested that the "wish-picture" of modern painters was contributing to mental and physical illness among the German people.

To apply this argument to architecture, Schultze-Naumburg began by declaring that "Houses have faces like men, and they wear a very definite expression." The "face" of German architecture up to the time of Goethe's death had been "to a very high degree harmonious in appearance; out of it there seemed to gaze the features of men upright, good and true."[51] But since that time a degradation of architecture had taken place, ending in the work of radical architects, which "expresses above all lack of clarity, disintegration and loathesomeness, and calls up an impression of men who look and act very differently."[52] Schultze-Naumburg denied that this change in architectural style was caused primarily by social or political changes, "although they have played a part," nor could it be explained by a natural process of cultural decline "as Spengler and others claim."[53] "We must," he wrote, "consider it as a biological phenomenon. . . . The only essential explanation [of the existence of the two architectural styles] is that they express two different types of men."[54] The "decline" of German architecture was thus, according to Schultze-Naumburg, the result of the racial decline of the German "people," a process which he believed had its origin in nineteenth-century industrialization when the "inferior" part of the population had multiplied and the "superior" part had not. But the threat of racial decline had only become pronounced since the war, "in which the best Germans were killed," and which had been followed by "an influx of foreigners who bring with them a different spiritual principle and probably also a different physical one."[55]

In *The Face of the German House*, Schultze-Naumburg sought to explain in more detail the way in which architecture acted upon race and culture. The book compared housing in the new style with older residental styles in order to prove that the former represented a threat to the German people. Schultze-Naumburg illustrated his text with pictures of houses resembling some of his own early work or that of Tessenow and Schmitthenner, and, claiming that they were "German" houses, argued that they helped to produce a sense of national or racial identity. The "German house," he wrote, "gives one the feeling that it grows out of the soil, like one of its natural products, like a tree that sinks its roots deep in the interior of the soil and forms a union with it. It is this that gives us our understanding of home [Heimat], of a bond with blood and earth [Erden] for one kind of men [this is] the condition of their life and the meaning of their existence."[56] Urban growth, he said, had forced such houses out of the cities so that they now remained only in villages and small towns, "where they give the form of the village and the landscape a German face."

To the "German" house Schultze-Naumburg contrasted the housing projects of radical architects "now so loudly admired, which look as if they were put together anywhere and set down anywhere by messenger and as if they could just as well be anywhere else. . . . They have really become stationary sleeping cars. . . . Actually they are the work of the nomads of the metropolis, who have lost entirely the concept of the homeland [Heimat], and no longer have any idea of the house as inherited, as a family estate."[57] To Schultze-Naumburg, such designs "make sleeping, eating, and drinking . . . into a business, [and] put the whole of life on a purely materialistic basis." He claimed that this "materialism" represented an attempt to destroy German culture: "For all who depend on their German heritage, on their home soil and their inherited cultural tradition, the threatening suppression of the German face represents a terrible danger. We feel that something irreplaceable is being annihilated, either intentionally or unintentionally, while as a substitute a soulless, godless, and mechanical world threatens to rise, in which life has lost its inmost meaning."[58] Only the "German house," with its "sense for the relationship between house and landscape" and its subordination of mere technology to "beauty and phantasy" could, according to Schultze-Naumburg, serve as a bulwark against racial and cultural decline.

Schultze-Naumburg's writings won increasing support within the architectural profession, and in 1928 he was able to form an organization called the "Block" in competition with the Ring. Although the Block was not particularly active as a group, it included among its members Professors Paul Schmitthenner and German Bestelmeyer, two of South Germany's most influential architects. Schmitthenner held the chair of architecture at Stuttgart's important Technische Hochschule and Bestelmeyer, who held the same position in Munich, was also President of the Munich Academy of Arts. From about 1930 Schmitthenner elaborated upon Schultze-Naumburg's arguments in the Württemberg press; and in 1931 he published *The German House,* a polemic against the "dwelling-machine" illustrated with pictures of his own designs, which he now claimed had a German "face."[59] Schultze-Naumburg's arguments also began to appear in the right-wing press from about 1929, but when they did it was usually in combination with charges of "bolshevism" which were not included in Schultze-Naumburg's works. Although Schultze-Naumburg had written that "it is precisely . . . the half and quarter men . . . who believe in the equality of man,"[60] he had for the most part ignored political questions and concentrated on the connection between culture and race.

Despite the occasional use of the term "bolshevism" by men like Högg, the revival of the political charges first made during the Bauhaus controversy had its principal origins in the writings of the conservative Swiss architect Alexander von Senger.[61] In two scurrilous tracts published in 1928 and 1931, *The Crisis of Architecture* and *Moscow's Torch,* Senger combined the notion of "art bolshevism" and Schultze-Naumburg's racist ideas into a full-scale attack on what he called "architectural bolshevism."[62] The theme of both books was that the new style acted as a tool of an international communist conspiracy against European culture and the "Nordic" race. *The Crisis of Architecture* presented Corbusier and his periodical *L'Esprit Nouveau* as the leading agents of the conspiracy, but the book attracted little attention in either France or Switzerland.[63] His arguments, however, achieved such immediate success in Germany that Senger revised the content of the book to give the German version of the new style more prominence, and published the result in serialized form in the fall of 1930.[64] *Moscow's Torch* followed this precedent of concentrating on German architecture and German architects. Senger's writings introduced into the debate over the new style the tone and methods of exposition which some of the Weimar opponents of the Bauhaus had used and which were also characteristic of Nazi propaganda: the manufacturing of quotes or their use out of context, the suggestion of guilt by association, and accusation by implication.

"It is well known," wrote Senger, "that communism smuggles its secret agents into foreign states under harmless titles like 'trade delegations' and spreads its teaching through 'art films.' This movement which is known harmlessly as 'the new architecture' is also nothing else than bolshevism."[65] All of Senger's writings were concerned with this conspiratorial theory of architecture, but it was *Moscow's Torch* which offered the most concrete explanation of the workings of the conspiracy.[66] In this book, Senger argued that radical architects' introduction of new materials and methods of construction represented a conscious attempt to level society. By encouraging mass-produced buildings or at least the use of mass-produced synthetic materials, he said, the new architecture "destroys and proletarianizes hundreds of thousands of self-sufficient building tradesmen; it liquidates the heart of the petty-bourgeoisie."[67] But since the use of mass-produced building products was clearly beneficial to large-scale industry, Senger was also compelled to state that the new architects were sponsored by capitalism as well as communism. He therefore claimed that radical architects were the agents of both "bolshevism" and "money-hungry capitalism," or "mammonism," acting together in a "new capitalist-bolshevist front." Typical of his argument is the following explanation of this sponsorship: "Marxism supports the new architecture because it creates new proletarian masses, and profit-hungry mammonism supports the new architecture because it creates a new market for exploitation. Thus . . . proletarianization has become a postulate of mammonism just as the new architecture has become a postulate of Marxism. Both postulates are the issue of a soulless, power-hungry . . . sub-humanity."[68]

But according to Senger, the effects of "bolshevist architecture" reached beyond the creation of a new proletariat to exert a profound influence upon culture and race. For to Senger as to the early opponents of the Bauhaus, "bolshevism" was not merely a political matter: "Bolshevism is not specifically Russian . . . , bolshevism is the modern word for an international condition of the spirit which is as old as the world; it is the breaking out of that which is animal in men. The old cultures were destroyed by bolshevism."[69] Bolshevism was thus the worship of material things, of technology and material gain rather than art, and in this sense, Senger said, "liberalism, Marxism, and bolshevism are variations on the same theme."[70] The new architecture was thus "bolshevist" in that it "makes function and utility the measure of all things," and represented an attempt "to deprive building of its soul . . . and men of theirs."[71] In order to support this contention, Senger made frequent reference to Corbusier's dictum that "man is a geometric animal," laying stress on the last word, and he claimed that this was what Gropius and Taut had meant when they predicted the evolution of a "new humanity."[72] Thus in the work of the radical architects "the appearance of a building . . . shall no longer inspire us and make us happy; rather the products of the new architecture are intended to impress upon us day after day that we are merely 'geometric animals' without past or future."[73]

With the same goal in mind, Senger argued, radical architects repudiated the art and culture of the past. Gropius was "quoted" as suggesting that the Louvre be torn down, while Martin Wagner was said to have planned the razing of the Brandenburger Tor, from which Senger concluded that they subscribed to Corbusier's "demand" that all the cities of the past be torn down in order to create a market for "concrete cells." This destruction of past traditions was to Senger not only "architectural bolshevism" but also "cultural bolshevism."

Although Senger emphasized the threat posed to society and culture by the new architecture, he also took over and adapted Schultze-Naumburg's claim that it caused racial decline by creating an unhealthy "wish-picture" for the race. Works of art, he wrote, "have a political-biological significance . . . which unfortunately is not recognized by anybody but the bolshevists. . . . They have a powerful effect upon the forms of states, on politics and on human selection. It was not Greece which made Homer, but Homer who through his poetry first really created Greece."[74] But while the "wish-picture" of Homer's poetry "created" Greece, the materialistic "wish-picture" established by the new style "destroys the desire for [racial] health and encourages the desire for [racial] illness."[75] The cultural tradition which radical architects had repudiated was, on the other hand, the only sure foundation for racial "health": "The whole of European culture, from the time of the Greeks and the Romans to the many national variations of the present, had a Nordic-antique character, and therefore contributed to the support and stabilization of this sort of attitude and favored [racial] selection in this sense. Our culture was thus shot through with yearning for the great health of the Antique."[76]

Unlike Högg and Schultze-Naumburg, Senger did not describe in detail the type of architecture he believed could oppose the destructive tendencies of the new style and merely said that it would be "building with a soul, filled with national, religious, racial . . . mythic and symbolic components."[77] But in implying that it would embody a "Nordic-antique character" he suggested the direction which some of Nazi architectural theory was to follow.

Schultze-Naumburg's and Senger's comprehensive attack on the new style as a threat to culture and race began to find its way into the right-wing press shortly before the onset of the depression. In mid-1929, both the neoconservative journal *Der Ring* and the more traditionally conservative *Neue Preussische Kreuz-Zeitung* published articles on "bolshevism" in architecture, quoting at length from *The Crisis of Architecture*.[78] In early 1930, *Ludendorffs Volkswarte* printed an elaborate discussion of "The German Home and Modern Architecture," which combined Schultze-Naumburg's and Senger's arguments in the claim that radical architects were working toward "the extermination of the German home . . . the destruction of all folk character and the culture which expresses it . . . in favor of an international civilization which replaces the soul with the machine . . . [in order to] make the German man into a collective entity, a herd animal, the ideal type of bolshevism."[79]

Similar arguments appeared in Berlin's nationalist *Deutsche Tageszeitung*, which wrote that Gropius' housing designs "schematize men and reduce them to collective beings," and in Munich's *Münchner Zeitung* which said that May's housing was "intended for geometric animals" and represented a "bolshevist conspiracy."[80] Arguments deriving from Senger's books appeared in *Der Jungdeutsche*, the newspaper of the right-wing of the youth movement, in 1932, while the Hugenberg papers described the Bauhaus as "bolshevist" and the new style as a "bolshevist" threat to the "German race."[81]

Similar charges also found an appreciative audience in the press of those heterogeneous, radical right-wing groups which were usually described as the "völkische Bewegung." Such ardently nationalist and anti-Semitic organizations as the Bartelsbund, the Deutschbund, and the Deutschvölkische Schutz- und Trutzbund contributed throughout the late twenties and early thirties to the support of a syndicated newspaper column on the arts, the *Deutsche Kunstkorrespondenz,* which was published in a number of small "völkische" newspapers and which devoted most of its space to attacks on modern art and architecture.[82] The author of the column, Bettina Feistel-Rohmeder, collected excerpts from it and published them in 1938 as *In Terror of Art*

Bolshevism, a title which indicates the conspiratorial and inflammatory tone of her writing. The column was filled with mottoes like "art is the flower of the folk and stems from its blood,"[83] and consisted, in addition to these, of fragmentary quotes from other writers' judgments on modern art and architecture. Högg's "flaming protest against the architecture of the enemies of the folk," was reproduced in part in mid-1928,[84] and subsequent articles quoted at random from Nonn, Schultze-Naumburg, and Senger. Feistel-Rohmeder called the Ring "foreign" and "ruled by Corbusier"; the Bauhaus "[a part of] the war against the trades and crafts and destructive of the family," and the new style "nihilist, oriental . . . and bolshevist."[85] She also said that the Ring was "Jewish," a claim which even the racist writings of Schultze-Naumburg never made.[86] Aside from their anti-Semitism, her articles were neither original nor coherent, but they indicated a tendency among the "völkische" organizations to adopt the catchwords of political, cultural, and racist attacks on the new style.

In a very few instances before the Nazis adopted them, the theories of Schultze-Naumburg, Senger, and their precursors also found political support. This support came chiefly from the DNVP, which occasionally used their arguments in its attacks on the public housing program. At a meeting of the party's "National Committee on Cities" in January of 1928, Hermann Schluckebier, the chief speaker, declared that the public housing policy of the Republic represented a "Marxist" attempt at "an internationalization of housing which will force foreign dwelling forms . . . upon the German family."[87] He described Britz, Weissenhof, and May's Frankfurt developments as products of the "Socialist utopia," where "there are no more family dwellings. Married couples are to keep house in a sort of hotel with a great central kitchen. The children are to be interned and educated in institutions." The DNVP had long opposed many aspects of the public housing program and had sought the greater participation of private capital in housing construction. Schluckebier now claimed that the achievement of this goal would "uphold the German home . . . the bulwark of family life . . . [which] has made us a strong home-loving race . . . and has formed the foundation for the development of our German culture." This type of attack on the new style never became established policy in the DNVP, but it did reappear in Hugenberg's address to the Party Congress in 1930, in which he called for "a new Germany . . . built on the land, where the family still grows." Using Senger's terminology, Hugenberg described the public housing policy of the previous decade as "Socialist cultural bolshevism . . . which has devoured the marrow of the German soul."[88]

Although the controversy over the new architecture often degenerated into scurrilous character assassination and garbled racism, it had nevertheless developed around the high claims of radical architects to serve a new culture and a new society. Their claims had early met with the countercharge that their work was destructive of German culture and the product of an era of decline. As the Ring architects began to build great public housing projects, Schultze-Naumburg and the other opponents of the new style made the additional argument that the new architecture represented a new society, not of joint cooperation and spiritual progress, but of the mass man and the dominance of the metropolis and the machine. And like their predecessors in the Bauhaus controversy, Senger and Schultze-Naumburg also elaborated a cultural theory of politics according to which the materialism of radical architects' methods of planning and construction represented the "bolshevist" ideology and constituted an assault by foreign powers on national and racial identity.

But although these arguments began to gain an audience in the right-wing press at the end of the twenties, they were not supported by the type of strong and vocal popular antagonism to the new architecture which was present in Weimar between 1919 and 1924. And though right-wing political parties, particularly the DNVP, showed an almost instinctive opposition to the new architecture in both local and national politics, they employed ideas like Schultze-Naumburg's only rarely. It was only the Nazi party which, at a very late stage in the controversy, recognized the propaganda value of opposition to the new style and adopted its arguments as part of a political program.

VI / The New Architecture and National Socialism

Long before the Nazi party began its propaganda against the new architecture, it had incorporated theories of art and culture into its political program. Hitler's writings and speeches criticized the Weimar Republic for its alleged cultural weaknesses as well as for its lack of political and military strength. He repeatedly described both Weimar democracy and the military defeat of 1918 as the product of a process of cultural decline, itself caused by "racial" decline. Hitler saw evidence of this decadence not only in the "materialism" and "lack of an heroic ideal" of Weimar society, but also in modern art. In *Mein Kampf,* he described modern art as "bolshevist art," adopting the language of the Bauhaus controversy.[1] Earlier he had warned against forms of art which "poison" the nation, while Point 23 of the "Twenty-five Points" promised "a legal battle against tendencies in the arts and literature which exercise a disintegrating influence on the life of the people," a promise Hitler repeated in 1922 and 1923.[2]

Among the arts, Hitler singled out architecture for special attention, for this was the profession to which he had once aspired. As early as 1920 he told his small audience at the Hofbräuhaus that a strong Germany must have a great architecture, since architecture was a vital index of national power and strength. In *Mein Kampf* he lamented the disappearance of a tradition of monumental building in Germany, and in a passage reminiscent of Taut's *Stadtkrone* he spoke of the symbolic significance of the urban monumental architecture of antiquity. The lack of similar monuments in contemporary cities was, he said, a sign of cultural decay; in 1929 he promised that when the party took power, "out of our new ideology and our political will to power we will create stone documents."[3]

The Nazi party was thus more disposed than any other major political party in Germany to use architecture and the arts for political propaganda. But although Hitler bitterly denounced modern painting in the early twenties, he never made a direct attack upon modern architecture, and in any case his views on

147

the arts had for many years no significant influence upon party propaganda as a whole. Early party propaganda, largely restricted to Versailles and anti-Semitism, wholly neglected the Bauhaus controversy and took notice of contemporary art only insofar as it could be used as a basis for anti-Semitic attacks. The character of Nazi propaganda began to change around 1928 when the party press began to discuss literature, music, and the drama in a relatively sophisticated manner, in a conscious effort to broaden its appeal. But the Nazi party did not enter the debate over the new architecture until 1930, long after the controversy had become a question of national significance. And when the party did take up the issue, it was not Hitler, who never publicly criticized modern architecture before 1933, but Rosenberg, the party's other frustrated architect, who took the initiative.

When the party finally did begin to attack the new architecture, it found in the controversy over the new style a powerful weapon with which to play upon the economic distress and the despairing mood of the depression years. The propaganda organs under Rosenberg's control, including the *Völkischer Beobachter* and the party cultural front which he founded in 1928, took over the arguments of the conservative architects who had previously attacked the new architecture and used them to wage ever more bitter war upon the "Ring" group during the last three years before the Nazis came to power. Under Rosenberg's influence, the party used the new architecture as a symbol of a disintegrating culture which had lost contact with the traditions of German art, and as a symbol of a mass society whose members had lost their identity through urbanization and their economic security through proletarianization and unemployment. And in Nazi propaganda the new style began to be described not merely as the symbol of these cultural and social ills, but also as their cause — as a tool of the republican government in bringing about the decadence of the German nation and the German "race." Nazi architectural propaganda thus provided an effective means of denouncing the Weimar Republic as a whole, for it condemned the republican regime and blamed upon it an entire era in economic, political and cultural development.

The basis for the Nazi attack upon the new architecture began to be laid in Nazi propaganda around 1928. During that year, the *Völkischer Beobachter* greatly expanded its coverage of artistic questions and began to develop the arguments which would be directed against the new style from 1930 onward. At about the same time, Rosenberg founded the Kampfbund für deutsche Kultur, a group of intellectuals who he hoped would help to extend the cultural influence of the party.

The initial impetus for the new emphasis on the arts in Nazi propaganda probably came from Rosenberg's organization, for many of the *VB*'s attacks upon modern art in 1929 and 1930 can be traced directly to the statements of speakers sponsored by the Kampfbund. Moreover, the group itself became an important propaganda organ of the Nazi party since its public lectures and its publications reached a relatively wide audience. Yet information about this significant organization is extraordinarily scarce. The Kampfbund encountered official disfavor and eventually boycott after 1933, so that few records of its origin and development remain.

The Kampfbund had its obscure beginnings in South Germany in 1928,[4] but its formal establishment as a national organization dates from February 26, 1929.[5] Its earliest statements of purpose were cast in very general terms. Rosenberg's standard speech at the initial organizational meetings, called "Today's Cultural Crisis," described contemporary culture as "fragmented" and promised to bring about "a new [cultural] bond, in the form of the dawn of a national Myth."[6] The organization's first published membership appeal called upon the German people to uphold "the holiest religious belief — the honor of the nation" against "conscious subversion . . . by international powers" and by "the so-called world press." "In the midst of today's cultural decline," the Kampfbund would "inform the German people about the interconnection of race, art, learning [Wissenschaft] and moral . . . values."[7] As examples of contemporary cultural decline, its early publications quoted pacifist and antireligious passages from the writings of Ernst Toller, Kurt Tucholsky, and Georg Grosz; they also included warnings against the prevalence of "pornography" in public entertainment.[8] As an antidote to these conditions, the Kampfbund promised to "support every characteristic expression of German cultural life."[9]

Both in the vague cultural pessimism of its original aims and in the obscurity of its original membership, the Kampfbund resembled a large number of other small local "cultural" organizations formed in Germany in the twenties to combat "modernism" or to preserve "German" tradition. Bettina Feistel-Rohmeder, editor of the *Deutsche Kunstkorrespondenz*, described about twenty of these groups scattered throughout Saxony, Bavaria, and Baden, of which a few, such as Nürnberg's Feierabendgesellschaft and Munich's Verein für künstlerische Interessen, concentrated upon opposition to contemporary tendencies in the arts.[10]

But unlike these organizations, the Kampfbund had strong political backing and large ambitions. From the beginning, Rosenberg's group made a conscious effort to enlist the support of a wide variety of prominent conservative intellectuals. Men of such radically different views as Othmar Spann, Viennese sociologist and theorist of the corporate state; Adolf Bartels, head of the virulently anti-Semitic Bartelsbund and prophet of the "völkische Bewegung"; and Hans Johst, "expressionist" playwright, spoke at Kampfbund meetings or wrote for its publications during the first two years of its existence.[11] By the middle of 1930, the members of the Bayreuth circle were active in the Kampfbund's cause;[12] and Robert Mielke, well-known art historian and founder of the influential Bund Heimatschutz, had increased the prestige of the group by his endorsement of its goals.[13] This kind of support enabled the Kampfbund to extend its membership very rapidly, particularly in academic circles, and to absorb its rivals among local organizations with similar aims.[14] By 1932 the Kampfbund had acquired more than thirty-three subchapters and published a magazine called *Deutsche Kultur-Wacht*.[15] By 1933, when it reached the height of its power and influence, the Kampfbund had set up branches for the visual arts, literature, the theater, radio, and film; through these it attempted, although without lasting success, to become the chief organ of control of the creative professions within the Nazi state.

In keeping with the generality of its claims and the heterogeneity of its membership, the Kampfbund's activities touched upon a wide variety of cultural questions. The public lectures which the organization sponsored with increasing frequency ranged in their subject matter from education and sports to radio and the film. A very high proportion of the early meetings, however, dealt with literature, music, and the drama; and attacks upon contemporary tendencies in these fields dominated the Kampfbund's propaganda up to 1930. In March of 1929, for example, Alfred Heuss, publisher of the *Zeitschrift für Musik,* gave a series of lectures for the Kampbund attacking the works of Krenek and Kurt Weill.[16] Rosenberg's favorite targets at this date were Max Reinhardt, the great Berlin theater director and producer, and Heinrich Mann, whose pacifism earned him the epithet "art bolshevist" in Rosenberg's speeches.[17] Rosenberg and Heuss used the works of these men as examples of the "chaos" which threatened German "form" and which had its twin sources in American "mechanism" and Russian "bolshevism."

In the attacks of Kampfbund speakers upon contemporary tendencies in the arts, racism played a prominent part. Rosenberg constantly called attention to the fact that Reinhardt was a Jew and hinted at a connection between Reinhardt's avant-garde productions, his politics, and his race. But the Kampfbund speakers did not restrict themselves to anti-Semitism, as earlier party propaganda had. Heuss dwelt on the fact that Krenek's Berlin revue, "Jonny spielt auf," had a Negro as its principal actor, a clear indication, he said, of the racial basis of Weimar's cultural decline. Later Kampfbund lecturers liked to speak of the Republic's "Nigger-Culture" because of the popularity of American jazz, often performed by Negro entertainers.[18] Moreover, the racist theme in Kampfbund propaganda was always part of a broader cultural argument, so that it took a relatively sophisticated form.

Although these attacks upon contemporaries predominated among the Kampfbund's activities up to 1930, the organization also made an effort from the start to display a positive side. Thus the Dresden chapter endowed a literature prize for the state of Saxony, proposing, among others, Hans Johst, Ernst Jünger, Adolf Bartels, Richard Strauss, and Siegfried Wagner as its recipients.[19] The Kampfbund also held chamber music concerts, at which the works of "German" masters were performed, and "artistic evenings," at which Bartels and Baldur von Schirach read their poetry.[20] Later on it set up its own theater in Munich which the party took pride in keeping open when the depression forced other Bavarian theaters to close.[21] Here the most familiar German classics were performed.

After 1928 the activities of Rosenberg's organization began to be reflected in the policy of the party's chief propaganda organ, the *Völkischer Beobachter*.[22] The paper began at this time to publish attacks upon writers like Karl Krauss and Walter Hasenclever, and its many references to the Reinhardt productions closely paralleled Rosenberg's.[23] In 1929 the *VB* printed several shrill editorials on Paul Robeson and Josephine Baker at the time of their appearances in Berlin, and in January of 1930 it published an article which summed up the party's entire cultural policy as "Against Negro Culture."[24] At the same time, crude anti-Semitism became less prominent in the *VB*'s discussions of the arts, and the tone of many of the articles on cultural questions became more sophisticated than had earlier been the case. Its editorials began to talk of cultural decline in terms reminiscent of *Mein Kampf*, and the paper began to make frequent references to such earlier and relatively respectable writers on culture and race as Paul de Lagarde or Houston Stewart Chamberlain.

In the late twenties, the party was thus beginning to adopt in its propaganda many of the ideas expressed by the critics of the new architecture. In January of 1929 the *VB* even began to use the term "cultural bolshevism" as a slogan to describe all that it opposed in contemporary culture.[25] Yet despite the new role which Rosenberg's activities gave to the arts in Nazi propaganda and despite the VB's willingness to use the terminology of the debate over the new style, before 1930 both the Kampfbund and the VB were strikingly reluctant to join in the attacks upon the new architecture. Except for a brief passage on the paintings of George Grosz in one of its early pamphlets, the Kampfbund made no reference to any of the visual arts during the first two years of its existence. The VB, on the other hand, made a clear effort during 1929 to give broader coverage to the visual arts, but its articles on painting and sculpture consisted chiefly of reviews of exhibitions of which it approved. 1928 and 1929 also saw a considerable increase in the VB's treatment of architectural questions, and these articles help to explain why Nazi propaganda was so tardy in attacking the new architecture. For up until 1930, the VB's articles on architecture reveal a certain admiration for this type of design. In articles on public housing in 1927 the paper commended the work of Gropius, Wagner, and May, praising in particular the standardized plans and building methods employed in their developments and the kind of built-in mechanical equipment which had created a "housewife's paradise."[26] A Munich housing official was quoted with approval when he admired the uniform appearance of the new developments, important, he said, in overcoming "the false individualism of the prewar period."[27] In mid-1928 on the occasion of an exhibition of very modern interior furnishings and mechanical equipment in Munich, a series of articles described enthusiastically "the penetration of our homes, and thus of our lives and thoughts, by the essence of [modern] technology, by the technical spirit of Sachlichkeit."[28] Tentative admiration for the urban planning of radical architects is evident in some of these articles, and even as late as June 1929, the paper published a sympathetic discussion of the city planning of Corbusier, the archenemy in Senger's writing.[29]

These instances of sympathy for the new style, though relatively infrequent, reflect what might be termed the "socialist" strain in Nazi ideology. The VB constantly supported programs for large-scale, low-cost public housing in an attempt to appeal to the working classes, and the radical architects won its approval for their concern with this question. In addition the editors often wrote about Germany's industrial development and how it could be improved. The VB did not, to be sure, express admiration for every aspect of modern industrial society, but it frequently described rapid technological development as a means toward renewed national power, and it was only gradually and reluctantly that the paper began to adopt the argument of conservative intellectuals that technology can represent a threat to "culture." Finally, the *VB* was probably influenced by the admiration for great cities which Hitler frequently expressed in his writings and speeches, and this made the paper willing occasionally to endorse radical architects' urban planning. These attitudes naturally militated against the acceptance of the views of conservative architects.

But around 1930, two events helped to overcome the party's grudging admiration of the new style and to bring conservative architects into the forefront of the Kampfbund's propaganda. The first was a change in party ideology itself, as a result of the new influence of Richard Walter Darré within the party hierarchy. Darré introduced a strong antiurban tendency into Nazi thought and Nazi propaganda, a tendency which came to be known by the catchwords "blood and soil." The second was the ministry of Wilhelm Frick in Thuringia in 1930. Frick instituted a short-lived new cultural program in that state, employed Schultze-Naumburg as Bartning's successor, and brought him directly to the attention of the Kampfbund leadership.

Although Darré achieved great influence in the party after 1930, he was a latecomer to Nazi politics.[30] Born in Argentina and trained in Germany in agronomy and animal husbandry, he began his career in 1927 as a consultant to the Prussian Ministry of Agriculture.[31] He entered the Nazi party toward the end of the decade and quickly became its leading expert on agricultural problems. Darré was an outspoken opponent of the agricultural methods employed by the Junkers on the great estates of east Germany and proposed to Hitler the creation of new small and medium-sized peasant landholdings in this area. Hitler incorporated this and others of Darré's proposals into a Nazi peasant program, which he issued over his own signature in March of 1930.[32] From this point onward, Darré's rise to power within the party was extremely rapid. He set up and headed a new argicultural section of the party in August of 1930 and successfully built it up into an effective rival of the national agrarian league, or Landbund. He became one of Hitler's closest associates, and by the end of 1933 he shared control of the party's political organization only with Goebbels and Ley. Darré supplanted Hugenberg as Minister of Food and Agriculture in the summer of 1933 and retained this post until 1942.

The cost of this increasing political power was, however, the failure of his programs. The party implemented neither his plan for the dissolution of the Junker estates nor his later proposals for decreased interest rates on agrarian debts. This failure may have provided part of the motive for Darré's close friendship with Himmler, who was deeply impressed with Darré's program and hoped to achieve the establishment of what Darré called "the new peasant aristocracy" in a new SS-controlled empire in the east. Darré's racial views also inspired Himmler, for Darré was the party's principal advocate of selective breeding, on the analogy of animal husbandry, in order to preserve the purity of the race. Beginning in 1931, Himmler carried out this idea in the series of ordinances governing the marriages of members of the SS. Himmler's admiration for Darré led him to make the Minister of Agriculture chief of the Rasse- und Siedlungs-Hauptamt within the SS, the organization initially in charge of Himmler's resettlement plans and eventually deeply implicated in the execution of "the final solution."[33]

Both Darré's agricultural proposals and his racial views were based upon a nearly mystical idealization of the peasant way of life. An extremely prolific writer, Darré propounded this peasant mysticism in a long series of books and pamphlets between 1929 and the middle thirties; but his principal arguments are clearly formulated in his first work, *The Peasantry as the Life Source of the Nordic Race*, published in 1929.[34] In this book Darré traced the origins of the "Nordic" race back to the first Germanic settlers of Europe. In his view, the earliest peoples of Europe could be divided into two categories: the "settlers" and the "nomads." The former provided Europe with warriors and aristocrats and spawned the Nordic race; the latter in his thinking were the source of all the other races, and especially of the Semitic, oriental, and Indian "races." In Darré's writing this division between settlers and nomads represented a cultural division as well as a racial one. Nomadic peoples are always "materialistic," because originally they had to concentrate all their attention upon the hard business of feeding and clothing themselves. Thus the nomadic races became, at a later stage in history, Europe's peddlars and tradesmen. Nomadic peoples, moreover, have no respect for property; they therefore become communists; Lenin was thus a product of the nomadic racial strain. Nomads are, in addition, sophists in philosophy and uncreative in art, since, always on the move, at least spiritually, they never see into the true reality of things.[35]

The "settlers" who produced the Nordic race represent in their culture the antithesis of all these qualities. "True peasant thought," Darré wrote, perceives both the essence of reality and the process

of organic growth and change, since the peasant, at least spiritually, remains on his property, tending his corn and pigs. Thus
the peasant people have produced both German idealism and
natural philosophy. Unlike the nomads with their communism,
the peasant has given the Nordic race a belief in individualism
and the free development of the personality, which can only grow
out of the identity which settled property-holding creates. Since
this belief in personality is also a principal source of "Nordic"
culture, the sanctity of (peasant) property and cultural creativity
are indissolubly bound together. The peasant too has been the
source of success in both arms and statesmanship throughout
European history.[36] Thus all the virtues of European civilization,
in Darré's writing, derive from the Nordic race, which is itself
rooted in the peasant way of life.

This doctrine of "blood and soil," as it came to be called,* never
won over the entire party hierarchy. Hitler exploited it in his
appeals to the peasantry; Rosenberg accepted some parts of it;
Goebbels none. But it had a great deal of influence upon party
propaganda from 1930 onward, and it began to influence the treatment of architecture in Nazi writing even before that. For Darré's
idealization of the peasantry involved an emphatic condemnation
of modern technology and the modern city. The Nordic race "has
never been successful in founding cities," since "the idea of separ-
ation from the land was so foreign to the Germanic [peasants]."
Only nomads could successfully live and spread their cultural
values in the cities, because they do not need to provide for the
future. But the Nordic race can only be propagated on the soil,
and the modern city is therefore an "infertility machine [Un-
fruchtsbarkeitsmaschine]." The rapid urbanization which began
at the end of the nineteenth century has nearly destroyed the
Nordic peasantry and must be halted. Darré saw the cause of this
urbanization in industrialization, which he deplored, and he
claimed that the only hope for the Nordic race and its cultural
values was to repatriate new generations of racially pure Nordic-
peasants to the soil.[37]

This view of the city began to influence the *VB* in 1928 and
1929, when the paper published a column called "News from the
Asphalt Deserts." The column describes the "metropolis" as "the
melting pot of all evil . . . of prostitution, bars, illness, movies,
Marxism, Jews, strippers, Negro dances, and all the disgusting
offspring of so-called 'modern art.' "[38] Berlin becomes "the most
infertile city in the world."[39] By the end of 1930 these ideas had

*After Darré's second book, *Neuadel aus Blut und Boden* (Munich, 1930).

supplanted every trace of sympathy for urbanization in the VB's pages, and by June of 1931 the paper had specifically endorsed Darré's proposals for the repatriation of urban populations to the soil.[40] The Kampfbund too gave Darré its endorsement: he was one of the principal speakers at the organization's national congress in June of 1930. He attacked urbanization at the meeting and explained to the Kampfbund's members how the peasant way of life could provide a new basis for German culture.[41] By 1930, then, Darré's teachings had supplanted the nascent admiration for modern technology and the modern city evident in Nazi propaganda before that date and had begun deeply to influence the policies of the Kampfbund. This antiurbanism fitted in very closely with the kind of attacks Schultze-Naumburg had been making upon the new architecture; when Kampfbund propaganda began to concentrate upon the visual arts, the organization turned first to Schultze-Naumburg as its spokesman.

It was not, however, either Rosenberg or Darré who introduced Schultze-Naumburg to the Nazi party, but Wilhelm Frick, who as a member of the Thuringian coalition government of 1930 was the first of his party to hold a state ministry.[42] Because of his long record of service to the party and to Hitler, Frick, a Bavarian, was nominated to leadership in Thuringia after the local Nazi party won a sizeable plurality in the state elections of January 1930. This plurality allowed Frick to demand two ministries, and he chose the ministries of Interior, which gave him supervision of the Thuringian police, and of Education. The latter choice was the result of a decision to emphasize cultural policy. Frick and his advisers, as the Gauleiter Fritz Sauckel later explained, knew that they were not strong enough to effect far-reaching political and economic changes, "but they were convinced that they had finally found the opportunity to turn this state into a cell . . . from which the forces of moral and spiritual renewal could reach out into the Reich."[43] Frick's cultural policy was thus intended from the start as a substitute for other types of political action.

The basis of Frick's program for "moral and spiritual renewal" was his "Ordinance against Negro Culture" of April 1, 1930, which proposed to rid Thuringia of all "immoral and foreign racial elements in the arts."[44] His first and most important step in carrying out this program was to dissolve Bartning's architectural school and, ignoring the candidates proposed by the other conservative parties, to appoint Schultze-Naumburg to head a new "united school," offering training in painting, applied arts, and architecture.[45] Schultze-Naumburg's term of office lasted only a little more than a year, for Frick rapidly came into conflict with both the federal government and the Thuringian Landtag, and his ministry was brief. Frick's artistic policy aroused considerable local opposition, and many of his other actions — his introduction of racist prayers into the schools, his appointment of Hans F. K. Günther to a professorship at Jena over the protests of university officials, and his police purges — violated state and federal law. In April of 1931, the other right-wing parties withdrew their support from Frick's ministry and repealed his ordinances; a few months later they discharged Günther and Schultze-Naumburg.[46]

Schultze-Naumburg therefore had little time to work out any kind of positive policy in his new position, and his actions were almost entirely destructive. At his instigation the paintings of Barlach, Kandinsky, Klee, Schlemmer, and Schmidt-Rottluff were removed from public view in Weimar, as representative of "eastern or otherwise racially inferior subhumanity."[47] Schlemmer's murals in the buildings which had housed Gropius' school were painted over. Most important, Schultze-Naumburg discharged the entire faculty of Bartning's school, explaining that it still included too many teachers who were sympathetic to Gropius' ideas; he had hardly begun to collect a new staff when his appointment was terminated.[48] Schultze-Naumburg's policies in Weimar therefore took on the appearance of a latter-day attack upon the Bauhaus, revived the interest of the national press in the Bauhaus controversy, and for the first time identified the Nazi party with opposition to Gropius' school.

Frick's ministry in Thuringia represented merely a brief interlude in the rise of the Nazi party. But for the duration of his term in office, Frick became the hero of party propaganda and his cultural policy was extravagantly praised throughout the party press. The *VB*, which had praised the Bauhaus occasionally and had previously paid no attention to Schultze-Naumburg's ideas,[49] now began to provide very thorough coverage of his speeches and books and to defend him against his critics. It now described the Bauhaus as "that infamous . . . stronghold of art bolshevism," and represented Schultze-Naumburg as the apostle of "true German architecture."[50]

As soon as these developments in Thuringia had begun to give Schultze-Naumburg an important reputation in Nazi circles, the Kampfbund enlisted his services. Early in 1930 the organization began to publish his writings.[51] In June the Kampfbund held its annual congress in Weimar, in recognition of the accomplishments of Frick's ministry. In addition to Darré, Frick and Rosenberg spoke at the congress, and each of them paid tribute to Schultze-Naumburg's racial theories of art and his attacks upon "rootless," "urban" architecture.[52] Schultze-Naumburg now rapidly became the Kampfbund's principal spokesman on artistic questions, and with his help the organization began a very active, virulent, and highly publicized campaign against the new architecture. As such other prominent opponents of the new style as Konrad Nonn, Paul Schmitthenner, Eugen Hönig, Alexander von Senger, and German Bestelmeyer gathered around Schultze-Naumburg, the Kampfbund founded a daughter organization for them designed to "carry on the battle against architectural bolshevism" and to impart a "nationalist education" to German architects. By the end of 1932, this group, which was called the Kampfbund deutscher Architekten und Ingenieure (KDAI), played as prominent a role in Nazi cultural propaganda as the parent organization itself.[53] The Kampfbund's propaganda effort against the new style reached its peak during 1933: in that year it founded a new magazine to which such distinguished and universally respected architects as Theodor Fischer, Fritz Schumacher, and Fritz Höger contributed, and held a series of large public meetings at which Rosenberg and Gottfried Feder joined with the conservative architects in attacking the new architecture as "cultural bolshevism."[54]

The Kampfbund launched its propaganda campaign against the new architecture at the beginning of 1931, when it sponsored Schultze-Naumburg in a series of lectures entitled "The Struggle over Art." Schultze-Naumburg presented these lectures in six major cities during the course of the year, and his tour contributed more than any other Kampfbund activity to the organization's notoriety. On the whole, the lectures repeated the arguments and methods of presentation which Schultze-Naumburg had worked out in *Art and Race* and *The Face of the German House,* but some elements of his earlier arguments now received more emphasis. As in *Art and Race,* he tried to show the resemblance between the figure-style of modern painting and the appearance of the physically deformed or the mentally deficient. Again Schultze-Naumburg compared the worst examples of modern painting he could find with the masterpieces of the German middle ages, in particular with the famous statue of the Bamberg Rider. And he now extended this comparative technique to his architectural discussions, juxtaposing shabby rear views of modern apartment blocks with slides of Gothic cathedrals on the one hand and with pictures of Schmitthenner's elaborate villas on the other.

These illustrations were accompanied by the racist arguments about art which Schultze-Naumburg had developed earlier, but he now devoted the larger proportion of the lectures to his attacks on the new architecture, and his claim that the new style symbolized social disintegration and cultural decline received a new emphasis. Again and again Schultze-Naumburg compared "the work of the nomads of the metropolis . . . who have lost the concept of the homeland [Heimat], to "the German house . . . rooted in the soil." The new architecture symbolized, and at the same time helped to produce, an "uprooted people." The lectures gave, in addition, a greater emphasis than before to the dangers of the "mechanical functionalism" of the new style. In glorifying technology, radical architects threatened the German "soul" with an "unlimited materialism." To these older arguments with their new emphases, Schultze-Naumburg now added a political plea, urging his audience to support the Kampfbund's work: "For, just as in German politics, a battle over life and death rages in German art today. Alongside the struggle for power, the struggle for art must be fought through with the same earnestness and the same decision, if we do not want to sacrifice the German soul."[55] He concluded: "Around us a new Germany must rise, which can find a home in dwellings embedded in foliage, whose government buildings no longer look like factories, nor its churches like movie houses, but instead bear the signature of the majesty and the power of the people . . . This evil, tormenting dream must cease. And when dawn comes, then will resound the cry: Deutschland erwache!"[56]

Schultze-Naumburg's lectures created a sensation wherever they were given. Usually he appeared at universities or Technische Hochschulen, and he filled their largest lecture halls to capacity. Each lecture — at Munich, Dresden, and Berlin; Wiesbaden, Darmstadt, and Frankfurt — was introduced by Rosenberg and protected by a full complement of SA guards. The Storm Troopers often proved to be necessary; during at least two of the lectures, catcalls drowned out the speaker and fights broke out.[57] But despite the hostility of many members of his audiences, the lectures were enormously popular, and in Munich public demand made a repeat performance necessary. The liberal newspapers and many professional journals were scandalized by Schultze-Naumburg's arguments and his methods, and their bitter attacks provided the Kampfbund with unexpected, and, from Rosenberg's point of view, very desirable, publicity.[58] As far as the Kampfbund was concerned, therefore, Schultze-Naumburg was an extraordinary success; from the time of his tour, the Kampfbund publicized his speeches and writings more widely than those of any other member except Rosenberg himself.

The publicity which the Kampfbund gave to Schultze-Naumburg's teachings caused the other conservative architects who had attacked the new architecture to come to the support of Rosenberg's organization. Between the beginning of 1931 and the spring of 1933, Schmitthenner, Bestelmeyer, Senger, and many others followed Schultze-Naumburg's example in joining the Kampfbund and lecturing under its auspices. These men continued, of course, to offer their own characteristic arguments against the new style, which were often quite different from Schultze-Naumburg's. Paul Schmitthenner, for example, liked to warn against the radical architects' departure from tradition: "It just won't do, simply to throw our entire inherited tradition overboard. We stand on the shoulders of those who go before us." Or, as he frequently argued, "That which is truly spiritual in architecture cannot be international."[59] German Bestelmeyer, on the other hand, usually attacked the uniformity of design created by the new style, a uniformity which "prepares the way for bolshevism."[60] Alexander von Senger continued to point to the revolutionary political associations of the new style and to speak and write about the "communist conspiracy" in architecture.[61] But such was the overwhelming influence of Schultze-Naumburg within the Kampfbund that it was his warnings against the tyranny of the machine and the metropolis which took precedence in the organization's official attacks on the new architecture. When the KDAI was founded for the architects who wished to support the Kampfbund, Schultze-Naumburg repeated "The Struggle over Art" at each of the organizational meetings of its subchapters.[62] The first statement of purpose issued by the new organization included the assertion that "the revivification of agriculture [Reagrarisierung] is the principal need of our time."[63] Winfried Wendland, one of the directors of the Berlin chapter of the KDAI, described the work of the Kampfbund as an attack upon the "worship of the metropolis." To oppose "bolshevist" urban architecture, Nazism must, he said, encourage young architects to create an architecture based upon "nature and the soil," using Handwerk rather than machine technology.[64] The same kind of arguments gradually began to dominate the thinking of the Kampfbund's politicians as well as its architect members. When Gottfried Feder became head of the architects' Kampfbund in 1932 he took over Schultze-Naumburg's warnings against the city and the machine.[65] And the same views influenced Rosenberg himself. Long after the Kampfbund had lost most of its power in both party and state, he continued to speak of an architecture "uprooted from blood and soil" as the chief focus of "the struggle over art" and "the struggle over culture."[66]

Because its members were artists and intellectuals and because their speeches were generally presented in an academic setting, the Kampfbund's propaganda reached a limited audience. But at the same time the attack on the new architecture was conveyed to a much larger public by the *Völkischer Beobachter*. Around the beginning of July 1930, the *VB* reversed its former policy and launched a virulent campaign against the new style.[67] Articles recording opposition to the new architecture began to take up more and more space in its pages, until by 1932 the paper was publishing an average of three major articles on architecture each month. In early 1933, six out of the last ten issues of the *VB* appearing before the elections of March 5 contained full-page attacks upon radical architects and their work. Moreover, by 1933 opposition to modern architecture had nearly supplanted the kind of criticism of contemporary tendencies in the other arts which the *VB* had begun to publish in 1928. The paper's many articles on contemporary culture still occasionally contained some discussion of literature or drama, but architecture now took the most prominent place. Insofar as modern art was discussed, the Ring architects were almost invariably blamed for its development and popularity.[68] The editors explained this new emphasis on architecture by explicitly adopting the old argument of the radical architects that architectural style "reflects" much broader developments in culture and society: "In building as in no other area [of life] the cultural, economic, and racial powers of the Volk are bound together."[69] Thus in the last few years before the Nazis took power, the *VB* came to regard the new style as the equivalent of what the Nazis had begun to call "cultural bolshevism": as a symbol not only of all that was "modern" in the visual arts, but also of all that the party condemned in contemporary society as a whole.[70]

The *VB*'s attacks upon the new style took a very great variety of forms. The policy of reviewing art and architectural exhibitions, initiated in 1928 as part of the paper's attempt to broaden its appeal, now began to play a part in the *VB*'s tactics against the radical architects. The exhibitions of the radical architects were punctually reviewed after 1930 and used as occasions for sweeping denunciations of the cultural dangers inherent in the new style.[71] On the other hand, cases of local opposition to the new style were treated as ordinary news stories — they received a good deal of space, under inflammatory headlines, but were reported with a minimum of editorial comment.[72] For the most part, the attacks of professional journals and the building trades were used in a similar way. The *VB*'s election appeals also frequently provided the occasion for an attack upon the new architecture. These appeals contained a number of subsections, each of which urged a specific group to vote the Nazi ticket. The sections directed toward artists, architects, or members of the building trades usually attacked the radical architects and their work.

In addition to these reviews, reports, and election appeals, the *VB* also reprinted the writings and speeches of the most prominent conservative opponents of the new style. From April of 1930, the paper regularly published Schultze-Naumburg's speeches and lengthy quotations from his books; a few months later it began to publish excerpts from the writings and speeches of other opponents of the new style, in many cases even before these men had enlisted in the Kampfbund. Bestelmeyer, for example, became a favorite of the *VB* in October of 1930, Schmitthenner in December, while in October and November revised portions of Senger's *Crisis in Architecture* reappeared under the title "Bolshevism in Building."[73] Senger's articles were accompanied by full-page companion articles by the editors on such related topics as "Blood as the basis of all true art," "Sweden too rejects the new architecture," and "The essence of the Germanic world-view."

But the largest proportion of the *VB*'s architectural propaganda was neither geared to a specific occasion nor wholly dependent upon the arguments of conservative architects. Most of the paper's attacks upon the new style took the form of elaborate critical articles which exploited at length all the symbolic implications of the new style. Schultze-Naumburg's and Senger's arguments played an important role in these articles, but their ideas were imbedded in a broader argument. These attacks drew comprehensively upon every variety of criticism which had been made in the past: upon the arguments arising from the Weimar controversy, upon the articles which had appeared in national conservative newspapers, upon the pamphlets published by the building trades or by professional journals, as well as upon the ideas of the conservative architects. The editors and their columnists interlarded these arguments with personal invective against the radical architects themselves, and put the whole together in a patchwork fashion which lacked logical structure but which by a process of suggestion and shrill insinuation achieved an effectiveness of its own.

The character of the *VB*'s architectural propaganda emerges most clearly in direct quotation. The following example appeared during the election campaign of November 1932 as part of a series of articles on architecture entitled "The Purpose of our Cultural-political Struggle."

The Bauhaus — that was "the cathedral of Marxism," a cathedral, however, which damned well looked like a Synagogue. To the "inspiration" of this "model school" we owe not least those oriental boxes which we have described before, [and] which are repugnant to good taste. That they also deserve the scorn of all experienced builders, we have recently established. After just a few years these buildings, prized as today's highest accomplishments, began to develop great cracks at every edge and corner. Yes, whole blocks of dwellings were so full of damp that the health authorities had to intervene. . . . The protests of good German architects have remained unheard for a long time, because certain industries had financial interests in the experiments of the Bauhaus — we speak of the Bauhaus here always as a concept — and the international [political] parties expected a lot from the cultural bolshevism which they carried on openly. . . . And they were right, for this architecture came to be the spiritual expression of their spirit. . . . They believed that "the house is an instrument like an automobile." . . . Thus these men reveal their character as typical nomads of the metropolis, who no longer understand blood and soil. . . . Now their secret is known! The new dwelling is an instrument for the destruction of the family and the race. Now we understand the deeper sense of that architectural nonsense which built housing developments in the style of prison cells, and perpetrated an asiatic interlude on German soil. . . . Bolshevism, the arch-enemy of all mature culture, works toward the victory of this [architectural] desolation and horror![74]

These are familiar phrases. Konrad Nonn's "cathedral of Marxism" is jumbled together with *Deutschland*'s "oriental boxes" and *Deutsche Bauhütte*'s allegations of construction failures in radical architects' housing. There follow hints derived from Senger about the corruption of German industry and radical architects' own claim to express the "spirit of the age." Schultze-Naumburg's refrain is amplified by a reference to "blood and soil," a term he himself had not used, and the conclusion that the new architecture threatens "the family" is borrowed from *Ludendorffs Volkswarte*. The anti-Semitism of the völkische papers, never present in the arguments of conservative architects, reappears in the opening lines. These ideas and insinuations had never been put together in quite the same combination before, nor had they ever been so clearly focussed in a political attack upon the republican regime. Like the opponents of the Bauhaus, like Senger, like some of the conservative newspapers, the *VB* condemns all the sins of the new style as "bolshevism." But these sins are now described as part of a conscious political policy of "cultural bolshevism" carried on by "the international parties" which control the Weimar government in Germany.

This combination of ideas appeared in each of the *VB*'s major articles on the new architecture. But the emphasis in these articles often varied. During the depression years, the *VB* made a concerted effort to appeal to the unemployed in the building trades, and many of its articles argued that it was the Ring architects who had deprived these men of jobs:

> The bolshevisation of architecture has gone so far today that native German architects, dependent on the Fatherland, are pressed to the wall and hundreds emigrate or commit suicide. . . . Architects colored with Marxism, who know their way around [die die Lage erfasst haben] and have the right connections, get the fattest commissions. . . . The so-called leaders of the trades [Handwerk] too have one-sided political connections . . . The young artisan is ever more proletarianized and pushed into the arms of the communists.[75]

The *VB* invariably took the opportunity to put the blame for this situation on the patronage which the Ring had obtained from local and national governments under the republican regime:

> Instead of earnestly beginning the task of practical reconstruction, this state founded a "Reichsforschungsgesellschaft," . . . a society of "prominent" men who have been friendly to the spirit of this Republic since its "brilliant" beginning. . . . It is only to be expected that people favored by their connections with the leaders of the red parties have taken over these "experiments." . . . The buildings [of these men] have only one virtue, that they show the next generation that foreigners, rather than their fathers, are responsible for this mixture of steel, glass, and flat roof. . . . These excrescences would not have occurred had the state . . . driven the communists from the country at the outset. . . . But all the old parties were too weak and degenerate, too timid, to make even one energetic effort against this "propaganda studio" and the harm it brings to all honorable architects. . . . From such a state, nothing further should be demanded or expected . . . for a state which is not able to value and care for . . . the inheritance of history, for a native environment, can be dismissed from its duties without compunction.[76]

Because of this emphasis on the privileged position of the "Marxist" Ring architects and the consequent sufferings of "German" architects and builders, the *VB*'s articles often gave a great deal of space to personal attacks upon the most prominent radical architects. In July of 1931, for example, in a long article on the Reichsforschungsgesellschaft, the paper devoted several columns of invective to "the members of the Jewish-bolshevist architectural organization, the Ring."[77] Gropius was described as "that elegant salon-bolshevist," who "had to leave Weimar because he misappropriated government funds"; Bartning "builds churches for evangelical groups who do not realize that he is a follower of atheistic bolshevism"; May "went to Russia after the buildings he built with public funds had to be closed"; Wagner "is responsible for the fact that neither private architects nor most members of the building trades receive work in Berlin's housing developments." The article continued in this vein with some twenty more members of the Ring (or men whom the editors thought were members), among them Döcker, Häring, Haesler, Hilberseimer, Hans and Wassily Luckhardt, Mendelsohn, Mies, Poelzig, Karl Schneider, and Bruno and Max Taut. As a conclusion to this kind of attack, the VB promised that the party would "settle accounts" with these men when it came to power; occasionally it spoke of the "extirpation [Ausrottung]" of their work as well.[78] The Third Reich would also "take care of the thousands of architects, engineers, and technical personnel who graduate from the technical schools each year . . . revivify the crafts . . . support private architects . . . and restore building activity."[79]

But whatever the emphasis of the VB's articles, almost all were very broad in scope. If a passage emphasized the favoritism of republican patronage, it often went on to accuse the "foreigners" sponsored by the government of attempting systematically to do away with the traditions of "German" art: "German architects! Never forget that in the postwar era everything built up over centuries by the German creative impulse has been arrogantly, criminally treated by men without conscience — reviled and denigrated by constructivists, psychopaths, and foreigners in order to win the favor of unscrupulous patrons, while you have been treated as traitors and have found no tasks with which to test your skill and your spiritual power."[80] Those articles which concentrated upon character assasination nevertheless commonly included attacks upon the style of radical architects' buildings. Most often these attacks centered around the charge that the Ring architects sought to impose social leveling:

According to the leaders of the Bauhaus . . . rooms must look like studios, like operating theaters; all warmth is banned from them. Therefore no wood; rugs and upholstery are sins against the holy ghost of "Sachlichkeit." Glass instead, all kinds of metal, or artificial stone — these are the stylish materials! The new man is no longer a man, he is a "geometric animal." He needs no dwelling, no home, only a "dwelling-machine." This man is not an individual, not a personality, but a collective entity, a piece of mass man. And therefore they build "housing developments," apartment blocks of desolate uniformity, in which everything is standardized. These are tenements, built not as a necessity, as in the rapidly growing cities during the second half of the nineteenth century, but as a matter of principle. They want to kill personality in men, they want collectivism, for the highest goal of these architects is Marxism, communism.[81]

And particularly in connection with this kind of warning about the social effects of the new style, the *VB* liked to invoke the image of Jewish conspiracy:

Now is revealed the picture of Jewish monopoly-art already only too well known: the unclean collaboration of certain branches of great industry, dominated by Jews, with the Marxist parties and with the fuzzy ideologues of certain bourgeois circles. The result: the proletarianization and nullification of the German man, his denigration to a domestic pet of the Jew, who is permitted only the minimum necessities for his physical existence, but is denied even the smallest room for his spiritual needs.[82]

The *VB* used the term "cultural bolshevism" to describe each of these sins of radical architects in turn, and usually ended its articles with some such conclusion as: "Only National Socialism has the power to protect the cultural traditions of the nation and to secure the birth of a new German creativity."[83]

Despite the incoherence of the *VB*'s patchwork arguments and the crudity of its invective, the paper's attacks upon the new style, taken as a whole, present a clear composite picture. In the *VB*'s pages, the new style came to epitomize the social and economic changes caused by the new wave of industrialization since 1914 and acute during the depression years, changes which had produced a sense of rootlessness in the German middle class. In its architectural propaganda, the *VB* was able to ascribe these feelings of economic and social distress to both cultural and political causes. The paper's editors stigmatized the social and economic changes of the postwar period as part of a process of "cultural decline" and succeeded in turn in ascribing this cultural deterioration to the conscious political purpose of "the international powers," of "bolshevism," and above all of the Weimar Republic itself — "the present state." The implication was, of course, that the "extirpation" of "architectural bolshevism" by political initiative would strike decisively at economic and social "bolshevism" — an implication which helps to account for the continuing prominence of architectural propaganda after the Nazis took power. The elements of this picture of the new architecture had all been present in public debate before 1930, but the party press succeeded in welding them together into a new and politically effective whole.

It is important to remember that every aspect of the Nazi attack upon the new architecture involved a positive implication; that every condemnation of the values which the new style allegedly represented committed the party, at least in theory, to foster their opposite. Not only a program for national strength, but also admiration for individualism and nostalgia for a hierarchical society and a preindustrial economy, emerge from the party's architectural propaganda between 1930 and 1933. These values are not only contradictory among themselves; many of them are also wholly incompatible with the character of the Nazi state as it evolved after 1933. Nevertheless, support for some kind of architectural style which would symbolize these contradictory values was implied in party propaganda, and attacks upon the new style often referred to the "great" styles of the German past. Yet these were variously defined: as the "architecture of around 1910" by the conservative architects sponsored by the Kampfbund, as the art of classical Weimar in the age of Goethe by Frick and by many writers in the VB, as the German Gothic, and even in some cases as the "folk" style of the German peasant in late medieval times. Thus the greatest political virtue of Nazi opposition to the new syle — the fact that it was able to appeal to a wide variety of economic, social, and cultural concerns — also created potential sources of dissent once the party took power and launched its own building program. The contradictions implied in this architectural propaganda were never solved, but took the form of a continuing debate within the Nazi party after it came to power.

VII / The Evolution of Architectural Control under the Nazi Regime

Despite the many contradictions implicit in Nazi architectural propaganda before 1933, this propaganda appeared to make two clear and consistent promises to the supporters of the party. On the one hand, the Ring architects and their followers were to be deprived of their influence upon German architecture; on the other hand, the party would work to support a "German" or "national socialist" style in building. These promises led the opponents of the new style to expect not merely a purge of the Ring architects from all public office, but also the establishment of official organizations which could regulate the styles which architects would be permitted to use. Many of the articles in the *Völkischer Beobachter* encouraged these expectations, and the Kampfbund was insistent on both points. Several months before the Machtergreifung, the leaders of the Kampfbund began to think of their organization as the natural vehicle for exerting artistic regulation and control of this type. They hoped to see the architects' Kampfbund (KDAI) enlarged into a professional society which, while excluding the radical architects, would educate the rest of the profession along "national socialist" lines. To the group of conservative architects who had gathered together in Rosenberg's organization this demand meant, of course, the restoration of the influence of the progressive historicist traditions of the prewar period, with an emphasis on architecture of a rural, rather than an urban character.

The party fulfilled only a part of these promises after it came to power, and it frustrated nearly all of the specific ambitions of the Kampfbund leadership. In the spring of 1933 the new government began a systematic attack upon the creators of the new style, depriving them of their jobs in schools, building societies, and municipal governments, and of their positions of leadership in the national professional organizations. But no law was passed which prevented the radical architects from obtaining new commissions, nor were they excluded from ordinary membership in the professional societies. Moreover, the purges stopped short at the first rank of radical architects: many men who had been associated with the new style as assistants and students retained positions of influence under the new regime. The Nazi government did carry out the demand of the Kampfbund for the creation of a single professional organization which would be able to regulate the character of its members' work. But the Kampfbund itself was not permitted to dominate this organization, which did not, in the event, act as an effective instrument in controlling architectural style.

The inconclusiveness of the measures taken to purge the architectural profession and control its future output was in part the product of rivalries among the Nazi leadership. During the purges, it became apparent that the party officials who interested themselves in architecture held widely varying views, both about architectural style and about the degree to which the state should impose stylistic control. These differences of opinion emerged particularly clearly in the power struggle between Rosenberg and Goebbels which took place during the summer of 1933. Rosenberg, hoping to transform the Kampfbund into a state rather than a party organ, was the strongest advocate of the establishment of a single government organization to control cultural affairs. But when this body, the Reichskulturkammer, was established, it was placed under the authority of Goebbels' Propaganda Ministry, and Goebbels refused to make extensive use of the organization for cultural control. In the process of jockeying for power, the two men repeatedly attacked one another and publicly expressed very different conceptions of the goals of Nazi cultural policy.

Thus although the demands of the Kampfbund and of party architectural propaganda before 1933 were accomplished in general outline, they were satisfied more in the letter than in the spirit; and in the process the Kampfbund lost most of its power and influence. While the leading radical architects suffered from the initial purges, their principal opponents from the pre-Nazi era suffered from the accession of Goebbels to power in cultural affairs. The failure of the regime to set up a single set of stylistic canons for the regulation of Nazi architecture was a double failure from the point of view of the spokesmen and leaders of the Kampfbund. They did not secure the dominance within the architectural profession which they had expected, and the architectural styles which they had favored did not dominate the Nazi building program.

The story of Nazi architectural policy after 1933 thus falls into two phases. The way in which the mechanisms for state control and regimentation of the architectural profession were established and then inhibited in their effect illustrates in a negative way the rivalries among the party leaders. The development of the Nazi building program itself, described in Chapter VIII, illustrates the positive issue of these rivalries in a series of conflicting styles.

The Bauhaus was of course the first target of the Nazi purges, and the party made a successful attack upon the school even before it took control of the national government in 1933. From 1925 onward, the Bauhaus encountered very little local opposition in its new home in Dessau, where it was supported by funds from both the city and the state of Anhalt. Mies van der Rohe, who had succeeded Gropius and Hannes Meyer as Director, won such broad support that he was able to carry on with most of the activities at the school during the first years of the depression.[1] But this situation changed suddenly at the beginning of 1932, when the Nazis won a plurality in the Dessau City Council and enough seats in the Landtag to enable them to form a coalition ministry with the DNVP.

The Nazi candidates for the City Council had promised in their campaign to dissolve the Bauhaus and tear down the famous Bauhaus buildings: "with the closing of the so-called 'Hochschule für Gestaltung' one of the most prominent centers of the Jewish-Marxist art program [Kunstwillens] will disappear from the German soil. Let us hope that total demolition will follow, and that, where today the . . . oriental glass palace stands . . . there will soon be homesteads or parks, which will offer German men a home and recreation."[2]

In January of 1932 the Nazi representatives attempted to accomplish this program in the City Council, threatening to reject the city budget because of its provision of funds for the Bauhaus. The combined opposition of the Democrats, SPD, and DNVP within the City Council obstructed the Nazi demands until the summer; but in August, despite Mayor Hesse's continuing defense of the school, the SPD yielded to increasing pressure from the state government and abstained on the crucial vote.[3] The city government was thus forced to carry out the Nazi demands and on October 1 dissolved the school, discharging faculty and students. But as it turned out, the party did not tear down the Bauhaus buildings. Instead, party officials had a sloping wood roof added to the studio wing and converted the buildings into a school for party leaders. This forgetfulness of campaign arguments and unwillingness to waste valuable buildings, no matter what their style, was to be very typical of Nazi architectural policy after 1933.[4]

Meanwhile, a remnant of the student body and faculty moved to Berlin, where the school continued to operate for a few more months under Mies's direction. But, as soon as the party gained control of the Prussian government, the Gestapo staged a raid on the new quarters of the Bauhaus and arrested a number of the students for possessing "illegal communist propaganda material."[5] The new government "provisionally" shut down the school on April 12 with the promise that it might be reopened if Kandinsky and Hilberseimer were discharged and if the school's plan of instruction were approved by Rust's Ministry of Education.[6] Mies's appeals for assistance, directed to Rosenberg and to Winfried Wendland, at that time a member of Rust's ministry, produced prolonged and ultimately fruitless negotiations, while the Bauhaus, operating unofficially and without funds, neared bankruptcy.[7] Its faculty dispersed by common consent on the tenth of August, 1933.[8]

Outside the Bauhaus the radical architects did not hold many teaching positions, and of this relatively small number only a few suffered in the regime's purges of educational institutions. Ernst Wichert, who as director of Frankfurt's School of Arts and Crafts had worked closely with Ernst May and had been one of his most vigorous supporters, was discharged toward the end of May.[9] Shortly thereafter Hans Scharoun and Adolf Rading, designers of some of the most radical housing developments built during the Weimar Republic, lost their positions in the "Meisteratelier" of Breslau's art academy.[10] Aside from these few instances, the regime's intervention in the architectural faculties was relatively slight at first and usually confined to those cases where attacks upon specific individuals had called them to the attention of the authorities. For example, when the Kampfbund attacked Hans Poelzig's appointment as Director of Berlin's Vereinigte Staatschulen für Architektur, Malerei, und Kunstgewerbe because of his friendship with Wagner and Gropius, Rust's ministry forced him to resign and replaced him by Paul Schmitthenner, again at the urging of the Berlin Kampfbund.[11] Similarly, when Robert Vorhoelzer, who had been responsible for the very modern buildings executed by the Bavarian post office department in the twenties, lost his professorship at Munich's Technische Hochschule in October of 1933, he was the victim of the attacks of German Bestelmeyer. Bestelmeyer and the local chapter of the Kampfbund used their influnce with Bavarian Minister of Culture Hans Schemm to secure Vorhoelzer's replacement by Alexander von Senger.[12] In general the regime's policy in regard to teaching by modern architects followed no consistent principle, for although a few radical architects were discharged from their posts, many others, only a little less well known, continued to teach without much interference.[13]

A second method of attack upon the modern architects was through the "Gleichschaltung" of the municipal building adminstrations and building societies. These bodies had been far more deeply influenced by the radical architects than the schools, and their reorganization by the new regime was more thorough and consistent. Purges of the municipal building administrations began in Prussia immediately after the state and municipal elections of March 13, 1933, when Goering took over the Prussian Ministry of the Interior. The principal objects of his attacks were the building administrations of Berlin and Frankfurt. Within two weeks, Martin Wagner and all of his associates in Berlin who had administered the capital's public housing program were summarily discharged.[14] In Frankfurt the toll was smaller, since May had taken most of his staff with him to Russia; but his former second-in-command, Martin Elsaesser, lost his position. Walter Curt Behrendt, an official in the Prussian state building administration and one of the new style's more active publicists, was discharged at about the same time.[15] In April the purge was extended to the entire country, and other important officials were discharged, including Johannes Göderitz and Konrad Rühl.[16]

The purges of the building societies themselves were still more comprehensive. Between March and May the entire administrative staffs of all the Prussian building societies were discharged, and new men who could prove their sympathy with the party were "elected."[17] At the same time most of the nation's building societies were joined in a central organization under direct government supervision, while the Gehag, which came to be the most important building society of the Nazi regime, was taken over by the Labor Front.[18] These measures were clearly not restricted in their effect to the radical architects — in fact, few prominent modern architects had served on the permanent staffs of the building societies and the most important of them, Taut and May, had left the country by 1933. Of the first rank of the Ring architects, only Martin Wagner lost his position as a result of the purges of the building societies. But these purges of the administrative staffs made it certain that the societies would no longer hire the radical architects for individual projects, and close government supervision of the work of the permanent architectural staffs of the societies influenced the style in which they built from then on.[19]

While the Gleichschaltung of municipal administrations, schools, and building societies removed radical architects from many positions of influence in public life, the reorganization of professional organizations sought to deprive them of their influence on the profession as a whole and to regiment the rank and file for the future. Needless to say, the creation of a single professional association which could deny architects the right to work and dictate to them on stylistic questions represented a far greater threat to the radical architects than any of the measures so far described, and this appeared to be the purpose of the changes which took place in Germany's professional organizations during the spring and summer of 1933.

At the beginning of the year there existed three major organizations which could claim leadership within the architectural profession. The Bund deutscher Architekten (BDA), similar to the American Institute of Architects, had been Weimar Germany's chief professional society for architects; but more influential in many ways was the Deutscher Werkbund, in which architects were predominant though it also included industrialists, painters, sculptors, and craftsmen. During the first few months of 1933, both organizations were thoroughly reorganized and their leadership taken over by loyal Nazis. But at the same time, they were challenged by the architects' Kampfbund (KDAI), daughter organization of Rosenberg's Kampfbund für deutsche Kultur, which sought to supplant the older associations. For nearly a year, these three groups competed for leadership in the reorganization of the architectural profession. Eventually, however, all three were forced to submit to the control of Goebbels' Propaganda Ministry.

The reorganization of the BDA was begun early in March, when Wilhelm Kreis was replaced as President by Eugen Hönig, professor of architectural history in the Munich Academy of Art and director of the Munich chapter of the Kampfbund.[20] Hönig announced that the Bund would serve as the chief organization for German architects and would operate "along National Socialist lines."[21] The meaning of the latter phrase was soon clarified by the Bund's new membership qualifications, which required evidence of non-participation in either the SPD or the KPD and of a non-Jewish racial heritage.[22] Membership was, in addition, to be restricted to those who "respect the cultural and völkische principles of the Kampfbund."[23] The implications of this restriction for architectural style were spelled out in the indoctrination meetings which the organization began to hold for its members. The official speakers attacked the work of the Ring architects because it "renounced spiritual things and valued only technology," and called for a "new architecture rooted in the Volk . . . in blood and race."[24] The implementation of these provisions, however, proceeded rather slowly. By the fall of 1933, only twenty-five architects had been excluded from the BDA, primarily on the basis of the political and racial clauses in the new membership requirements rather than because of the character of their work.[25]

The reorganization of the Werkbund also began in March. Toward the end of the month, Ernst Jäckh, Executive Secretary of the Werkbund, met with Hitler and Rosenberg, who ordered him to set up a new governing board.[26] At this news, Gropius and Wagner resigned from the Executive Council in protest. The purge itself followed on the tenth of June, when the remaining members of the Council met and voted themselves out of office.[27] Wagner was then expelled from the organization entirely, although Gropius was not, and a new Council was chosen in July, headed by Karl Lörcher, an official in the Kampfbund, with Winfried Wendland his second-in-command. Schmitthenner, Richard Riemerschmid, and Jäckh also occupied positions on the new Council.[28] Like the reorganization of the BDA, these changes in the Werkbund leadership were carried out on the basis of the "Führerprinzip": a single director was "elected" under pressure from the Nazi government, and he then selected his subordinates. According to its new leadership, the Werkbund was to continue to "foster quality production" and the "unification of all areas of the visual arts" as a member of "the great cultural front of National Socialism."[29] Like the new directors of the BDA, Wendland and Lörcher made it clear that the Werkbund's new tasks involved a rejection of the new style. Wendland employed the reorganized *Die Form* to announce that "not the new dwelling . . . the fanatic dream of the worshippers of the metropolis, but the relationship of men to the earth, to the Volk . . . must provide the basis for new forms."[30]

By the summer of 1933 there thus remained little doctrinal difference among the three professional organizations. The directors of the BDA and the Werkbund were members of the Kampfbund für deutsche Kultur, although Lörcher and Wendland, younger men as yet uncommitted to any particular style, had a reputation of greater friendliness to modern architecture than the leading architects of the KDAI. And while the attacks of the Kampfbund and the KDAI upon radical architects were more virulent than those made by the reorganized Werkbund and BDA, all three organizations rejected the new architecture and called for a national socialist style founded on "blood and soil." The competition among them was thus a matter of personal and organizational rivalry, and not a question of conflicting ideas. In April the KDAI began negotiations toward setting up an organization to which all practicing German architects would be legally required to belong, and although the BDA appeared to be the party's candidate for this function during May, the NSDAP's Central Commission announced in June that the KDAI was the only organization approved by the party for German architects and engineers.[31] Both the BDA and the Werkbund were incorporated into the Kampfbund during the course of the summer, and both subsisted for a time as parallel, but subordinate, to the KDAI within the Kampfbund. Once this had been achieved, the KDAI, now directed by Gottfried Feder, could proceed unimpeded by organizational problems to "carry on the battle against architectural bolshevism."

But before the Kampfbund had time to extend the purges further or to take the initiative in determining a "National Socialist" style, it encountered the powerful competition of Goebbels and his Propaganda Ministry, which set up its own rival organization. This was the Reichskulturkammer, established on November 15, 1933 as a branch of the Propaganda Ministry under Goebbels' presidency.[32] The Kulturkammer was intended to "create a new relation between culture and state," by "assembling creative persons of all professions under the leadership of the government [Reich] toward a uniform creative attitude."[33] It was divided up into "chambers" for film, literature, theater, music, press, radio, and the visual arts on the national level, each with a president named by Goebbels; and on the regional level, into thirty-one regional offices, each with a local administrator for each chamber, directed by a regional "co-ordinator."[34] The various chambers became, by successive laws, the only legal organizations for members of the creative professions.[35] By 1935, as a result of the competition of the Kulturkammer, the Kampfbund had wholly lost its status as a professional organization.

The Kulturkammer represented, in part, the natural evolution of Nazi government, for it incorporated into the new state the machinery of cultural control first sought by the party through the Kampfbund. But it was also the product of personal rivalries and conflicting points of view. From the beginning of 1933, Goebbels had shown himself to be unsympathetic to the more vigorous opponents of modern art. In April he promised that "every genuine artist is free to experiment" in attempting to create a suitable art for the new regime, and in June he spoke of the Nazi victory as a "spiritual revolution," which would produce a "new feeling for style."[36] His speech at the opening of the Reichskulturkammer was nothing less than an open attack upon the conservatism of the Kampfbund: "German art needs fresh blood. We live in a young era. Its supporters are young, and their ideas are young. They have nothing more in common with the past, which we have left behind us. The artist who seeks to give expression to this age must also be young. He must create new forms."[37]

While these speeches showed Goebbels' apparent opposition both to the imposition of artistic control by the state and to official encouragement of any kind of historicist revival in the arts, he often seemed to go farther and to support the most modern tendencies in the arts. A number of his speeches were susceptible of this interpretation: at a meeting of German theater directors on May 10, for example, he defined the "new" German art as "sachlich" and without sentiment, phrases which had frequently been used in defense of the new architecture.[38] It was well known, moreover, that Goebbels' personal taste in painting ran to expressionist works; and he chose as one of his chief aides in the propaganda ministry Hans Weidemann, a young expressionist painter. One of Weidemann's first official tasks was to prepare the exhibition of German religious art which the Propaganda Ministry sent to the Chicago "Century of Progress" exposition in mid-1933. He included a few of the works of Ernst Barlach and Emil Nolde in the exhibition, an action which attracted a great deal of attention and helped to reinforce the growing impression that Goebbels was willing to foster the development of modern art and architecture.[39]

It is easy to see, in retrospect, that this impression was mistaken — that despite his personal tastes Goebbels had no intention of setting himself up as the official protector of modern art and architecture. His *Angriff* had had its share in the attacks on architectural "bolshevism" and his encouragement of "every genuine artist" at the same time referred disparagingly to recent "experiments" which had gone too far and had been "dominated by a foreign spirit." His main concern in 1933 was that the Nazi state appear to be creative, rather than restrictive, and that its cultural activities be protected from the stigma of reaction aboard.[40] Yet the revolutionary tone of his utterances, so reminiscent of the writings of radical artists and architects in 1918, led the supporters of modern art to hope that the new regime might, after all, be persuaded to endorse the new style. These hopes produced a debate over style within the party itself, which lasted nearly a year and contributed significantly to the development of Nazi cultural policy.

Very shortly after Goebbels' appointment to the Propaganda Ministry, a few defenders of the new style began to appeal to the new regime for support. On March 26 Wassili Lückhardt published an article in Berlin's *Deutsche Allgemeine Zeitung* which described the new architecture as the embodiment of Moeller van den Bruck's "Prussian style."[41] Luckhardt argued that "this generation [of radical architects] expects to be given essential tasks and an essential place in the political refashioning of the Volk." A few days later Bruno Werner, the art critic for the *Deutsche Allgemeine Zeitung*, addressed an article to Goebbels which urged that "the fresh youthful strength of the Nazi movement conquer in the artistic field," so that artists like Barlach, Marc, and Nolde would no longer be attacked as Jews, nor architects like Poelzig or Mies van der Rohe as bolshevists. Werner had long been a supporter of modern art and architecture, and his appoinmtent in the middle of March as chairman of the Verband deutscher Kunstkritiker seemed itself to be an indication of the liberalism of the Propaganda Ministry.[42] The radical architects' journals too were encouraged by Goebbels' apparent progressiveness. In May, just after his speech to the theater directors calling for "sachlich" and "unsentimental" art, *Die neue Stadt* addressed an open letter to him, claiming that "only the new architecture . . . fits your prescriptions, Herr Minister, and can form the stone monument[s] of bold statesmanship over centuries."[43]

For a few weeks these attempts to win the Propaganda Minister's support for modern art and architecture produced no response among the opponents of the new style. But by June Rosenberg's supporters had begun to be very sensitive to the rumors about Goebbels' artistic sympathies. On June 21, the *VB* published a four-column rebuttal of Werner's article, describing it as evidence of "a crisis in our view of art" and as part of an effort to reestablish that "cultural bolshevism" which had earlier deprived the true representatives of German art of their proper position in the state.[44] At the end of June, the KDAI held a national meeting of its directors, at which the speakers came rather close to direct criticism of Goebbels. Schultze-Naumburg delivered the major speech and warned the delegates against those who claimed that Nazi art could be the expression of a new or revolutionary era.[45] This meeting probably brought the friction between Goebbels and Rosenberg to a head, for within the next week open controversy broke out within the party. The occasion was a debate over the merits of Nolde and Barlach, in which some of Goebbels' supporters succeeded in involving Rosenberg himself. Narrow in its focus, this debate nevertheless called into question the entire artistic policy of the regime.

At the beginning of July, the "National Socialist Students' League" at the University of Berlin organized an exhibition of the works of Barlach, Nolde, Schmitt-Rottluff, and Hans Weidemann and entitled it "German Art." The leader of the students' organization, Otto-Andreas Schreiber, a friend of Weidemann and later his associate in the Labor Front, then sent a letter to the *Deutsche Allgemeine Zeitung* which was not only a defense of expressionism but represented a full-fledged attack upon historicism in art.[46] The letter, entitled "Youth defends German Art," condemned "the erection of historicism into a dogma," as the work of obscurantists who "don't even know enough to understand what they don't understand." Their reactionary efforts "weigh like a mountain upon all the young artists of our Movement who still believe wholeheartedly in the strength of their own blood and the possibilities of their own talents." Alluding to Goebbels' public statements about artistic "revolution," Schreiber concluded: "The National Socialist student has therefore described these efforts as art-reaction; he demands a revolutionary view of art. . . . Long live the complete National Socialist revolution!"

Never had any Nazi dared publicly to challenge Rosenberg in this way. But, although he responded at once, Rosenberg attempted at first to adopt a moderate tone. During the second week of July he published two long articles in the *VB* on "the revolution in the visual arts." The first commented upon the students' exhibition and discussed the work of Nolde and Barlach in detail. It admitted that "since the visual arts have stood so long at the center of bitter controversy, it is easy to understand that politically like-thinking National Socialists may often differ on questions of art."[47] Nolde and Barlach were indeed talented men, but they did not display in their works the "Nordic ideal of beauty," and thus could not truly represent the Nazi movement. Rosenberg's second article, written after Schreiber's letter, revealed a much angrier man. "This cultural Otto Strasser," he said, "claims that I am merely a politician and know nothing about art. I have never heard that this writer has concerned himself with the visual arts, whereas I have been fruitfully engaged in painting and architecture since my fifteenth year."[48] The rest of the article attacked the idea of "revolution for its own sake," which "will destroy all the values of the past in order to appear the more revolutionary." Rosenberg compared the defenders of expressionist art to Otto Strasser's Black Front "which we have already vanquished in political affairs, to the benefit of the Movement," and his concluding words, given the usual euphemism of Nazi prose, clearly represented a warning: "We would offer these cultural literati some good advice. Let them confine themselves to the cultivation of their own inner maturity, and limit their discussions. By launching a public storm against a so-called artistic reaction, they identify themselves as defenders of those personalities whom we already know as the heroes, both political and cultural, of the old system." In other words, revolutionary tendencies within the party were to be identified either with Strasser's rebellion or with the "old system." By implication, Rosenberg had put himself on record here as opposed to the "revolutionary" artistic views of Goebbels, one-time follower of the Strassers.[49]

On July 15, immediately after these articles appeared, Rosenberg held a public rally of the Kampfbund on the subject of revolution in art; here he brought architecture more obviously into the debate. After condemning expressionism in the terms he had already used in the *VB*, Rosenberg turned the meeting over to Paul Schmitthenner. Schmitthenner repeated passages from his earlier speeches attacking the new architecture and defending "the traditions of 1900" as "true German art." But, in addition, Schmitthenner made an attempt to identify the Nazi "revolution" with conservative historicism through a new argument which took the form of a parable. He called it the story of "the unknown stonemason." During the last generation, a "wonderful old building" (the German Reich) had been allowed to decay. But then came an unknown stonemason (Hitler), who gathered together, not new unknown talents, but the good old workmen who had earlier been unable to protect the old building. Together "they chased out the false masters and shored up a firm scaffold around the building and began to clear away its fake decorations and vain tinsel, so that the old pure form could arise again."[50] In the context of public debate over the arts, Schmitthenner's sentimental phrases may be recognized for what they were: an appeal to Hitler to support Rosenberg and the KDK against those of less reactionary artistic views.

On the day of Schmitthenner's speech, Rust's ministry, reflecting the party's rising concern over the open split between Rosenberg and Goebbels, prohibited further public discussion among artists on these disputed questions.[51] The ruling did not end the debate, but neither Rosenberg nor his opponents renewed it until after the "Address on Culture" which Hitler gave at the opening of the Party Congress six weeks later.

This speech, the first of the long, rambling discussions of culture which were to become an annual feature of the Party Congresses, was delivered on September 1, 1933. Entitled "German Art as the Proudest Justification of the German People," it represented both Hitler's first official pronouncement on the role of the arts in the Nazi state, and his first full-scale discussion of the arts since the appearance of *Mein Kampf*.[52] The variety of Hitler's statements on this occasion permitted the supporters of both factions to attempt to find justification for their positions in the speech. But although the VB in particular was to claim that Hitler had endorsed Rosenberg's views, the overall effect of his words was to urge a compromise. It is true that Hitler condemned "those who think that the representatives of the cultural decadence, which now lies behind us, can be the standard bearers of the future," and in the VB the same week one columnist interpreted this sentence as a clear-cut rejection of the radical architects and of modern art.[53] But Hitler's words could also be supposed to apply to the conservatives of the Kampfbund, and some contemporaries interpreted them in this way.[54] Moreover, Hitler also said that "today's tasks require new methods," a statement closely paralleling Goebbels' speeches of the previous five months. Most important, he demanded for Nazi architecture a "crystal-clear functionalism," a declaration which, if taken at face value, clearly repudiated the Kampfbund's suspicion of modern technology. The rest of the speech was couched in vague generalizations, and it is clear that Hitler's main concern was to preserve within the party an appearance of consensus on artistic matters. He returned to this point in his next speech on the arts, only a few weeks later, when he insisted that "there be no wrangling or small selfish quarrels among the brothers of the great German fatherland."[55]

Although Hitler was careful to avoid pronouncing clearly in

favor of either of the contending factions, his ultimate decision was, of course, in favor of Goebbels, whom he authorized to set up the Reichskulturkammer and thus to assume authority over all the arts. But even after this step was taken, the controversy over the question of "revolution" versus "reaction" in the arts continued, although with greatly diminished intensity. The *Deutsche Allgemeine Zeitung*, which had published the appeals to Goebbels in the spring, continued for several months to express guarded approval for the work of the Ring architects;[56] and Gropius, Wagner, and Häring, still hoping for aid from Goebbels, addressed private appeals to the Reichskulturkammer as late as June of 1934.

Gropius, who initiated and inspired these appeals, tried to defend the "Germanness" of the new architecture:

> Shall this strong new architectural movement which began in Germany be lost to Germany? Must we be forced to stop our work, when the entire world has begun to accept our initiative and to carry further our inspiration? . . . Can Germany afford to throw overboard the new architecture and its spiritual leaders, when there is nothing to replace them? . . . The new architecture offers vast opportunities for creative development. But above all I myself see this new style as the way in which we in our country can finally achieve a valid union of the two great spiritual heritages of the classical and the Gothic traditions. Schinkel sought this union, but in vain. Shall Germany deny itself this great opportunity?[57]

Wagner, on the other hand, responded directly to the revolutionary theme in the controversy:

> You will have to decide . . . which forces you will use to lead the battle for a new life and a new way of life in this Reich; youth and the old youths, or the "young" oldsters, who are artificially prolonging their lives with new make-up. The choice is of course harsh and one-sided, but revolutionary times are always harsh and one-sided. The tasks which our era sets us are not those of the middle ages and not those of the Biedermeier period, but those of men striving for freedom, and their machines [sic]. . . . The state cannot solve [these tasks] with a renaissance of the Biedermeier; it cannot solve them . . . with thatched peasant cottages.[58]

Häring defended the Ring as a professional organization by stressing its roots in the prewar Werkbund, which had been both progressive and nationalist in its aims.[59] All three men begged for an opportunity to defend their work in public. But whatever their arguments, these communications, the last effort of the Ring publicists in defense of the new style, were wholly fruitless. When the officials of the Kulturkammer answered at all, they urged silence, warning that public controversy would endanger the architectural profession as a whole.[60] Gropius, at least, now began his preparations to leave the country.

On the other side of the controversy, the hopes of the Kampfbund leaders persisted much longer. In December of 1933 the architects' Kampfbund held a rally at which Feder complained that Nazism's artistic victory was not yet won, and Nonn deplored the weakness of the Kampfbund, which must, he said, be permitted "uncompromisingly to make clear the cultural destructiveness of the Ring."[61] On the following day Hinkel, representing the government, publicly rebuked the Kampfbund for thinking that culture could be created "by laws and organizations," and announced the incorporation of the entire Kampfbund für deutsche Kultur into Kraft durch Freude, where it would "carry on the ideological education of the members of this organization."[62] Despite this drastic downgrading of his organization, Rosenberg continued to attack the work of the Bauhaus and the new architecture for another eighteen months in a series of speeches in which he still spoke of a "struggle over art."[63] But by the middle of 1935, the Kampfbund für deutsche Kultur had lost the last remnants of its significance as an organization within the Nazi system. It had undergone another metamorphosis in June of 1934, when it became the "NS Kulturgemeinde" within the Labor Front, still dedicated to the ideological education of Kraft durch Freude in theory, yet in fact greatly restricted in its activities.[64] After 1935, although the organization may have continued to exist, all reference to its activities disappeared from the Nazi press. From 1935 onward, Rosenberg no longer referred to the visual arts in his speeches; and the conservative architects whom he had protected were forced, like the radical architects before them, to address their complaints privately to the officials of the Reichskulturkammer.[65]

Yet if Hitler had sided with Goebbels, who in turn excluded Rosenberg from effective control in cultural affairs, Rosenberg received considerable compensation. When he became head of the party's foreign policy bureau, this helped, for a few years at any rate, to distract his attention from his ambition to control the regime's cultural policy.[66] Early in 1934 Hitler gave him the meaningless post of "Custodian of the entire intellectual and spiritual training and education of the party." At the "culture days" which began each Party Congress, it was Rosenberg, not Goebbels, who was permitted to give the principal address following Hitler's "culture speech." And when in 1937 Hitler initiated a prize "for art and learning" as a substitute for the Nobel prize, Rosenberg was the first to receive it, while Goebbels made the formal presentation.[67] In the development of Nazi cultural policy, although Goebbels was able to appropriate the tools of power, the honors which Rosenberg received lent an appearance of influence to his ideas and those of the Kampfund. Rosenberg was thus willing to give his tacit agreement to the consensus which Hitler sought.

After his victory over the Kampfbund, Goebbels' artistic policy developed along the lines of the compromise suggested in Hitler's speeches. He neither rehabilitated the Ring nor completely repudiated the ideals of the Kampfbund, but rather pursued a middle course, while assuming firm control over artistic organizations. Between November 1933 and 1935, the Kulturkammer took over all the architectural functions of the Kampfbund, absorbing both the BDA and the Werkbund into its architectural division, and taking over the membership requirements devised by the BDA and the Kampfbund.[68] A few of the men who had gained positions of influence within the Kampfbund retained them within the Reichskulturkammer: Goebbels made Eugen Hönig president of the Reichskammer der bildenden Künste (RDBK) within the Kulturkammer, and German Bestelmeyer a member of the governing body of the entire organization (Reichskultursenat), but these men had been among the least active opponents of "architectural bolshevism."[69] Schmitthenner and Lörcher were dismissed from their offices in the RDBK in 1935, after that chamber's legal framework had been completed, and neither Senger, Nonn, nor Schultze-Naumburg ever held any office in the organization.[70] The great majority of Goebbels' deputies in artistic control were "new men," neither deeply involved in the previous activities of the Kampfbund nor closely associated with the historicist tradition.

Although it adopted the membership requirements for architects devised by the Kampfbund, the Kulturkammer did not proceed to use these regulations in the way intended by the Kampfbund leadership. The idea that all practising architects must in their work "respect the cultural and völkische principles of the Kampfbund," which had formed part of the membership requirements of the BDA, disappeared, to be replaced by a law which required them to design buildings which "express proper architectural views [anständige Baugesinnung]."[71] This professional code, to be sure, not only permitted sweeping regulation of style, it seemed to require it, since by its terms "higher officials" were intended to issue rules defining "proper architectural views" and to see that the local building officials carried them out. Yet neither Goebbels nor his subordinates ever set forth any such definition, and there is no evidence that local officials ever employed the law except to preserve a uniform roof line in the historic sections of the oldest cities or occasionally to prevent the erection of ugly signs and billboards.[72] Certainly no architect was excluded from the RDBK on the basis of the style of his work since, for example, both Peter Behrens and Mies van der Rohe retained membership. Insofar as can be determined today, the membership requirements for architects, intended originally as a means to control architectural style, were used by the RDBK only to exclude Jews from practice.[73] The Reichskulturkammer, so often described as the channel of "totalitarian" control of culture because of its insistence upon a "uniform creative attitude" among its members, made no attempt, at least in architecture, to enforce this attitude.

But if the establishment of the Reichskulturkammer cut short the purges of 1933 and prevented the original leaders of the Kampfbund from gaining control of architectural style, Goebbels' organization never explicitly repudiated the Kampfbund's attacks on the new architecture; and these attacks had a profound effect upon the careers of the radical architects. Neither threatened with imprisonment or terrorism nor legally deprived of the right to practice, radical architects nevertheless received no new commissions after 1933. Gropius, Mendelsohn, Mies van der Rohe, Wagner, and Ludwig Hilberseimer, entirely without work, emigrated to England and America, Gropius and Mendelsohn at the earliest opportunity and the others between 1935 and 1938. May and Taut were of course already in Russia, and for that reason were officially prevented from returning to Germany.[74] The second rank of radical architects, although they remained, fared very little better. Martin Elsaesser, having lost his important position in Frankfurt's building administration, was able to teach but received no notable commissions.[75] Otto Haesler, no longer employed by Celle, retired from the profession until 1945.[76] Göderitz taught for a time in Berlin after leaving Magdeburg, until local party officials had him discharged; and neither he, Häring, the Luckhardts, nor Richard Döcker could find work.[77] A few architects who had worked primarily in industrial architecture and who had never been attacked in the Nazi press received and held influential teaching positions,[78] and a number of younger men, not yet well known, were able to take subordinate positions in large firms which stood under the protection of important party officials.[79] After the end of 1933 no modern architect was able to publish any defense of the new style. Although they did not themselves win control of German architecture, the early opponents of the new architecture thus succeeded in excluding the most prominent of their adversaries from architectural patronage under the Nazi regime.

VIII / Nazi Architecture

The political involvement of architecture in Germany reached its culmination in the building program of the Nazi regime. The propaganda campaign against the new style and the purges of 1933 had committeed the party to a positive architectural policy. The new government accepted this committment willingly — again and again its leaders expressed the view that Nazi culture and society must find a reflection in a specifically "National Socialist" architecture. On the basis of these views, the new regime instituted a huge building program and accompanied it with an intensive propaganda campaign which constantly stressed the ideological significance of Nazi architecture. In this way, architecture achieved unprecedented political significance in the Nazi state.

But despite the overwhelming ideological importance assigned to architecture after 1933, the Nazi building program proved to be in many ways inconsistent with earlier party propaganda. Nazi architecture did not return to the historicist manner advocated by the Kampfbund, nor did it by any means reject all the teachings of the radical architects. The official buildings of the new regime were designed in an extraordinary variety of styles, some of which drew upon older architectural traditions, but in a way very different from that favored by the conservative architects of the Kampfbund, while other buildings displayed the marked influence of the modern movement.

This diversity in Nazi architecture reflected the widely differing views of the party's leaders, who, after Goebbels had prevented the establishment of centralized mechanisms of stylistic control in 1933, assumed initiative, individually, in deciding questions of architectural style. Despite Hitler's many pronouncements on the subject, Feder, Schirach, Ley, Goering, and the other officials who became the regime's principal architectural patrons never agreed upon a consistent theory of what Nazi architecture should be. Some of these men favored the modernized neoclassicism of Speer's Party Congress buildings, conceived as a new gathering place for the masses of the party faithful; others, the neo-Romanesque style of the castle-like Ordensburgen, quasi-military schools for a "heroic" party leadership; still others, the rustic appearance of government housing projects, intended to symbolize the repatriation of urban workers to the soil. A few commissioned buildings as radically modern as any constructed in the twenties; these were advertised as evidence of the revolutionary and "modern" character of the Nazi regime.

The varying stylistic preferences of Nazi patrons reflect very clearly the fundamental conflicts in Nazi ideology as it affected architecture. Some of these conflicts were already implied in the vacillation of the *Völkischer Beobachter* between urbanism and antiurbanism in its early articles on architecture in 1928 and 1929, and they were more clearly stated in the debate between revolutionaries and historicists in the summer of 1933. After 1933 these conflicts persisted in the ideological committments of the party's leaders, which differed both in kind and in degree. Men like Ley, Darré, Schirach, Feder, and Rosenberg continued to contradict one another in their statements about architecture and thus, by implication, in their views about the proper form of Nazi society. In addition, many others involved in establishing architectural policy disregarded all official ideological pronouncements. The buildings which Goering commissioned for the Air Force, although often free of the most striking features of the new architecture, were usually executed in a very progressive manner which neither referred to tradition nor evoked the military virtues. And most of the men concerned with public housing were either not interested in such concepts as wholesale repatriation of urban populations to the soil or else, under the pressure of practical circumstance, soon came to accept more conventional solutions to the problem of mass housing.

After Goebbels had succeeded in preventing the Kampfbund from taking control of cultural policy, there existed no effective legal hindrance to these disagreements among party officials. Nor did Hitler provide the control lacking in Nazi law. Hitler of course had his own stylistic preferences, but they were expressed chiefly in the limited group of monumental buildings which he commissioned directly. Moreover, in his speeches on art he praised each type of architecture in turn, seeing each as an index of national creativity and denying any conflict among them. Hitler's attitude and the diversity in style and ideological commitment which it permitted demonstrates again the essential opportunism of the Nazi party. This opportunism had allowed Nazi propaganda to attack the new style when controversy over it was at its height, despite the presence of elements in Nazi thought which were relatively sympathetic to the work of the radical architects. After 1933 the same spirit led to the development of a permissive attitude about style and ideology once the attack had ceased to be so useful politically.

This opportunism was further displayed in Nazi propaganda after 1933, for neither the lack of a consistent architectural theory nor the variety of style apparent in new building prevented the party propagandists from waging ideological warfare with the aid of architecture. A mammoth propaganda campaign ceaselessly publicized all the diverse architectural accomplishments of the regime and surrounded them with elaborate ceremonies and celebrations. The most blatantly ideological styles were publicized most energetically, but buildings without much ideological significance were also prominent in Nazi propaganda. The regime's most modern buildings were often praised in terms drawn from the arguments of the radical architects.

The Nazi architectural program thus had three components: an ideology, torn by internal contradictions, which the party leaders sought to embody in architecture; a propaganda campaign which was itself lacking in consistent ideological direction; and a building program which sometimes followed the prescriptions of ideology, more often ignored them, and occasionally stood in considerable contradiction to them.

From the fall of 1933 onward, it was Hitler who took the lead in emphasizing the importance of architecture to the new state. This was a central theme in his annual "culture speeches," in his major addresses at the "House of German Art," and in a number of speeches on less specifically cultural occassions. During the early years of the Weimar Republic, Hitler had absorbed the idea, either from the writings of the cultural pessimists of the turn of the century or perhaps from the radical architects, that great art is the product of national and political greatness. This view, so prominent in *Mein Kampf,* emerged again after Hitler's long silence on artistic questions as the foundation of all his pronouncements on architecture and the arts. By 1933 Hitler was able to derive all his other statements about the arts from this central idea, because he had come to think of art and politics as essentially the same. This was so, he explained at the Party Congress of 1936, because both art and the state are the products of a creative force which he termed variously "the authoritarian will [autoritäre Wille]" or the "political power of creating forms."[1] Out of this political will grew both the form of the state and the forms of the arts, and its prerequisite was a unified people or nation.[2] The interpreters of this creative force were, according to Hitler, the artist on the one hand and the politician on the other. Characteristically, he often spoke of the two in almost interchangeable terms.[3]

Among the arts which he saw as the products of the political strength and creative personality of the body politic, Hitler again assigned architecture a special place. Like the radical architects writing in 1919, he described architecture as the unifier of the arts, whose forms "determine" the forms of painting and sculpture.[4] To Hitler, architecture was thus better suited than any other art to express national greatness: "Every great period," he said, "finds the final expression of its value in its buildings."[5] And he believed, again echoing some of the arguments of the earlier defenders of the new style, that architecture not only "expressed" the unity and power of the nation but could also help to create it. Great buildings, he told the assembled party members in 1937, could create the kind of common "will" which he had earlier called their necessary prerequisite. They would awaken national consciousness and thus "contribute more than ever to the political unification and strengthening of our people; in German society they will become an element in the feeling of proud togetherness [Zusammengehörigkeit]."[6] Lastly, it was the function of architecture to impress the ideas of its creators upon other nations and, even more important, upon posterity: "Such visible demonstration of the higher qualities of a people will, as the experience of history proves, remain for thousands of years as an unquestionable testimony not only to the greatness of a people, but also to their moral right to exist."[7]

But if Hitler continually stressed the imporance of architecture both as an index and a source of national unity and power, his attempts to define in greater detail the architecture appropriate to the Third Reich were vague and contradictory and produced no clear guide for the building program of the regime. The Kampfbund's frequent criticisms of the revolutionary character of the new style probably influenced Hitler to deny that each new era requires a radically new style, for then "every political revolution would immediately destroy the great works of past cultures," and "every great work of art contains an absolute value."[8] He claimed, futhermore, that architecture must represent the nation or the "race," lasting entities, and he jusified his own admiration for Greek art and architecture with the argument that they were the eternally valid work of "Nordic" or "Aryan" peoples. On the other hand, like Goebbels, Hitler repeatedly emphasized that National

Socialism had ushered in a "new era" and argued that when "the general life of peoples fashions itself anew [it] . . . seeks after a new expression."[9] Posterity must be able to recognize Nazi architecture "as a work of the German people and of this our epoch."[10] Nazi architecture must therefore be "up-to-date" and must employ "new means of expression."[11] In some of his speeches, Hitler even went so far as to describe "functionalism" and "practicality" as the sources of architectural beauty.[12] But he always combined this kind of argument with a condemnation of the "functionalism" of the new architecture, whose creators had "confused animalistic primitiveness with harmonious beauty."[13] Nazi architecture, he said, would be "sachlich" in a manner similar, not to the work of radical architects, who had "worshipped newness for its own sake,"[14] but to the "Greek spirit" which in its architecture combined beauty and function.[15]

In considering whether Nazi architecture would be "modern" or "traditional," Hitler thus attempted to take advantage of both arguments by equivocation. In the process he often made use of a slogan, devised in answer to the question "What is German art?" which had arisen out of the controversy of 1933. "Deutsch sein heisst klar sein [Germanness equals clarity]," the slogan ran, which meant, Hitler explained, "that to be German means to be logical, and above all to be truthful."[16] He became so fond of this euphemism that he used it again and again, not only to describe the "Germanness" of Nazi art and architecture, but also to characterize the structure of the Nazi state.[17]

Only one point in Hitler's description of the architecture of the new regime was stated unequivocally. Nazi architecture must be "heroic." But heroism in Hitler's speeches referred to monumental scale rather than to specific features of architectural style. Of the public buildings of the Nazi regime he said, "if they are to have a lasting significance and value, they must conform to the largeness of scale prevalent in the other spheres of national life."[18] "We must build as large as today's technical possibilities permit; we must build for eternity."[19] These views led Hitler to commission a number of improbable projects during the last years of his regime, such as a party monument 750 feet high and a new railroad station for Munich nearly a mile in diameter.[20] They led also to his frequent endorsement of large-scale urban planning. Particularly when he talked about his plans for the reconstruction of Berlin, Hitler condemned the idea that big cities were the cause of racial or cultural decadence, "for without the city of Rome, there would never have been a Roman empire."[21] But none of these projects was executed, and Hitler's predilection for the gigantic in architecture imposed few restrictions upon the style of the smaller, more feasible projects which became the actual showpieces of Nazi propaganda.

In leaving such latitude for interpretation, Hitler thus permitted a number of different views of Nazi architecture to exist unchallenged. After the controversy of 1933 and Hitler's demand for consensus at the end of that year, party and government officials expressed their views in guarded fashion, cloaking them in the kind of euphemism Hitler himself employed. Yet both the program for a rural type of architecture and the hope for a more "revolutionary" style continued to have their strong supporters. Gottfried Feder,[22] the housing officials of the Labor Front, and Darré's Agriculture Ministry all followed the main themes of the Kampfbund's propaganda in calling for an architecture rooted in "blood and soil," closely related to regional landscape and customs, "in which men can again find roots in the soil and which gives them a true feeling for their home."[23] Many others, perhaps under the influence of Goebbels' statements or of Hitler's references to "up-to-date" styles, urged a policy of architectural "modernity." Baldur von Schirach, for example, who as head of the Hitler Youth was responsible for a large amount of building, defended the right of his organization to build in a "youthful" style using steel, glass, and concrete, and attacked the monumentality preferred by many Nazi officials.[24] Similarly, the organization within Robert Ley's Labor Front which supervised the construction of workers' assembly halls constantly urged its architects to employ functional and efficient styles.[25]

These views, stubbornly held but cautiously expressed, are even more clearly apparent in the diversity of style which characterized the Nazi building program. This program was comparable in size to that of the Weimar Republic and just as decentralized in its direction. But it was now the officials of the party and central government and their agencies, rather than the municipalities, who were responsible for its development.

Hitler himself commissioned a number of the regime's most important projects: the party buildings and an art museum (the "House of German Art") in Munich, a new chancellery in Berlin, and the complex of parade grounds and assembly halls for the Party Congresses in Nürnberg. Aside from the construction of the Autobahn, Hitler's architectural interests were confined to these "Führerbauten." Planned by his personal architects, whose designs he closely supervised, these buildings were intended to express "the largeness of scale . . . of national life" and were carried

89. Paul Ludwig Troost, House of German Art, Munich.

out in a modernized neoclassical style which conformed to Hitler's
desire to bring the "Greek spirit" up to date.

The earliest of Hitler's projects and the one for which he took
most credit as codesigner was Paul Ludwig Troost's "House of
German Art" in Munich, begun in 1933 (fig. 89).[26] Troost had been
a minor participant in the progressive historicist movement of the
prewar period, and his use of limestone as a surfacing material
and the dominant classical colonnade which he set along the front
of the museum reflected the same desire to derive a massive
masonry style from historical precedents which had motivated
men like Behrens and Bonatz before 1914. At the same time, the
museum's blocky masses and flat surfaces, free of all ornament
save minimal base and cornice projections, and the horizontal
orientation of the building, proclaimed its debt to the radicals of
the twenties.

90. Albert Speer, Party Congress Grounds, Nürnberg, model.

The combination of modernity with neoclassicism which characterized Hitler's first commission was carried further in the work of Albert Speer, the young architect who succeeded to Hitler's favor after Troost's death in 1934.[27] Speer, later one of the most powerful men in Nazi government, first came to Hitler's attention through Goebbels, who discovered his particular talent for designs suited to party ceremonial.* As a result Hitler asked Speer to plan the immense parade fields and auditoriums for the Nürnberg Party Congresses (fig. 90). The Zeppelinfeld, the first unit in this group and the only one to be completed, displays Speer's style and Hitler's architectural interests in their most striking form. Used for parades of the Hitler Youth and the SA and for the more general meetings of the Congresses, it accommodated more than 100,000 people. The stand surrounding the field framed the party flags and emblems, and the entire backdrop was set off at night by searchlights, like a stage.[28]

Across the front of the field was the review stand, a long low structure which to an even greater degree than Troost's museum used its classical motifs in a very modern spirit (fig. 91). Its dominant feature was the great colonnade at the back of the stands which ran across the width of the structure, broken only by the cubic mass of the central podium. The terminal elements clearly derived from the entrance pylons of classical antiquity, but Speer handled them as free-standing cubic masses framing the horizontal pattern of the continuous colonnades. On the entrance side (fig. 92), the colonnade appeared as an unbroken horizontal band set into the great flat surfaces of the masonry walls. Although Speer's design was symmetrical and unmistakably neoclassical, it was deeply influenced by the abstract formal compositions of the twenties. This type of design initiated a rather considerable neoclassical revival among the architects employed by the regime.[29]

Although they were elaborately publicized, these buildings commissioned by Hitler represented only a very small proportion of total official construction under the new regime. Of the party agencies involved in new construction, Schirach's Hitler Youth movement and Ley's Labor Front were responsible for the largest volume. Robert Ley was also Reichsorganisationsleiter of the

---

* Speer, born in 1905, was Heinrich Tessenow's assistant in Berlin from 1929 to 1932. He joined the party in 1931 and did architectural remodelling jobs for party officials between 1931 and 1933. In 1933 Goebbels gave him his first major commission: the design for the decorations of a party rally at Tempelhof. See Rudolf Wolters, *Albert Speer* (Oldenburg, 1943).

91. Albert Speer, Zeppelinfeld, Nürnberg.

92. Zeppelinfeld, entry side.

93. Clemens Klotz, Ordensburg Vogelsang.

party, and in this capacity he and his staff commissioned the several Ordensburgen, or leadership schools, and perhaps a hundred local party office buildings and community centers, called "Gemeinschaftshäuser."[30] These party buildings, equally influential and nearly as widely publicized as those commissioned by Hitler, departed radically from the monumental neoclassicism which he preferred and attempted to appeal to the nationalist sentiment associated with the German middle ages. They revived not the traditions of the Gothic styles, but the military architecture of the medieval fortress or rural and regional motifs dating back to the later middle ages, which fitted into party propaganda about "blood and soil."

Of these party buildings, the three Ordensburgen constructed by Ley's Organisationsleitung were the largest in scale (figs. 93–95). Intended as training schools for a new leadership elite, the Ordensburgen were named after the castles of the medieval knightly orders, and the style in which they were carried out represented a conscious attempt to recall an era of crusades and military colonization.[31] Each of the schools employed rusticated masonry battlements and towers, and Ordensburg Vogelsang, the first of the group, was impressively situated on a hill after the manner of a medieval fortress. But despite their deliberate evocation of a Romanesque tradition* the Ordensburgen were, like

* Most of the "real" Ordensburgen were of course constructed long after the Romanesque period, in the Gothic or late Gothic manner.

Speer's and Troost's work, deeply influenced by the modern movement. The stone surfaces of the buildings were bare of ornament and unencumbered in outline in the manner of progressive architecture around 1910, and at Vogelsang and Crössinsee the architects incorporated into their romantic masonry buildings the asymmetrical window patterns and continuous window bays of the radicals of the twenties. The Ordensburgen were among the most aesthetically successful of the official buildings of the Nazi regime.

But if the monumental Ordensburgen romanticized a military tradition from the medieval past, many of the more modest buildings of the regime returned to the main themes of the Kampfbund's propaganda and attempted to evoke the image of a rural society through the use of regional "folk" styles. The thatched roofs of the North Sea region; the half-timbering and gable roofs of Lower Saxony; and the "Tyrolean" roofs, carved balconies, and white stucco of South Germany's mountain regions had been in use in rural farmsteads and small villages since the later middle

94. Clemens Klotz, Ordensburg Crössinsee.

95. Hermann Giesler, Ordensburg Sonthofen.

96. Hitler Youth Hostel.

ages, although during the twentieth century they had been employed in new buildings only in particularly remote and rural areas. Now, however, various branches of the party and government urged the adaptation of these traditions to other types of buildings; and despite the predilection of Schirach and many members of Ley's organization for modern styles, the Hitler Youth and the Labor Front took the lead in this policy for a time. As a result many youth hostels and a number of the Labor Front's "Kameradschaftshäuser" came to resemble alpine chalets and thatched or half-timbered cottages (figs. 96 and 97).[32] The folk style was also inflated for the use of such larger buildings as the hotels on the Autobahn, the exhibition halls of Kraft durch Freude in Berlin, and the federal Post Office administration buildings. It was employed, moreover, in practical kinds of buildings which had previously been considered the special province of modern architec-

97. Hitler Youth Hostel.

ture, such as the broadcasting station and garage shown in figures 98 and 99. The folk style was thus the most widespread of the officially encouraged styles, and for many Nazi officials it reflected a genuine ideological commitment. But in many cases it also reflected the cynical side of Nazi architectural propaganda; for when it was used indiscriminately, without much reference either to location or function, the folk style was intended to create an impression of rural life where none existed.

98. Air Force Ministry, Weather Service Broadcasting Station.

The buildings erected by the party, either on direct commission from Hitler or by party organizations such as the Hitler Youth and the Labor Front, received wider publicity than any other type; but the largest portion of public building during the Nazi period was financed from other sources. The new regime sponsored a large public housing program, supervised in part by the Labor Front and in part by the Ministry of Labor. A number of other branches of the government, like Darré's Food and Agriculture Ministry, which financed the construction of farm buildings and housing for agricultural laborers, entered into building programs of their own. But the largest volume of building was carried out by the armed services, particularly by Goering's Air Force Ministry. The Air Force planned airfields, laboratories, office buildings, and barracks; the Army also needed new barracks and administrative facilities in the process of preparation for war.

The types of buildings commissioned by Goering, either through the Air Force or through industrial concerns which he controlled, were far less historicist in style than any other Nazi building; and in a few cases Goering extended his patronage to designs quite as modern as anything built by the radical architects. The most important of the larger Air Force buildings, the new Air Force Ministry in Berlin, ignored even the very moderate historicism of the Führerbauten; only its surfacing material and the orientation of its windows suggested a tie to traditional styles (fig. 100). More-

99. Autobahn Garage.

100. Ernst Sagebiel, Air Force Ministry, Berlin.

101. Air Force Ministry, Offices.

over, unlike the more formal buildings of the other branches of party and government, most of the Air Force buildings were small in scale. The modest stucco building shown in figure 101, with its clean lines and surfaces and low proportions, was typical of the great majority of Air Force construction. This kind of design gradually became very popular among all the armed services and among many other public agencies as well. It appeared in many variations, looking more "modern" in the district hospital shown in figure 102, and somewhat more conservative in the Bavarian school building shown in figure 103. These simple buildings, like the rest of Nazi architecture, represented a stylistic compromise. Their sloping roofs and relatively low proportions distantly resembled folk architecture with its "applique" removed, thus faintly suggesting a rural association. At the same time, though they lacked the most striking features of the new style, the flat roof and the banded window pattern, they derived from it their flat stucco surfaces, regular unbroken outlines, and their antimonumental character. As in many other types of Nazi building, the result was a style which lacked the brilliant originality of the earlier period, but which often issued in pleasing and successful designs.

102. District Hospital, Vaihingen-Enz.

103. School at Allach, Bavaria (dedication ceremony).

While the smaller office buildings of the Air Force were deeply indebted to the modern movement, Goering also commissioned buildings which showed no trace of traditional influences. In the assembly plants of the Air Force's "German Experimental Station [Deutsche Versuchsanstalt für Luftfahrt]," for example, the flat surfaces and finely detailed patterns of glass, brick, and exposed structural members represent an elegant refinement of the most radical industrial designs of the twenties (fig. 104). A similar vernacular was employed by the designers of the Hermann-Goering-Werke.[33] Work of this type found its way into Nazi publications, which explained that it represented the "true practicality" and "crystal-clear functionalism" called for by Hitler in 1933.[34]

104. Air Force Ministry, Deutsche Versuchsanstalt für Luftfahrt.

More than any other segment of the Nazi building program, public housing under the new government had a powerful ideological motivation and purpose. Since the focus of the controversy over the new architecture had been the mass housing developments designed by radical architects, the regime paid particular attention to housing in its propaganda and initiated a housing program which it claimed was radically different from the housing program of the Weimar Republic. It proposed, not so much a particular style in dwelling design, but a new housing policy, involving the repatriation of city dwellers to the soil and thus fulfilling the promises implicit in "blood and soil" propaganda. At the same time, the planning and style of Nazi public housing diverged from these standards set for it by Nazi ideology far more widely than did any other type of Nazi building. For although the regime could point to a few Siedlungen actually built around the concept of repatriation, no systematic effort was made to transform the housing program as a whole according to this pattern. The majority of Nazi housing remained without ideological content, and official propaganda was left with the job of glossing over for the public the difference between housing policy and housing practice.

The housing program of the regime made use of the legal and administrative machinery set up during the Weimar period; but as in other areas of Nazi administration, the central government assumed direct responsibility for what had previously been state and municipal functions. The transference of authority from the states, municipalities, and building societies began during the process of Gleichschaltung in 1933, when the directorates of the building societies were replaced by party members. In 1934 a new law removed the building societies entirely from municipal control by merging them in a national organization under the direction of the federal government and entirely dependent upon it for funds.[35] At the same time, Gottfried Feder was made "Reichssiedlungskommissar" with full administrative powers over the building societies, while the power of allocating funds and establishing federal housing standards was given to the "Reichsheimstättenamt" of the Labor Front.[36]

Upon assuming his office, Feder made public his ambitious plans for the redistribution of the urban populations. The main purpose of his housing program was, he said, "The dissolution of the metropolis, in order to make our people be settled again, to give them again their roots in the soil [Wiederbodenständig- und Sesshaftmachung]. . . .The metropolis has destroyed men's feeling for their homeland [Heimat]. . . .The reincorporation of the metropolitan populations into the rhythm of the German landscape is one of the principal tasks of the National Socialist government."[37] The new housing policy would be, he explained, one of the chief elements in "National Socialist population policy," for in an urban society, "families die out after the third generation . . . having lost the desire for children. . . . The metropolis is the death of the nation."[38] Under Feder's influence the Reichsheimstättenamt issued pamphlets containing the slogans "Away from the metropolis!" and "Heimatlicher Hausbau!"[39] and announced that the new housing policy would "strengthen the race."[40]

But during his brief term of office, which lasted only one year, Feder never translated these promises into a concrete and comprehensive program, nor did the Reichsheimstättenamt itself do so. Most of the housing built by the new nationalized building societies did not reflect his desire to provide Germany's city dwellers with rural "homesteads" but continued instead to conform to the Weimar practice of constructing row housing and apartment buildings on the periphery of urban population centers. The building societies did abandon the major innovations made by the proponents of the new architecture; they did not, for example, seek to construct new satellite cities like May's Nidda valley project in Frankfurt, and they discarded, along with the hated flat roof, such prominent features of "the new dwelling" as elaborate mechanical equipment, the "open" floor plan, large glass areas, and the use of irregular massing and balcony patterns to break up the facade. But the plain stucco buildings which they built, like most of the rest of the regime's architecture, represented a compromise with the tradition of design created by the new style. Their vertical windows, often with shutters, and their steep tile roofs proclaimed their "German" character, while their unbroken lines, plain surfaces, and their open "finger plans" drew upon the progressive housing of the twenties (figs. 105 and 106).

Only one type of housing development, representing a small minority of total housing construction under the regime, conformed at all closely to the demands of Feder's program. Near the major cities, but usually located at a very considerable distance beyond their outer suburbs, the regime built a number of small housing developments consisting of single-family houses with large garden plots. It was this type of project which Nazi publications often described as the characteristic form of Nazi housing. A few small developments of single-family dwellings had of course been built throughout the Weimar period, but such groups of detached houses were expensive and were usually occupied by the moderately well-to-do. The housing officials of the Republic did not find that this type of dwelling offered a practicable method

105. Apartment Buildings, Nürnberg.

106. Apartment Buildings, Braunschweig.

of relieving metropolitan congestion, and public funds were seldom used for dwellings of this type. In 1931, however, the Brüning government used its emergency powers to initiate a program for the construction of "Kleinsiedlungen," housing developments of single-family dwellings for the unemployed, as an antidepression measure.[41] On the basis of a series of ordinances issued in 1931, the Brüning government provided unemployed workers with land and materials to build small houses which they would thereafter own. Each plot had room for a garden which would yield the owner a partial subsistence.

The Nazi government took over the outlines of the Kleinsiedlung program from its predecessors. It retained the favored status given to minimum-size dwellings with truck gardens under the Brüning program, but it did away with the idea of self-help and required that the residents of the projects be employed.[42] Several hundred of these small developments, each consisting of one to two hundred dwellings, were erected after 1933, frequently for the use of workers in the new factories being built in outlying industrial areas (fig. 107).[43] The houses were tiny; they usually had only 600 square feet of floor area, much of it in the second story under the sloping roof. The plots were, however, enormous by German standards, typically about a quarter acre when truck gardens were included.

107. Housing Development, Aachen.

108. Siedlung Heddernheim, Frankfurt am Main.

The exteriors of the houses in these projects occasionally displayed some reference to the "folk" tradition — a little half-timbering or vertical wood siding, a thatched roof, or a roof overhang with exposed beams (fig. 108) — and these practices were strongly encouraged by the Reichsheimstättenamt as a part of its program of "Heimatlicher Hausbau."[44] But the great majority of dwellings in the Kleinsiedlungen were executed in either whitewashed brick or white stucco with steeply sloping tile roofs and no ornament (fig. 107). Even without the employment of the bits of "folk" applique, the small cottages on their large plots presented a striking contrast to the streamlined apartment buildings at Britz and even to May's row housing in Frankfurt, and this contrast supported the Nazi claim to sponsorship of a "rural" housing program. But the new regime had not invented this type of housing, and the small number of dwellings actually constructed in the Kleinsiedlungen did not represent a significant step toward "the dissolution of the metropolis."

This housing program was accompanied by a costly propaganda effort which side-stepped the shortcomings of Nazi housing and sought to create for it a favorable public image through the construction and publicizing of model housing exhibitions. This plan had its origin in 1933, when the reorganized Werkbund decided to build a new housing development in Stuttgart near the Weissenhof Siedlung as a rival to it. The project, called the "Kochenhof Siedlung," was intended by the Werkbund leaders to be the first example of true Nazi architecture and was carried out in wood construction under the direction of Schmitthenner. But by the time the Siedlung was completed late in 1934, the Werkbund, the Kampfbund, and Schmitthenner himself were out of favor, and the project received no official publicity. The idea of a housing development which would act as a permanent exhibition of Nazi housing policy was instead taken over by the regime in the "Ramersdorf Siedlung," built early in 1934 in a southeastern suburb of Munich.

The Ramersdorf exhibition consisted of two parts. The housing development itself contained some 150 single-family houses of relatively generous size, sited on very large and lavishly landscaped plots which were in turn arranged around a long strip of open parkland (fig. 109). The development thus had the appearance of a small rural village, although no real German village had ever had such an extensive endowment of parks and vegetation. Adjacent to the settlement was a permanent exhibition hall which contained standard plans for small cottages, models of prospective developments in rural areas, and examples of recommended interior decoration. The latter included an entire room from "the new farmstead," panelled in wood and furnished with heavy wooden furniture and brightly colored cushions and curtains. Such furnishings were far too expensive ever to be incorporated into the Kleinsiedlungen.

The exhibition was opened with great fanfare and publicity, with representatives of both the international and national press attending. The *VB* published a special edition of pictures and comment, and remembering the Weissenhof Siedlung, it described the Ramersdorf housing as representative of "the German dwelling of the future."[45] The principal speaker at the opening ceremonies, Feder's deputy Wilhelm Ludovici, attempted to set the tone for

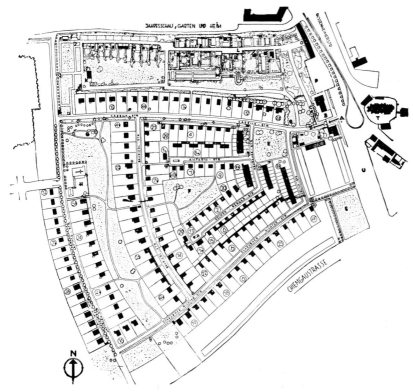

JAHRESSCHAU, GARTEN UND HEIM

CHIEMGAUSTRASSE

N

109. Siedlung Ramersdorf, Munich.

all this publicity by describing Ramersdorf as an example of how the regime's housing policy would "lead Germans back to the soil."[46]

At least two more of these exhibitions were constructed during the next four years, each attended by ceremonial and wide publicity.[47] It was these model developments, rather than the far less attractive normal products of the Nazi housing program, which appeared most often in official publications where they were described as typical of Nazi housing in general. The developments were invariably constructed in suburban areas, but official propaganda described them as models for the rural resettlement which would immediately ensue. They therefore served as symbols in Nazi propaganda for that "return to the soil" which never took place.

The methods employed in Nazi housing propaganda were characteristic of Nazi architectural propaganda as a whole. Through repeated official ceremonies and elaborate exhibitions, the principal official buildings of the regime were kept continuously in the public eye during their construction, which often lasted many years; and similar publicity was given even to those projects which were never executed. These ceremonies and exhibitions were fully reported in the daily press, under Goebbels' supervision. The press was also filled with pictures and articles about the buildings erected for party and government use, and provided running accounts of the progress of the construction of particularly important buildings such as Troost's House of German Art. Because of their centralized control of the newspapers, the Nazis did not need to depend upon the professional journals for their architectural propaganda. But the government did issue an official architectural magazine edited by Speer, and various organs of government and party published a large number of lavish picture books.[48]

Through these methods the new regime was able to surround its building program with a volume of publicity as great as or greater than that achieved by the radical architects through their own efforts. But the purposes of this publicity were, of course, very different. Insofar as Nazi architectural propaganda had an ideological content, it reproduced the conflicting ideas of the regime's principal architectural patrons. But even more important, Nazi architectural propaganda also served to create a public impression of a far greater volume of construction than was actually taking place. And as in the case of the publicity attending the model housing developments, some of it was intended to make the official building program appear different than it actually was.

In this massive program of architectural propaganda, Hitler played a central role. He appeared as the principal speaker at cornerstone ceremonies for many important buildings, and he spoke at the openings of most of the major architectural exhibitions. Hitler's part in the propaganda program is perhaps best illustrated by the history of Troost's House of German Art in Munich. Troost's building had a special importance in Nazi architectural propaganda, because it was the first of Hitler's own buildings, and also because it was intended as a showcase for Nazi painting and sculpture. It was therefore consistently described in the press and in party publications as Hitler's "work"; and in Nazi propaganda it served as a symbol, not only of the architectural, but also of the artistic, creativity of the new regime.[49]

The first of the ceremonies which attended the progress of the House of German Art was held on October 15, 1933, when Hitler participated in laying the cornerstone of the building.[50] Representatives of the party and press from all over Germany, of the foreign press, and of the various embassies were invited to witness a lavish and ingenious pageant. Before the ceremony itself, columns of Hitler Youth, SS, and SA paraded along the Prinzregentenstrasse toward the building site. When Hitler arrived, he was greeted by the masons' foreman and other members of the building trades dressed in medieval costume. After the Prelude to *Die Meistersinger* had been performed, Hitler spoke of Germany's great cultural mission: in the midst of the depression, when other countries concerned themselves with merely material concerns, Germany would initiate a new era of creativity and show them that "man lives not by bread alone." He concluded by endowing Munich with the title of "the capital city of German art." That evening at Munich's Rathaus, the "masterbuilder of the Third Reich" accepted a medal of honor from German Bestelmeyer, President of the Academy of Art. The next day Munich celebrated a "day of German art" with a series of ceremonies and parades which the Bavarian Minister of Culture heralded as "the Christmas of the German soul."[51]

During the course of the construction of the Haus der Kunst, the official propaganda effort constantly reminded the public of its significance. The *VB* and other publications printed frequent articles on the progress of construction, and guided tours regularly visited the building site.[52] Munich continued to celebrate a "day of German art" in each successive year with ceremonies which centered around the idea that the new building represented both a restoration and a rebirth of German culture. When the museum finally opened in July of 1937, the party again organized two days of celebrations, and the national press was filled with articles on the building itself and on the works of sculpture and painting exhibited in it. Hitler presented another major speech on art and architecture at the opening ceremony, and Munich contributed another series of spectacles commemorating the "day of German art" and its own honorary status as the capital city of German art.[53]

The publicity attending the other Führerbauten was less extensive but similar in kind. There was generally a cornerstone ceremony at which Hitler appeared, accompanied by the Minister of Culture and the local Gauleiter. After turning the first spadeful of dirt, Hitler would speak, stressing at length the importance of monumental building to the new regime. At the Party Congresses, Hitler took every possible additional occasion to refer publicly to Speer's Congress buildings, which he described, rather inaccurately, as "gigantic," "prodigious," "colossal."[54] Party officials took delegates and foreign observers on tours through the Nürnberg building sites and emphasized again and again the monumentality of the buildings: "the spirit of our times is embodied here . . .

in this eternal monument to German rebirth, in this stone symbol of German greatness, German vitality, and German culture."[55] Since the construction of all the Führerbauten was a lengthy process and was in many cases not completed, pictures of the designs were published at frequent intervals in official publications, and drawings and models were displayed at the official architectural exhibitions.

There were three of these architectural exhibitions, held in the House of German Art in 1938 and 1939. Hitler, accompanied by Goebbels, and on one occasion by the Yugoslavian Prime Minister,[56] opened each exhibition with a major speech about architecture. The exhibitions gave a high proportion of their space to pictures and large-scale models of the monumental buildings of the regime — to the Führerbauten, the Ordensburgen, and the war memorials — although buildings by the Labor Front and the Hitler Youth in the "folk styles" and pictures of the model housing developments were also very prominent. The buildings of the armed forces, though less prominent, were also displayed; and these included some executed in the most modern manner as well as modest stucco buildings entirely devoid of any monumental character. Hitler praised each type of building in his speeches and described them all as "documents of the beginning of a new era."

The pattern of propaganda at the architectural exhibitions also characterized the general architectural publications of the regime. In these collections of pictures of "modern German architecture," a few buildings appeared again and again.[57] The Führerbauten and the Ordensburgen, often photographed from ten or fifteen points of view, came first in every book published by Speer and other Nazi officials; in Speer's periodical, *Die Kunst im Deutschen Reich*, the same buildings appeared in nearly every issue. Almost invariably, the pictures of these buildings were accompanied by quotations from Hitler's speeches emphasizing the importance of monumentality in creating a "common will" while symbolizing renewed national strength. Next followed a variety of examples of the "folk" styles and pictures of model housing developments and projected rural settlements, each accompanied by appropriate references to "blood and soil." But like the architectural exhibitions, official publications also included a wide sampling of pictures of every type of official building, from the Wehrmacht barracks to the most modern buildings at the Hermann-Goering-Werke, as examples of the "modernity" of Nazi building. Even the homes of private individuals and the buildings of private industry were often reproduced as evidence of the "National Socialist will to build."[58] The party press employed the same methods

in its architectural propaganda. While the principal official building occupied the most prominent place in its pages, no post office
was too small or Hitler Youth Hostel too obscure to escape the
notice of the *VB*.[59] Whatever their style, these buildings were described as "national socialist architecture."

Like the structure of architectural control in the Third Reich
and like the Nazi building program itself, Nazi architectural propaganda represented a compromise among contradictory ideas and
purposes. The minority of explicitly "ideological" buildings, to
which it gave great prominence, reflected two conflicting ideas of
the character of the new society. The monumental buildings, described by Hitler as symbols of the "heroic scale of life," were
intended to reflect the power of the dictator and his modern state
over his subjects in the mass. This view was wholly incompatible
with that represented by the Kleinsiedlungen and folk styles,
which, symbolizing an individualistic preindustrial society, conformed more closely to the ideals of the Kampfbund and the
earlier critics of the new style. But not only did Nazi propaganda
ignore this conflict, it also publicized nearly every other type of
building construction after 1933 and often praised those styles
which closely resembled the work of the radicals of the twenties.
The exception to this permissiveness in Nazi propaganda was the
historicist architecture of the original critics of the new style.
There was in fact no large-scale revival of the historicism of 1910
under the new regime. Schmitthenner, Schultze-Naumburg, and
members of their school executed a few minor works, but these
were almost completely ignored in the Nazi press.[60] The "folk"
styles which carried on the blood and soil thinking popularized
by the earlier conservative critics did not resemble the kind of
architecture they themselves believed in. The chief element of
continuity between the controversy of the twenties and Nazi
architectural propaganda after 1933 was thus a belief in the symbolic meaning of architecture. The Nazi regime was content to
exploit this belief in its propaganda without attempting to resolve
the conflicts implied in its building program or to dictate questions of architectural style.

Like the new architecture of the twenties, the official building
of the Nazi regime did not represent a deviation from the development of European architecture in general. In every European
country, and in America too, the thirties saw a resurgence of interest in monumental styles for which modified neoclassical forms
were employed. One architectural historian has even described
the Führerbauten as manifestations of a "Trocadero style," thus
emphasizing the French contribution to this type of architecture.[61]

The folk revival too had its parallels in other countries, where the experiences of the depression turned men's affections from urban to rural themes. Nor, as we have seen, did the Nazi regime go very far along the road toward establishing "totalitarian" control of architectural style, although it did effectively prevent the leaders of the radical movement from following their profession. Thus style in Germany remained to a large extent the product of the taste of those who paid for it, as in the rest of western Europe. What differentiates the development of Nazi architecture from the rest of European architectural history is the degree of ideological significance attached to it by the Nazi leaders and the intensity of the political propaganda which surrounded it. These characteristics of Nazi architecture can only be understood in the light of the fierce political controversies over architecture which took place during the Weimar period. That the architectural policy of the Nazi regime emerged out of this background determined both the general character of its architectural program and its political significance. Thus, although the political involvement of architecture reached its height in Germany under Hitler, it began in 1918.

Selected Bibliography

Note: This bibliography is essentially a check list of titles, without annotation, because so much space is devoted in the notes to discussing the character of the source materials. It includes only the more important primary and secondary materials used in the preparation of the book, and it excludes all anonymous magazine articles and almost all newspaper articles, anonymous or not, since their citation would render it unreadable. Where the texts of speeches were drawn from newspaper sources, reference is made to the chapter in which the speeches are quoted. Few of the materials in public and private archives are listed individually, since the archives are described in a separate section. The lists of newspapers and periodicals do not include those consulted only in excerpt form in the private collections of press clippings.

PRIMARY SOURCES

1. COLLECTIONS OF DOCUMENTS AND PRIVATE PAPERS

a. *Walter Gropius, Lincoln, Massachusetts:* When it was complete, as it was when the work for this book was begun, the Gropius Archive was probably the richest existing source for the study of twentieth-century German art and architecture. In his capacity as director of the Bauhaus, Gropius collected all the school's prospectuses, catalogs, and publications, together with the legal documents having to do with its relations with the Thuringian and Anhalt governments. Moreover, he and his staff compiled scrapbooks of all press notices on the school (cited in the notes as the "Zeitungsarchive"). The material on the Bauhaus, however, made up only a small portion of the Archive. Gropius' papers include approximately 5,000 pages of his correspondence, dating from 1910 to the present and touching upon every aspect of modern art and architecture. They include, in addition, thirty letter file volumes of press clippings relating to Gropius' own wide-ranging career and several volumes of his manuscripts.

Early in 1961, Gropius donated the bulk of the material on the Bauhaus to the new Bauhaus Archive then being set up in Darmstadt under the direction of Hans-Maria Wingler. Most of the documents in the Lincoln Archive now concern Gropius' own career. But before the Bauhaus documents were sent to Germany, the "Zeitungsarchive" were microfilmed by Widener Library at Harvard University as a part of its program to copy all the press clippings among the Gropius papers. This program is now complete, and microfilm copies of both the "Zeitungsarchive" and the letter files are on deposit in Widener.

I have cited only the original scrapbooks and letter files in the notes. But for the benefit of those who will want to use the microfilm copies in Widener, a brief description of the relevant rolls of film is appended. *Microfilms of press clippings in the Gropius Archive, Widener Library:*

·Roll # 1 — "Zeitungsarchive" 1-5.

Roll # 2 — "Zeitungsarchiv" 6, two scrapbooks on the Bauhaus exhibition of 1923, a letter file on the later history of the Bauhaus entitled "Presse-Bauhaus 1928/34," and files on Gropius' own work entitled "Presse 1913/27" and "Presse 1925/27."

Roll # 3 — File "Presse 1928" and miscellaneous.

Roll # 4 — "Presse 1929," I and II; "Presse 1930," I, II, and III; and "Presse 1931," I, II, and III.

b. *Ernst May, Hamburg — Gross Flottbeck*: Like Gropius, May collected newspaper and magazine articles, both favorable and unfavorable, relating to his work in Frankfurt between 1925 and 1930. His Archive contains several hundred pages of these clippings, which were of central importance to the survey of public opinion on his work given in Chapter IV.

c. *Hans Eckstein, Munich*: Hans Eckstein, now director of the Neue Sammlung, Munich's museum of modern art, was a free-lance art critic during the twenties and thirties. He has saved copies of all his articles, including a very large number in which he surveyed the artistic policies of the Nazi regime. The latter, anonymous and published for the most part in Swiss newspapers, were particularly valuable for Chapters VI, VII, and VIII, since unbiased contemporary comment is very hard to find. The Archive also contains a number of extremely rare pamphlets published by the Kampfbund für deutsche Kultur.

d. *Ludwig Mies van der Rohe papers*: I have used copies of those of Mies's letters and manuscripts which have to do with the closing of the Bauhaus in 1933. Some of these are on file in the Busch-Reisinger Museum, Cambridge, Massachusetts; others were lent to me by Hans-Maria Wingler.

e. *Gerdy Troost papers*: The Troost collection includes both the private papers of Troost's widow and most of the business papers of her husband's firm. It consists of a large series of letter files, labeled by date and occasionally according to subject matter, but containing, nevertheless, very miscellaneous materials. The entire collection is on file in the Manuscript Division of the Library of Congress, Washington, D.C.

f. *Membership files of the Berlin division of the Reichskammer der bildenden Künste; U.S. Documents Center, West Berlin*: These files, though incomplete even for Berlin, are invaluable for any study of the policies of the RDBK. The folder of each member includes not only biographical information, but also correspondence with officials of the RDBK, memorandums from the latter on the suitability of the individual for membership, and, in some cases, the results of formal investigations made by the Gestapo. The scholar who wishes to use the files must first obtain permission from the Historical Division of the United States State Department.

2. PERIODICALS

Bauhaus. Walter Gropius and Laszlo Moholy-Nagy, eds. Dessau, 1927–1931.

Bauwelt. Paulsen, ed. Berlin, 1910 ff.

Der Cicerone. Leipzig, 1909 ff.

Die Denkmalpflege. Berlin, 1899 ff. Entitled *Denkmalpflege und Heim-atschutz* from 1923–1930; *Die Denkmalpflege* again from 1930–1932; *Deutsche Kunst und Denkmalpflege* after 1932. Konrad Nonn, ed., 1921–1927 and again from 1934.

Deutsche Bauhütte. Curt R. Vincenz, F. Rudolf Vogel, and H.A. Waldner, eds. Hannover: Curt R. Vincenz Verlag, 1897 ff.

Deutsche Bauzeitung. Berlin, 1867 ff.

Deutsche Kultur-Wacht: Blätter des Kampfbundes für deutsche Kultur. Berlin, 1932–1933.

Deutsche Technik. Gottfried Feder and Wolfgang Müller, eds. Berlin, 1933–1934.

Frühlicht: Eine Folge für Verwirklichung des neuen Baugedankens. Bruno Taut, ed. Magdeburg, 1921–1922. Recently reprinted in book form (Berlin: Ullstein, 1963).

Die Form. Walter Riezler, ed. Stuttgart, 1925–1935.

Die Kunst im Deutschen Reich. Albert Speer, ed. Munich, 1937 ff. From 1939, also issued in an "Ausgabe B": *Die Kunst im Deutschen Reich: Die Baukunst.*

Kunst und Künstler. Karl Scheffler, ed. Berlin, 1902 ff.

Das Kunstblatt. Paul Westheim, ed. Potsdam, 1917 ff.

Der Kunstwart und Kulturwart. Munich, 1886 ff. From 1925, *Der Kunstwart.*

Moderne Bauformen. Stuttgart, 1902 ff.

Nationalsozialistische Monatshefte. Berlin, 1931 ff.

Das neue Berlin. Martin Wagner, ed. Berlin, 1929.

Das neue Frankfurt: Monatsschrift für die Probleme moderner Gestaltung. Ernst May and Fritz Wichert, eds. Frankfurt am Main, 1926 ff. Subtitle varies. From 1932, *Die neue Stadt.* Joseph Gantner, ed. From 1933–34, published in Heidelberg and Zurich. Ceased publication 1934.

Siedlung und Wirtschaft. Berlin, 1919 ff.

Soziale Bauwirtschaft. Berlin: Verband sozialer Baubetriebe, 1921 ff.

Sozialistische Monatshefte. Berlin: Vorwärts, 1915 ff.

Stadtbaukunst alter und neuer Zeit. Cornelius Gurlitt, Bruno Möhring, and Bruno Taut, eds. Berlin, 1920 ff.

Wasmuths Monatshefte für Baukunst und Städtebau. Berlin, 1914 ff.

Das Werk: Die schweizer Monatsschrift für Kunst, Architektur, künstlerisches Gewerbe. Zurich, 1914 ff. Subtitle varies.

Wohnungswirtschaft. Martin Wagner, ed. Berlin, 1924 ff.

Zentralblatt der Bauverwaltung. Berlin: Preussisches Finanz-Ministerium, 1881 ff. Konrad Nonn, ed., 1921–1927, and again from 1934.

3. NEWSPAPERS

Der Angriff (NSDAP). Berlin.
Bayerischer Kurier. Munich.
Deutsche Allgemeine Zeitung. Berlin.
Deutsche Tageszeitung. Berlin.
Frankfurter Zeitung. Frankfurt am Main.
Fränkischer Kurier. Nürnberg.
Germania (Center Party). Berlin.
Leipziger Illustrierte Zeitung. Leipzig.
Ludendorffs Volkswarte. Munich.

München-Augsburger Abendzeitung. Munich.
Münchener Post. Munich.
Münchener Neueste Nachrichten. Munich.
Die Rote Fahne (KPD). Berlin.
Staats-Anzeiger für Württemberg. Stuttgart.
Stuttgarter Neues Tageblatt. Stuttgart.
Der Tag (DNVP). Berlin.
Tägliche Rundschau. Berlin.
Völkischer Beobachter (NSDAP). Munich. Unless otherwise noted, all references to the VB in the notes are to the Munich edition, except for the year 1933, for which I used the Berlin edition.
Volkstimme (SPD). Frankfurt am Main.
Vorwärts (SPD). Berlin.
Vossische Zeitung. Berlin.

4. BOOKS, ARTICLES, PAMPHLETS, MANUSCRIPTS

Die alte und die neue Regierung. Berlin: Reichszentrale für Heimatdienst, 1918.
An alle Künstler. Berlin, Spring 1919.
Bausünden und Baugeldvergeudung. Hannover: Deutsche Bauhütte, c. 1930.
Behne, Adolf. "Das Bauhaus Weimar," *Die Weltbühne,* Sept. 20, 1923.
———— "Bauhausresumee," *Sozialistische Monatshefte,* XXIX (1923), 542–544.
———— *Der moderne Zweckbau.* Munich, 1926.
———— *Neues Wohnen, neues Bauen.* Leipzig, 1927.
———— *Ruf zum Bauen.* Berlin, 1920.
———— *Eine Stunde Architekur.* Stuttgart, 1928.
———— "Weimar," *Sozialistische Monatshefte,* XXVI (1920), 69.
Behrendt, Walter Curt. "Geleitwort," *Die Form,* I (1925), 1.
Ein Beispiel aus der Siedlungsplanung. Berlin: DAF, 1934.
Bestelmeyer, German. "Baukunst und Gegenwart," *Deutsche Technik,* II (1934), 393–394, 444–445.
———— Speeches: see Chapters VI and VIII.
Bier, Justus. "Zur Auflösung der Staatlichen Bauhochschule in Weimar," *Die Form,* VI (1930), 269–274.
Brünninghaus, Erhard. *Heime der Hitler-Jugend.* Stuttgart, 1940.
Cetto, Max. "Briefe eines jungen deutschen Architekten an dem Herrn Reichsminister für Propaganda und Volksaufklärung Dr. Goebbels," *Die neue Stadt,* VII (1933/34), 26–28.
Darré, Richard Walther. *Das Bauerntum als Lebensquell der Nordischen Rasse,* 7th ed. Munich, 1938.
———— *Erkenntnisse und Werden: Aufsätze aus der Zeit vor der Machtergreifung,* 2nd ed. Goslar, 1940.
———— *Neuadel aus Blut und Boden.* Munich, 1930.
"Deutsche aller Berufe und Stände," *Flugblätter des Kampfbundes für deutsche Kultur,* nr. 1. Munich, c. 1929.
Die deutsche Heimstätten-Siedlung. Berlin: DAF, 1935.
Deutsches Kulturrecht. Hamburg, 1936.
Dietrich, Otto. "Adolf Hitler als künstlerischer Mensch," *Nationalsozialistische Monatshefte,* III (1933), 473.
Dorner, Alexander. "Walter Gropius," *Bauwelt,* April 10, 1930.

Eberlein, Kurt Karl. *Was ist deutsch in der deutschen Kunst?* Leipzig, 1934.

Feder, Gottfried. "Das deutsche Siedlungswerk," *Siedlung und Wirtschaft*, XVI (1934), 183–186.

Feistel-Rohmeder, Bettina. *Im Terror des Kunst-Bolschewismus.* Karlsruhe, 1938.

Freytag-Loringhoven, Mathilde Freiin von. *Das Staatliche Bauhaus und die Kunstschule im Staatshaushaltsplan für 1920.* Weimar, c. March 1920.

Gerstenberg, Kurt. "Revolution in der Architektur," *Der Cicerone*, XII (1919), 255–257.

Goebbels, Joseph. "Die deutsche Kultur vor neuen Aufgaben," *Signale der neuen Zeit* (Munich, 1934), 323–336.

———— "Die Deutsche Revolution," *Nationalsozialistische Monatshefte*, III (1933), 247.

———— Speeches: see Chapter VII.

Grebe, Wilhelm. *Gegenwarts- und Zukunftsaufgaben im ländlichen Bauwesen.* Berlin: Reichsnährstand, c. 1936.

Gropius, Walter. *Bauhausbauten Dessau.* Munich, 1930.

———— "Der Baugeist der neuen Volksgemeinde," *Die Glocke*, X (1924), 311–315.

———— "Baukunst im freien Volksstaat," *Deutscher Revolutions-Almanach* (Hamburg and Berlin, 1919), 134–136.

———— *Die bisherige und zukünftige Arbeit des Staatlichen Bauhauses in Weimar.* Weimar, March 1924.

———— "Flach-, Mittel- oder Hochbau," *Moderne Bauformen*, XXX (1931), 321–340.

———— "Das flache Dach; eine Entgegnung," *Deutsche Bauzeitung*, LX (1926), 188–192.

———— "Idee und Aufbau des staatlichen Bauhauses," *Staatliches Bauhaus in Weimar* (Weimar, 1923), 7–18.

———— *Internationale Architektur.* Munich, 1925.

———— *The New Architecture and the Bauhaus.* New York, 1937.

———— *Programm des Staatlichen Bauhauses in Weimar.* Weimar, April 1919.

———— "Systematische Vorarbeit für rationellen Wohnungsbau," *Bauhaus*, I (1927), 1–2.

———— "Wie wollen wir in Zukunft bauen?" *Wohnungswirtschaft*, I (1924), 152–154.

———— "Wohnungsbau der Zukunft," *Wohnungswirtschaft*, II (1925), 11–12.

———— Letters: see Chapters III, V, and VII.

———— Speeches: see Chapters II, III, and V.

Grundformen für Kleinsiedlungshäuser. Berlin: Arbeitsministerium, 1936.

Grundsteinlegung des Hauses der deutschen Kunst. Munich, 1933.

Günther, Hans F. K. *Rasse und Stil.* Munich, 1926.

———— *Rassenkunde des deutschen Volkes.* Munich, 1923.

———— *Ritter, Tod und Teufel.* Munich, 1924.

Gutkind, E., ed. *Neues Bauen.* Berlin, 1919.

Hager, Kurt. "Das flache Dach," *Deutsche Bauzeitung*, LX (1926), 151.

Häring, Hugo. "Nochmals Weimarer und Dessauer Bauhaus," *Zentralblatt der Bauverwaltung*, XXXXVII (1927), 171–172.

———— "Die Tradition, Schultze-Naumburg, und Wir," *Die Form*, II (1926), 180.

Hartlaub, Gustav. "Ethos der neuen Baukunst," *Die Form*, V (1929), 273–277.

Haug, Eugen. "Aufzeichnungen zur Vorgeschichte der Entstehung der NSDAP in Stuttgart." Manuscript, Institut für Zeitgeschichte, Munich, Gruppe VI, Stück 166.

Haupt, Albrecht. "Rasse und Baukunst," *Deutsche Bauhütte*, XXX (1926), 112, 134–135.

Herfurth, Emil. *Weimar und das Staatliche Bauhaus.* Weimar, Feb. 1920.

Heuss, Theodor. "Phantasie und Baukunst," *Der Kunstwart und Kulturwart*, XXXII (1919), 17–20.

Hilberseimer, Ludwig. *Groszstadt Architektur.* Stuttgart, 1927.

———— *Internationale neue Baukunst,* Stuttgart, 1928.

Hinkel, Hans. *Einer unter 100,000.* Munich, 1938.

———— *Handbuch der Reichskulturkammer.* Berlin, 1937.

Hitler, Adolf. *Mein Kampf,* ed. John Chamberlain, *et al.* 2 vóls. in 1. New York, 1940.

———— *Hitler: Reden und Proklamationen 1932–1945,* ed. Max Domarus. 2 vols. Würzburg, 1962.

———— *The Speeches of Adolf Hitler,* ed. N. H. Baynes. 2 vols. London, 1942.

———— *Adolf Hitler from Speeches 1933–1938,* ed. Richard Mönnig. Berlin, 1938.

———— Speeches, in the *Völkischer Beobachter:* See Chapters VI, VII, and VIII.

———— Speeches, published individually (listed chronologically):

    Rede im Hofbräuhaus zu München v. 13.8.1920. Copy in Institut für Zeitgeschichte, Gruppe I, Stück 62, Bl. 1–33.

    Die deutsche Kunst als stolzeste Verteidigung des deutschen Volkes (September 1933). Munich, 1934.

    Die Rede unseres Führers Adolf Hitler bei der Grundsteinlegung des Hauses der deutschen Kunst in München am 15. Oktober 1933. Munich, 1937.

    Liberty, Art, Nationhood; Three Addresses, Delivered at the Seventh National Socialist Congress, Nuremberg, 1935. Berlin, 1935.

    Die Reden Hitlers am Parteitag der Freiheit 1935. Munich, 1935.

    Reden des Führers am Parteitag der Ehre 1936. Munich, 1936.

    Reden des Führers am Parteitag der Arbeit 1937. Munich, 1937.

    Reden des Führers am Parteitag Grossdeutschland 1938. Munich, 1938.

Hoeber, Fritz. "Persönlichkeit und Volkstum in der Baukunst der Gegenwart," *Der Cicerone*, XI (1919), 76–82.

Högg, Emil. "Wege und Ziele deutscher Baukunst," *Deutsche Bauzeitung*, LX (1926), 653–656, 658–664.

Hübbenet, Anatol von. *Das Taschenbuch Schönheit der Arbeit.* Berlin, 1938.

Ja! Stimmen des Arbeitsrates für Kunst in Berlin. Berlin-Charlottenburg, 1919.

Jäckh, Ernst. *Der goldene Pflug: Lebensernte eines Weltbürgers.* Stuttgart, 1954.

———— "Idee und Realisierung der internationalen Werkbund-Ausstellung 'Die neue Zeit' Köln 1932," *Die Form,* V (1929), 401–421.

Ein Kampfbund für deutsche Kultur. Munich, c. 1930.

Kampffmeyer, Hans. *Friedenstadt,* 2nd ed. Jena, 1918.

Kandinsky, Wassily. *Über das Geistige in der Kunst, insbesondere in der Malerei.* Munich, 1912.

Klee, Paul. "Nocheinmal das Staatliche Bauhaus," *Die Hilfe,* August 1, 1924.

Klopfer, Paul. "Über Apollinisches und Dionysisches in der Baukunst," *Stadtbaukunst alter und neuer Zeit,* I (1920), 161–166.

Kremmer, Kurt. "Das ländliche Bauwesen im Dienst der Landfluchtbekämpfung und der Neubildung deutschen Bauerntums," *National-sozialistische Monatshefte,* IX (1939), h. 133.

Landmann, Ludwig. "Zum Geleit," *Das neue Frankfurt,* I (1926), 1–2.

Lotz, Wilhelm. "Neue Form und Heimatschutz," *Die Form,* VI (1930), 46–47.

———— *Schönheit der Arbeit in Deutschland.* Berlin, 1940.

Ludowici. "Das nationalsozialistische Siedlungswerk," *Wege zur neuen Sozialpolitik* (Berlin, 1936), 200–224.

May, Ernst. *Die Frankfurter Wohnungspolitik.* Frankfurt am Main, 1929.

———— "Grundlagen der Frankfurter Wohnungsbaupolitik," *Das neue Frankfurt,* III (1928), 113–153.

———— "Das neue Frankfurt," *Das neue Frankfurt,* I (1926), 2–7.

———— "Rationalisierung des Bauwesens," *Frankfurter Zeitung,* April 14, 1926.

———— "Der soziale Moment in der neuen Baukunst," *Das neue Frankfurt,* III (1928), 77–83.

Mortane, Jacques, ed. *Das neue Deutschland.* Zurich and Leipzig, 1928.

Die Neuordnung der Kleinsiedlung. Berlin, 1938.

Nonn, Konrad. "Die internationale Architektur-Ausstellung in Berlin," *Deutsche Bauhütte,* XXXII (1928), 210.

———— "Homunkulus-Architektur," *Deutsche Bauhütte,* XXXIV (1930), 142.

———— "Kritisches zur Reichforschungsgesellschaft," *Deutsche Bauhütte,* XXXII (1928), 156–157.

———— "Kurzlebige Moden für Wohnungsbauten?" *Deutsche Bauhütte,* XXXII (1928), 66.

———— "Das staatliche Bauhaus in Weimar," *Die Hilfe,* June 1, 1924.

———— "Das Staatliche Bauhaus in Weimar," *Zentralblatt der Bauverwaltung,* XXXXIV (1924), 42–44.

———— "Zusammenfassendes über das Weimarer und Dessauer Bauhaus," *Zentralblatt der Bauverwaltung,* XXXXVII (1927), 105–110.

Prinzhorn, Hans. *Bildnerei der Geisteskranken,* 2nd ed. Berlin, 1923.

Reform-Bauweisen für Siedlungsbau-Verbilligung. Hannover: Deutsche Bauhütte, 1930.

Reichsforschungsgesellschaft für Wirtschaftlichkeit im Bau- und Wohnungswesen e. V. *Sonderhefte,* 1–7, Berlin, 1928–1929.

Renner, Paul. *Kulturbolschewismus?* Munich and Leipzig, 1932.

Riezler, Walter. "Der Kampf gegen das Flache Dach," *Die Form,* III (1927), 26–27.

Rosenberg, Alfred. "Gesinnung und Kunst," *Nationalsozialistische Monatshefte*, V (1935), 607.

———— *Gestaltung der Idee*. Munich, 1939.

———— "Kampf um die Kunst," *Nationalsozialistische Monatshefte*, IV (1934), 1095–1099.

———— *Der Mythus des 20. Jahrhunderts*. Munich, 1930.

———— *Das politische Tagebuch Alfred Rosenbergs aus den Jahren 1934/35 und 1939/40*, ed. Hans Günther Seraphim. Göttingen, 1956.

———— *Memoirs of Alfred Rosenberg*, ed. and trans. E. Posselt. Chicago, 1949.

———— *Der Sumpf: Querschnitt durch das 'Geistes'-Leben der November-Demokratie*. Munich, 1930.

———— Speeches and newspaper articles: see Chapters VI, VII, and VIII.

Sauckel, Fritz. *Kampf und Sieg in Thüringen*. Weimar, 1934.

———— Papers on the history of the Nazi party and local völkische groups in Thuringia. *Microfilms of German War Documents*, prepared by the American Historical Association Committee for the Study of War Documents. Series T-81, Frames 136429–137002.

Scheffler, Karl. *Die fetten und die mageren Jahre*. Munich, 1948.

Schlemmer, Oskar. *Briefe und Tagebücher*. Munich, 1958.

Schluckebier, Hermann. "Unsere Stellung zum Wohnungsnot. Rede auf der Tagung des kommunalistischen Reichsausschusses der DNVP am 29.1.1928," *Flugschriften der Deutschnationalen Volkspartei*, nr. 316. Berlin, 1928.

Schmidt, Felix. "Der Kampfbund der Deutschen Architekten und Ingenieure im Kampfbund für Deutsche Kultur," *Deutsche Technik*, I (1933), 47–49.

Schmidt-Leonhardt, Hans. "Kultur und Staat im Recht des neuen Reichs," *Deutsches Kulturrecht* (Hamburg, 1936), 5–17.

Schmitthenner, Paul. *Die Baukunst im neuen Reich*. Munich, 1934.

———— *Das deutsche Wohnhaus*. Stuttgart, 1932.

———— "Tradition und neues Bauen," *Deutsche Kultur-Wacht*, II (1933), H. 17, 11–12.

———— Speeches: see Chapters V, VI, and VII.

Schönheit der Arbeit — Sozialismus der Tat. Berlin, 1936.

Schreiber, Karl-Friedrich. "Das geltende Reichskulturrecht," *Deutsches Kulturrecht* (Berlin, 1936), 17–33.

———— *Das Recht der Reichskulturkammer*. 5 vols. Berlin, 1934–1937.

Schreyer, Lothar. *Erinnerungen an Sturm und Bauhaus*. Munich, 1956.

Schultze-Naumburg, Paul. *Das ABC des Bauens*. Stuttgart, 1926.

———— "Aufgaben der Architektur im neuen Reich," *Deutsche Technik*, I (1933), 105–106.

———— "Zur Frage des schrägen und des flachen Daches bei unserem Wohnhausbau," *Deutsche Bauzeitung*, LX (1926), 761–766, 777–780.

———— *Das Gesicht des deutschen Hauses*. Munich, 1929.

———— *Kampf um die Kunst*. Munich, 1932.

———— *Kunst und Rasse*. Munich, 1928.

———— "Müssen wir in Zukunft in asiatischen Häusern wohnen?" *Das neue Deutschland*, I (1931), 88–91.

———— Speeches and newspaper articles: See Chapters V, VI, and VII.

Schumacher, Fritz. *Stufen des Lebens*. Stuttgart, 1949.

Senger, Alexander von. "Der Baubolschewismus und seine Verkoppel-
ung mit Wirtschaft und Politik," *Nationalsozialistische Monatshefte*,
IV (1934), 497–507.

———— "Bolschewismus im Bauwesen," *Völkischer Beobachter*, Oct. 22,
Nov. 5, 7, 21; 1930.

———— *Die Brandfackel Moskaus*. Zurzach-Schweiz, 1931.

———— *Krisis der Architektur*. Zurich, 1928.

Die Siedlung: Planungsheft der DAF. Berlin, 1938.

Das staatliche Bauhaus Weimar und sein Leiter. Weimar: Arno Müller,
n.d.

Staatliches Bauhaus in Weimar, 1919–1923. Weimar, 1923.

Steinwartz, Herbert. *Das Kameradschaftshaus im Betrieb*. Berlin: DAF,
1939.

————*Wesen, Aufgaben, Ziele des Amtes Schönheit der Arbeit*. Berlin: DAF, 1937.

Der Streit um das Staatliche Bauhaus. Weimar: Bauhaus, 1920.

Stürzenacker. "Die Revolution des Bauwesens," *Der Bauingenieur*, I
(1920), 192–197.

Taut, Bruno. *Alpine Architektur*. Hagen, 1919.

———— *Ein Architekturprogramm*. Berlin: Arbeitsrat für Kunst, Christmas 1918.

———— *Die Auflösung der Städte*. Hagen, 1920.

———— *Bauen. Der neue Wohnbau*. Leipzig, 1927.

———— "Bauwirtschaft," *Wohnungswirtschaft*, I (1924), 170–171.

———— "Beobachtungen über Farbenwirkung aus meiner Praxis,"
Bauwelt, X (1919), 12–13.

———— "Ersparnis im Wohnungsbau durch rationelle Einrichtung,"
Wohnungswirtschaft, I (1924), 20–23.

———— "Mein erstes Jahr 'Stadtbaurat,'" *Frühlicht* (Berlin, 1963),
215–221.

———— *Modern Architecture*. London, 1929.

———— "Neue Siedlungen," *Frühlicht* (Berlin, 1963), 121–124.

———— *Die neue Wohnung: Die Frau als Schöpferin*. Leipzig, 1924.

———— *Neues Bauen in Europa und Amerika*. Leipzig, 1929.

———— "Nieder der Seriosismus!" *Früchlicht* (Berlin, 1963), 11.

———— *Stadtkrone*. Jena, 1919.

———— *Der Weltbaumeister: Architekturschauspiel für symphonische
Musik*. Hagen, 1920.

———— *Ein Wohnhaus*. Stuttgart, 1927.

Utitz, Emil. "Zweckmässigkeit und Sachlichkeit," *Dekorative Kunst*,
XXVII (1923), 194–203.

———— *Die Überwindung des Expressionismus*. Stuttgart, 1927.

Der Verkehr: Jahrbuch des Deutschen Werkbundes 1914. Jena, 1914.

*Volk erwache! Was will die Deutschnationale Volkspartei? Die Rede
Dr. Hugenbergs im Berliner Sportpalast am 14. August 1930*. Berlin,
1930.

Wagner, Martin. *Neue Bauwirtschaft: Ein Beitrag zur Verbilligung
der Baukosten im Wohnungsbau*. Berlin, 1918.

———— "Neue Wege zur Kleinwohnungsbau: Ein Programm der Selbsthilfe," *Soziale Bauwirtschaft*, IV (1924), 21–33.

———— "Probleme der Baukosten Verbilligung," *Soziale Bauwirtschaft*,
IV (1924), 131–135.

———— *Städtische Freiflächenpolitik*. Berlin, 1915.

Waldner, H. A. "Über Herstellung von Wohnhäusern in Industriebetrieb. Zum Vorschlag des Bauhausdirektors Gropius," *Deutsche Bauhütte*, XXVIII (1924), 217–218.

Weber, E. "Die Reichsforschungsgesellschaft für Wirtschaftlichkeit im Bau- und Wohnungswesen e. V.: Ihr Werden und Wollen," *Schlesisches Heim*, VIII (1927), 425–434.

Weichen, Otto. "Grundsätzliches über die Gestaltung des Bauernhofes," *Architektur-Wettbewerbe: Bauernhofe*. (Stuttgart, n. d.), 5–9.

Vom Weimarer Bauhaus. Weimar, Dec. 31, 1919.

Wendland, Winfried. "Der Deutsche Werkbund im neuen Reich," *Die Form*, IX (1933), 257–258.

———— "Moderne Baukunst – Junge Baukunst," *Bauwelt*, XXIII (1932), 740–741.

———— "Nationalsozialistische Kulturpolitik," *Deutsche Kultur-Wacht*, II (1933), H. 24, 2.

Wenzel, Fritz. *Der Sieg von Blut und Boden*. Berlin, 1934.

Westheim, Paul. "Architektur-Entwicklung," *Die Glocke*, X (1924), 181–185.

Wichert, Fritz. "Die bildende Kunst und der soziale Staat," *Der Geist der neuen Volksgemeinschaft* (Berlin: Reichszentrale für Heimatdienst, 1919), 107–119.

Wienkoop, J. "Wandlungen der Baukunst im Lichte der deutschen Kultur," *Deutsche Bauzeitung*, LX (1926), 701–704, 718–720.

Wittmann, Konrad. "Von stattlichen Bauhaus in Weimar," *Deutsche Bauhütte*, XXVIII (1924), 49–51.

Wolf, Paul. "Die Architektur im neuen Deutschland," *Der Cicerone*, XI (1919), 3–7.

SECONDARY SOURCES AND REFERENCE WORKS

1. GENERAL BACKGROUND AND REFERENCE: POLITICAL, ECONOMIC, AND INTELLECTUAL HISTORY

Bracher, K. D. *Die Auflösung der Weimarer Republik*, 2nd ed. Stuttgart and Düsseldorf, 1957.

———— et al. *Die nationalsozialistische Machtergreifung*. Cologne, 1960.

Bullock, A. *Hitler: A Study in Tyranny*, revised ed. New York, 1962.

Drüner, Hans. *Im Schatten des Weltkrieges; zehn Jahre Frankfurter Geschichte von 1914–1924*. Frankfurt am Main, 1934.

Gordon, H. J. *The Reichswehr and the German Republic 1919–1926*. Princeton, 1957.

Hagemann, Walter. *Publizistik im Dritten Reich*. Hamburg, 1948.

Heiber, Helmut. *Joseph Goebbels*. Berlin, 1962.

Heiden, Konrad. *Der Führer*. Boston, 1944.

Hellwig, L. W. *Persönlichkeiten der Gegenwart; Luftfahrt, Wissenschaft, Kunst*. Berlin, 1940.

Hughes, H. Stuart. *Oswald Spengler: A Critical Estimate*. New York, 1952.

Mosse, George. *The Crisis of German Ideology*. New York, 1964.

Preller, L. *Sozialpolitik in der Weimarer Republik*. Stuttgart, 1949.

Reitlinger, Gerald. *The SS, Alibi of a Nation*. London, 1956.

Sington, Derick. *The Goebbels Experiment*, New Haven, 1944.

Sokel, Walter H. *The Writer in Extremis: Expressionism in Twentieth-Century German Literature.* Stanford, 1959.

Stern, Fritz. *The Politics of Cultural Despair: A Study in the Rise of the Germanic Ideology.* Berkeley, 1961.

Witzmann, Georg. *Thüringen von 1918–1933: Erinnerungen eines Politikers.* Meisenheim am Glan, 1958.

Wunderlich, Frieda. *Farm Labor in Germany 1810–1945.* Princeton, 1961.

2. HISTORIES OF ART AND ARCHITECTURE AND THEIR RELATION TO POLITICS

Bangert, Wolfgang. *Baupolitik und Stadtgestaltung in Frankfurt am Main.* Würzburg, 1937.

Banham, Reyner. *Theory and Design in the First Machine Age.* New York, 1960.

Bayer, Herbert, Walter Gropius, and Ise Gropius, eds. *Bauhaus 1919–1928.* New York, 1938.

Behne, Adolf. *Entartete Kunst.* Berlin, 1947.

Behrendt, Walter Curt. *Modern Building: Its Nature, Problems and Forms.* New York, 1937.

Brenner, Hildegard. *Die Kunstpolitik des Nationalsozialismus.* Hamburg, 1963.

Büge, Max. *Der Rechtsschutz gegen Verunstaltung.* Düsseldorf, 1952.

Dehlinger, Armand. "Architektur der Superlative: Eine kritische Betrachtung der NS Bauprogramme von München und Nürnberg." Manuscript, written under the auspices of the Institut für Zeitgeschichte, Munich.

Eckardt, Wolf von. "The Bauhaus," *Horizon, A Magazine of the Arts,* IV (November 1961), 58–77.

Eckstein, Hans, ed. *50. Jahre Deutscher Werkbund.* Frankfurt am Main, 1958.

Grautoff, Otto. *Die neue Kunst.* Berlin, 1921.

Hellack, Georg. "Architektur und bildende Kunst als Mittel nationalsozialistischer Propaganda," *Publizistik,* V (1960), 77 ff.

Herzog, Fritz. *Die Kunstzeitschriften der Nachkriegszeit.* Berlin-Charlottenburg, 1940.

Hitchcock, Henry-Russell. *Painting Toward Architecture.* New York, 1948.

———— and Phillip Johnson. *The International Style.* New York, 1932.

Jaffé, H. L. C. *De Stijl, 1917–1931: The Dutch Contribution to Modern Art.* Amsterdam, 1956.

Joedicke, Jürgen. *Geschichte der modernen Architektur.* Stuttgart, 1959.

Lehmann-Haupt, Hellmut. *Art under a Dictatorship.* New York, 1954.

Myers, Bernard S. *The German Expressionists: A Generation in Revolt.* New York, 1956.

Pevsner, Nikolaus. *Pioneers of Modern Design from William Morris to Walter Gropius,* 2nd ed. New York, 1949; 3rd ed. Baltimore, 1964.

———— "Post-War Tendencies in German Art-Schools," *Journal of the Royal Society of Arts,* LXXXIV (1936), 248–261.

Rassem, M. "Die Bayerische Post als Bauherr," *Der Zwiebelturm: Monatsschrift für das Bayerische Volk und seine Freunde,* VIII (1953), 345–347.

Rave, Paul Ortwin. *Kunstdiktatur im dritten Reich*. Hamburg, 1949.

Roh, Franz. *'Entartete' Kunst*. Hannover, 1962.

Schacherl, Lillian. "Die Zeitschriften des Expressionismus." Munich: Dissertation, 1957.

Schmalenbach, Fritz. "The Term 'Neue Sachlichkeit,'" *Art Bulletin*, XXII (1940), 161–165.

Sedlmayr, Hans. *Verlust der Mitte*. Salzburg, 1948.

Wernert, E. *L'art dans le IIIe Reich*. Paris, 1936.

Wingler, Hans-Maria. *Bauhaus — 1919–1933 — Weimar, Dessau, Berlin*. Bramsche, 1962.

Wulf, Joseph, ed. *Die Bildenden Künste im Dritten Reich: Eine Dokumentation*. Gütersloh, 1963.

Zevi, Bruno. *Towards an Organic Architecture*. London, 1950.

3. HOUSING AND HOUSING POLICY

30. Jahre Wohnungsreform 1898–1928. Berlin, 1928.

Fünf Jahre Wohnungsbau in Frankfurt am Main. Frankfurt am Main, 1930.

Gehag. Gemeinnützige Heimstätten-Aktiengesellschaft 1924–1957. Berlin, 1957.

Geschichte der gemeinnützigen Wohnungswirtschaft in Berlin. Berlin, 1957.

Gut, Albert. *Der Wohnungsbau in Deutschland nach dem Weltkriege*. Munich, 1928.

Mattutat, Hermann. "Die Krisis im Wohnungsbau," *Sozialistische Monatshefte*, X (1924), 441–445.

16,000 Wohnungen für Angestellte: Denkschrift hrsg. im Auftrage der GAGFAH anlässlich ihres zehnjahrigen Bestehens. Berlin, 1928.

Spörhase, Rolf. *Wohnungsunternehmen im Wandel der Zeit*. Hamburg, 1947.

Tremmel, Peter. "Die Wohnungsfrage," in Georg Schreiber, ed. *Politisches Jahrbuch 1927/28*. Gladbach, 1928, 491–494.

Wohnungsverhältnisse und Wohnungsbau in Köln. Cologne, 1929.

Das Wohungswesen der Stadt Frankfurt am Main. Frankfurt am Main, 1930.

Das Wohnungswesen der Stadt München. Munich, 1928.

Wutzky, Emil. "Wohnungswirtschaft," in Fritz Elsas, ed. *Die deutsche Städte, ihre Arbeit von 1919 bis 1928*. Berlin, 1928.

4. BOOKS OF ILLUSTRATIONS

Bauen im nationalsozialistischen Deutschlands. Munich, 1940.

Bauten der Bewegung. Berlin, 1938.

Bauten in der Stadt der Reichsparteitage Nürnberg. Nürnberg, 1942.

Berliner Architektur der Nachkriegszeit. Berlin, 1928.

Bau und Wohnung: Die Bauten der Weissenhof Siedlung. Stuttgart, 1927.

Deutschland Baut. Die Bauten und Bauvorhaben der Partei und des Reiches, der Arbeitsfront, der Hitler-Jugend, der Luftwaffe, des Heeres und der Marine. Stuttgart, 1939.

Dresler, Adolf. *Das Braunehaus und die Verwaltungsgebäude der Reichsleitung der NSDAP*, 3rd. ed. Munich, 1939.

Johannes, Heinz. *Neues Bauen in Berlin*. Berlin, 1931.

Müller-Wulckow, Walter. *Deutsche Baukunst der Gegenwart.* Leipzig, 1929.

München baut auf. Munich, c. 1937.

Neue Wohnhäuser im Gebirgsstil. Munich, 1939.

Neuere Postbauten in Bayern. Munich, 1925.

Platz, Gustav Adolf. *Die Baukunst der neuesten Zeit.* Berlin, 1927.

———— *Wohnräume der Gegenwart.* Berlin, 1933.

Raststätten an der Reichsautobahn. Berlin, n. d.

Rittich, Werner. *Architektur und Bauplastik der Gegenwart.* Berlin, 1938.

———— *New German Architecture.* Berlin, 1941.

Seeger, Hermann. *Öffentliche Verwaltungsgebäude.* Leipzig, 1943.

Speer, Albert. *Neue deutsche Baukunst.* Prague, 1943.

Troost, Gerdy. *Das Bauen im neuen Reich.* 2 vols. Bayreuth, 1943.

5. MONOGRAPHS AND BIOGRAPHICAL MATERIAL ON INDIVIDUAL ARCHITECTS AND ARTISTS

Cremens, P. J. *Peter Behrens: Sein Werk von 1909 bis zur Gegenwart.* Essen, 1928.

Eckardt, Wolf von. *Eric Mendelsohn.* New York, 1960.

Elsaesser, Martin. *Martin Elsaesser: Bauten und Entwürfe aus den Jahren 1924–1932.* Berlin, 1933.

Giedion, Siegfried. *Walter Gropius: Work and Teamwork.* New York, 1954.

Grohmann, Will. *Wassily Kandinsky.* New York, 1961.

Haesler, Otto. *Mein Lebenswerk als Architekt.* (East) Berlin, 1957.

Herbert, Gilbert. *The Synthetic Vision of Walter Gropius.* Johannesburg, South Africa, 1959.

Mendelsohn, Erich. *Erich Mendelsohn: Das Gesamtschaffen des Architekten.* Berlin, 1930.

Rühl, Konrad. "Erinnerungen an Bruno Taut," *Baukunst und Werkform,* XII (1959), 485–494.

Scheffauer, Herman George. "Bruno Taut, a Visionary in Practice," *Architectural Review,* London, LII (1922), 154–159.

Schultze-Naumburg, Paul. *Bauten Schultze-Naumburgs.* Weimar, 1940.

Wolters, Rudolf. *Albert Speer.* Oldenburg, 1943.

Endnotes

Introduction

1. P. O. Rave, *Entartete Kunst* (Hamburg, 1949); H. Lehmann-Haupt, *Art under a Dictatorship* (New York, 1954).

2. Recently Georg Hellack ("Architektur und Bildende Kunst als Mittel nationalsozialistischer Propaganda," *Publizistik*, V (1960), 77 ff.) and Hildegard Brenner (*Die Kunstpolitik des Nationalsozialismus*, Hamburg, 1963) have given considerable attention to the content of Nazi architectural propaganda, but neither explains satisfactorily the relative prominence of architecture in the Nazi artistic program.

3. F. Stern, *The Politics of Cultural Despair. A Study in the Rise of the Germanic Ideology* (Berkeley, 1961).

Chapter I / The Revolution in Style

1. This account follows Nikolaus Pevsner's *Pioneers of Modern Design from William Morris to Walter Gropius* (2nd ed., New York, 1949; 3rd ed. Baltimore, 1964) and Henry-Russell Hitchcock's *Painting toward Architecture* (New York, 1948) in emphasizing the formal, rather than the technological, development of modern architecture in Germany. But it differs from Pevsner and from most other writers in the prominence it gives to historicist architecture before the war and in its stress upon the break in stylistic development which the war produced.

2. These housing projects, constructed by semipublic agencies on suburban sites, are discussed in detail in Chapter IV.

3. The "garden city movement" originated in Ebenezer Howard's plans for the construction of suburban communities, separated from municipal, commercial, and industrial centers by open land. The version at Dresden-Hellerau centered around the famous Dalcroze school of modern dance and included, in addition to the school buildings, the workshops and small factories of the Deutsche Werkstätten (which produced house furnishings of modern design), and housing for the employees of the Werkstätten.

4. One version of the plan, illustrated in Walter Müller-Wulckow, *Bauten der Arbeit und des Verkehrs* (Leipzig, 1929), 116, employed a formal and asymmetric arrangement of the wings closely akin to the plan of the later Bauhaus buildings. But the scheme which was actually followed flanked the workshops with parallel warehouse wings, without integrating them into a unified architectural composition.

5. Hans Eckstein, ed., *50 Jahre Deutscher Werkbund* (Frankfurt am Main, 1958), includes brief sketches of the origins and development of the Werkbund, but there is as yet no comprehensive history of this extraordinarily influential organization. Nor is there, unfortunately, much prospect of one, since the central archives of the Werkbund in Stuttgart were destroyed during the second World War.

6. Including Karl Schmidt, owner of the Deutsche Werkstätten in Hellerau; Bruno Paul, director of the school run by Berlin's Museum of Arts and Crafts (Kunstgewerbemuseum); and Richard Riemerschmid, interior designer and influential educator. Riemerschmid helped to found the Münchner Werkstätten für Handwerkskunst, a group resembling the Deutsche Werkstätten in Hellerau, and became the director of Munich's applied arts school in 1913. For the broader influence of the arts and crafts movement, see Fritz Stern, *The Politics of Cultural Despair* (Berkeley, 1961), 173–174.

7. The activities and publications of the Werkbund before the war are described by Ernst Jäckh, the executive secretary, in "6. Jahresbericht des Deutschen Werkbundes 1913/14," *Der Verkehr: Jahrbuch des Deutschen Werkbundes 1914* (Jena: Diederichs, 1914), 87–102.

Chapter II / The New Architecture and the Vision of a New Society

1. Will Grohmann, *Wassily Kandinsky* (New York, 1961), 163; and Bernard Myers, *The German Expressionists* (New York, 1957), 215–216.

2. Gabo, Pevsner, and Kandinsky left Russia in 1921 because of the growing hostility of the government toward modern art. According to Grohmann, 172, the real attitude of the Bolsheviks began to be understood in Germany only in 1922.

3. Mann in *Professor Unrat*, 1905; Werfel in *Der Weltfreund*, 1911; Sorge in *Der Bettler*, 1912.

4. Wassily Kandinsky, *Über das Geistige in der Kunst, insbesondere in der Malerei* (Munich, 1912), Chapter III. Extracts reprinted in *Der Sturm*, nr. 106, April 1912.

5. Walter H. Sokel, *The Writer in Extremis: Expressionism in Twentieth-Century German Literature* (Stanford, California, 1959), 171–185.

6. Sokel, *ibid.;* Myers, 275–280.

7. Myers, 275–279; Otto Grautoff, *Die neue Kunst* (Berlin, 1921), 141–143; Fritz Hoeber, "Entwurf zu Kursen für Kunstbetrachtung, für Kunstkritik und Kunstpolitik," *Feuer*, Jan. 1920, 248–251. A statement of the aims of "Der Wurf" was published in the *Bielefeld Volkswacht*, Jan. 19, 1920, "Zeitungsarchiv 1," Gropius Archive.

8. On the radical art periodicals see Fritz Herzog, *Die Kunstzeitschriften der Nachkriegszeit* (Berlin-Charlottenburg, 1940), factually reliable but biased in interpretation, and the much more balanced treatment in the dissertation by Lillian Schacherl, "Die Zeitschriften des Expressionismus" (Munich, 1957).

9. Wilhelm Mommsen, *Die Deutschen Parteiprogramme, 1918–1930* (Leipzig, 1931), 45, 58, 66, 88.

10. Kurt Eisner, speech entitled "Der sozialistische Staat und der Künstler," reprinted in *An alle Künstler* (Berlin, Spring 1919), 25–36, a collection of essays by artists and politicians discussing the relationship of the arts — chiefly painting — to the new society and the new state.

11. Konrad Haenisch, "Das Kunstprogramm der Preussischen Regierung," *ibid.*, 37–38. See also the publications on art and art education of the "Reichszentrale für Heimatdienst," a cultural propaganda organ set up by one or more of the left-wing parties, with branches in Berlin and Munich. Grautoff, 132, 135, provides a general discussion of the attitude of the Socialists and the Independent Socialists to modern art.

12. See, for example, Paul Wolf, Stadtbaurat in Hannover, "Die Architektur im neuen Deutschland," *Der Cicerone,* XI (1919), 3–7; Stürzenacker, Ministerialrat in Baden, "Die Revolution des Bauwesens," *Der Bauingenieur*, I (Berlin, 1920), 192–197; and Erwin Gutkind, ed., *Neues Bauen* (Berlin, 1919), a collection of essays on the planning of suburban Siedlungen and the rationalization of building methods. In response to demands of the latter sort, the

federal government set up the "Reichsnormenausschuss" in 1922. It developed later into the "Reichsforschungsgesellschaft" described in Chapter IV, which sponsored housing in the new style.

13. Hans Kampffmeyer, *Friedenstadt. Ein Vorschlag für ein deutsches Kriegsdenkmal*, 2nd ed. (Jena: Diederichs, 1918). The first edition was published in January 1918, and sent to a large number of architects, educators, housing reformers, businessmen, and politicians. Their very laudatory answers form the second part of the second edition.

14. Gropius fought in the war; Taut did not. Biographical material on both men is relatively scarce. For Taut, I have relied upon Hermann George Scheffauer, "Bruno Taut: a Visionary in Practice," *Architectural Review*, LII (London, Dec. 1922), 154–159; and Konrad Rühl, "Erinnerungen an Bruno Taut," *Baukunst und Werkform*, XII (1959), 485–494; together with the verbal reminiscences of his brother, Max Taut, and his former assistant in Magdeburg, Johannes Göderitz. There are a number of books on Gropius, but they concentrate on his works rather than on his life. I have used Siegfried Giedion, *Walter Gropius, Work and Teamwork* (New York, 1954), and the materials in the Gropius Archive.

15. *Modern Architecture* (London, 1929), 92–93.

16. Essay in *Ja! Stimmen des Arbeitsrates für Kunst in Berlin* (Berlin, 1919), 32. Henceforth cited as *Ja! Stimmen.*

17. Introduction to the pamphlet *Ausstellung für [sic] unbekannte Architekten* (Berlin: Arbeitsrat für Kunst, April 1919).

18. *Die Stadtkrone* (Jena: Diederichs, 1919), 51, 60.

19. Bruno Taut, "Nieder der Seriosismus!" *Frühlicht 1920–1922: Eine Folge für die Verwirklichung des neuen Baugedankens* (Berlin: Ullstein, 1963), 11. Recently reprinted in book form as cited above, *Frühlicht* first appeared in 1920 as a section in *Stadtbaukunst alter und neuer Zeit*, a journal edited jointly by Taut, Cornelius Gurlitt, and Bruno Möhring. Taut left the staff of *Stadtbaukunst* when Gurlitt criticized his extremism, and began to publish *Frühlicht* as an independent periodical in Magdeburg, when he took office there. *Frühlicht* ceased publication at the end of 1922.

20. Reyner Banham, in *Theory and Design in the First Machine Age* (New York, 1960), 266, traces this imagery back to Paul Scheerbart's *Glasarchitektur* of 1914, which, he says, through Taut also influenced the design of glass curtain walls in Mies van der Rohe's early projects, and ultimately those constructed by other architects in the later twenties. Taut certainly admired Scheerbart, but since the latter's essay was first made public as a speech at the opening of Taut's Glashaus, it would be hard to say who influenced whom. There may be some connection between Taut's emphasis on glass and the development of glass curtain wall construction, but it is important to remember that Taut was less interested in transparency than in the patterns of light made by colored glass and in the beauty of crystalline shapes. These had a social significance for both Taut and Gropius, for the image of the crystal was used by both men to indicate the way in which architecture mirrors and gives structure to the characteristics of an age. See above, n. 17, and Taut in the same pamphlet: "Es wird einmal eine Weltanschauung da sein, und dann wird auch ihr Zeichen, ihr Kristall — die Architektur da sein."

21. *Alpine Architektur* (Hagen: Folkwang Verlag, 1919), drawing number 16 and text, which explains that materialism and boredom lead to war. The same idea appears in Taut's *Architekturprogramm* (Berlin: Christmas 1918), published in several periodicals and separately by the Arbeitsrat.

22. *Die Auflösung der Städte, oder Die Erde, eine gute Wohnung, oder auch Der Weg zur Alpinen Architektur, oder Weg zur Wahnsinn* (Hagen: Folkwang Verlag, 1920). The title page explains the purpose of the book as follows: "Es ist natürlich nur eine Utopie und kleine Unterhaltung . . . . Aber es dürfte doch gut sein, sich auf alle Möglichkeiten der Wiedergeburt gefasst zu machen, wenn man noch nicht reif zum Eingehen ist."

23. *Auflösung*, 11.

24. The latter part of the book forms a "Literatur-Anhang" containing quotes from critics of cities, ranging from Nietzsche to the Russian law socializing property. They are not arranged in any kind of a coherent argument; on the title page Taut describes them as "proof [Beweise]" of the first section.

25. Hellmut Lehmann-Haupt, in *Art under a Dictatorship* (New York, 1954), took the title of *Auflösung* to mean that Taut had in 1920 repudiated the interest in city planning which *Stadtkrone* displayed in 1919. In view of the fact that the opponents of the new style later charged its authors with an exaggerated enthusiasm for great cities, it is important to note here that Taut was everywhere consistent in rejecting the oversize metropolis, but always valued the middle-size city. In his *Architekturprogramm* he hoped that the "Groszstadt" would disappear; *Stadtkrone* does not contradict this, as the cities it describes are not large by modern standards. *Auflösung* contains plans for middle-size cities as well as small villages.

26. *Stadtkrone*, 58.

27. *Stadtkrone*, 67. For a later architectural formulation of the organic community, see "Natürliches Bauen—Organisches Siedeln," *Frühlicht* (Berlin, 1963), 88–89.

28. "Die sich zur Wundertat der gotischen Kathedrale aufschwang," *Ausstellung für Unbekannte Architekten*.

29. "Baukunst im freien Volksstaat," *Deutscher Revolutions-Almanach* (Hamburg, 1919), 135–136.

30. *Ja! Stimmen*, 32–33.

31. *Ibid.*, 31; and *Programm des Staatlichen Bauhauses in Weimar* (Weimar, April 1919).

32. *Ja! Stimmen*, 30.

33. *Ibid.*, 30, 31.

34. *Ibid.*, 30.

35. Kampffmeyer, *Friedenstadt*, 10.

36. *Stadtkrone*, 81.

37. Schmidt-Rottluff, in *Ja! Stimmen*, 91; Paul Wolf, 7.

38. Fritz Hoeber, "Persönlichkeit und Volkstum in der Baukunst der Gegenwart," *Der Cicerone*, XI (1919), 76–82.

39. Paul Klopfer, "Über Apollinisches und Dionysisches in der Baukunst," *Stadtbaukunst*, I (1920), 161–166, called for a "dionysian" architectural style, which would express the "might of wholeness, the power of the anonymous mass of the folk spirit," and would echo the "heartbeat of the masses" (165–166).

40. Peter Behrens, "Reform der künstlerischen Erziehung," *Der Geist der neuen Volksgemeinschaft; eine Denkschrift für das deutsche Volk* (Berlin: Reichszentrale für Heimatdienst, 1919), 93–107; Fritz Wichert, "Die bildende Kunst und der soziale Staat," *ibid.*, 107–119; Bruno Paul, *Erziehung der Künstler an staatlichen Schulen* (Berlin, 1918); Otto Bartning, *Unterrichts-Plan für Architektur und bildende Künste* (Berlin: Arbeitsrat für Kunst, 1919). Manifestoes of art and architectural students in Berlin and elsewhere are described in "Bestrebungen an deutschen Kunstschulen," an article of 1919 from an unidentified periodical, "Zeitungsarchiv 2," Gropius Archive. See also the "Memorandum zur staatlichen Kunsterziehung," of the "Arbeitsausschuss der bildenden Künstler Münchens," Feb. 1919, quoted by Grautoff, 141–143; and the report in the *Thüringer Landeszeitung "Deutschland,"* Dec. 12, 1920 ("Zeitungsarchiv 5," Gropius Archive), on the program of twenty-five artists' organizations in Berlin, presented to representatives of the federal government. The desire for reform in art education along the lines prescribed by Gropius is nearly unanimous among the opinions of members of the Arbeitsrat für Kunst published in *Ja! Stimmen*. An excellent general survey of the whole movement is Nikolaus Pevsner, "Post-War Tendencies in German Art-Schools," *Journal of the Royal Society of Arts*, LXXXIV (1936), 248–261.

41. Many of the trade unions, and particularly the Catholic ones, had sponsored building "guilds" among the building trades before the war, but the movement which Wagner led was carried on by the Socialist building trades unions, beginning in 1919, and the organizations were thus called "soziale Bauhütten." Wagner devised the organizational plan for these cooperatives and was influential in bringing them together into a national organization; the Verband sozialer Baubetriebe. It was his influence, too, which encouraged the soziale Bauhütten to employ new building methods and materials, a practice encouraged by other radical architects as well, so that the latter often hired the Bauhütten. The history of the movement is a complex one, being, for the most part, the history of individual cooperatives. August Ellinger, a majority Socialist active in the founding of the Verband, interprets the Socialist ideas of the movement in *Zehn Jahre Bauhüttenbewegung* (Berlin, 1930); and Alexander Garbai, in *Die Bauhütten, ihre Vergangenheit und Zukunft* (Hamburg, 1928), surveys the various types of cooperatives and traces them back to the medieval building guilds. The two German dissertations on the subject are very brief: Botho Hohn, "Die Entwicklung der sozialen Baubetriebe (Bauhütten) zu Unternehmungen der freien Gewerkschaften," (Göttingen, 1928), and Ludwig Lichtenberg, "Die neuere Entwicklung der Bauhütten und Bauproduktivgenossenschaften" (Göttingen, 1934). The periodical *Soziale Bauwirtschaft* (Berlin, 1920–1932), published by the Verband, gives statistics on the national movement, and notes on the vicissitudes of individual cooperatives and includes many articles on architectural construction and style.

42. The ideas on which Taut and Gropius based their plea for a revolutionary style had, of course, their prewar sources as well, which cannot be treated in detail here. In their belief that the arts, and architecture in particular, must be suited to their use, they made use of elements of the "functionalist" thought of the last quarter of the nineteenth century. The idealization of the arts and crafts of the middle ages rested upon a much older tradition dating back to Ruskin and Morris in England, while their notion that the medieval ideal of craftsmanship could be imported into the modern system of industrial production had been a part of the program of the founders of the Deutscher Werkbund. The best treatment of the origins of their thought is Pevsner, *Pioneers of Modern Design*. Reyner Banham's *Theory and Design* contains many very interesting observations on the development of architectural theory, although it is confusedly written and frequently inconclusive in its argument.

43. *Arbeitsrat für Kunst*, pamphlet, c. April 1919, File "Presse, 1913–1927," Gropius Archive. The programmatic part of the pamphlet without the membership list was printed in *Deutsche Bauhütte* (Dec. 22, 1919), 47.

44. April pamphlet, *ibid*. According to the same source, the first "Geschäftsausschuss," elected in March 1919, was led by Gropius, Taut, and Cesar Klein. The organization must have begun to take shape late in 1918, however, since its first publication, Taut's *Architekturprogramm*, was dated Christmas 1918. The correspondence contained in the file "Arbeitsrat für Kunst," Gropius Archive, indicates that Gropius at first took a leading part in organizational matters and that after he left Berlin for Weimar much of his work was taken over by Adolf Behne, the influential architectural critic who wrote frequently for left-wing periodicals and newspapers.

45. In addition to the pamphlet by Taut already cited, the group published Adolf Behne's *Ruf zum Bauen* (Berlin, 1920). The exhibitions included: "Ausstellung für unbekannte Architekten," Graphisches Kabinett, Berlin, April 1919; "Ausstellung neues Bauen," held in the same place on May 4, 1919; and an exhibition for workers held in Berlin early in 1920. The first-named attracted particular attention at the time, but little is known about it today. It was apparently an exhibition of drawings of "utopian" projects, but no student of the period has yet found reproductions of the drawings, and, as they were left unsigned in keeping with the Arbeitsrat's fondness for personal anonymity, the reviewers offer no information as to whose work was exhibited.

But from the reviewers' descriptions, it seems safe to assume that some of Taut's drawings from *Alpine Architektur* and probably some of the more fantastic projects of Poelzig, the Luckhardts, and Wenzel Hablik, all of which are illustrated in *Ja! Stimmen*, were shown. For favorable reviews see Kurt Gerstenberg, "Revolution in der Architektur," *Der Cicerone*, XI (1919), 255–257; Theodor Heuss, "Phantasie und Baukunst," *Der Kunstwart und Kulturwart*, XXXII (1919), 17–20, and the *Frankfurter Zeitung* of April 30, 1919. The Arbeitsrat also held public lectures, such as Erich Mendelsohn's "Das Problem einer neuen Baukunst," given in 1919, reprinted in *Erich Mendelsohn: Das Gesamtschaffen des Architekten* (Berlin, 1930), 7–21.

46. April pamphlet.

47. According to Wolf von Eckardt, *Eric Mendelsohn* (New York, 1960), 18, Mendelsohn himself, together with his friend Erwin F. Freundlich, raised the money for the building.

48. The many-angled planes of Behrens' chapel, illustrated in Paul J. Cremens, *Peter Behrens* (Essen, 1928), may reflect Taut's enthusiasm for faceted crystals. The house designs of the Luckhardt brothers in 1921, *Frühlicht* (Berlin, 1963), 123, which are entirely broken up into planes shooting off at different angles, probably derive from the same source; and the interesting and much published project by Otto Bartning, the Sternkirche of 1921, was probably influenced by Taut's "Domstern," *Alpine Architektur*, 26.

49. No satisfactory general history of the Bauhaus exists at the present time. Hans-Maria Wingler's *Das Bauhaus — 1919–1933 — Weimar, Dessau, Berlin* (Bramsche, 1962) reprints many of the documentary materials essential to an understanding of the school's history, and these, together with Wingler's brief comments on them, constitute the best introduction to the development of the Bauhaus. A useful brief survey of the program of the Bauhaus and the major events in its history may be found in Herbert Bayer, Ise Gropius and Walter Gropius, eds., *Bauhaus 1919–1928* (Boston, 1952); a retrospective summary of its founder's ideas is presented in Gropius' *The New Architecture and the Bauhaus* (New York, 1937). The *Bauhausbücher*, edited by Gropius and Moholy-Nagy, describe the various aspects of the school's teaching as well as the work of artists and architects whom the editors admired. A readily available contemporary source for the work of the Bauhaus is *Staatliches Bauhaus in Weimar* (Weimar, 1923), a lavish collection of essays and photographs published on the occasion of the school's first large exhibition.

50. As a stopgap project the Bauhaus leadership asked that the students be allowed to repaint the city hall in brightly colored patterns, but the plan, not surprisingly, foundered on the opposition of Weimar citizens. The school did succeed in decorating one small customs house in a combination of bright blue and red, an event which caused considerable adverse comment in the press at first, but which was eventually approved even by the school's opponents. See Mathilde von Freytag-Loringhoven, "Der Kornblumen Geleithaus," *Thüringer Landeszeitung "Deutschland"*, Feb. 26, 1922. These projects may have derived from Taut's concern for "colorful building"; see below.

51. Banham, *Theory and Design*, 285; Wingler, *Bauhaus*, 15.

52. The principal author of this very popular argument is H. L. C. Jaffé, *De Stijl, 1917–1931; the Dutch Contribution to Modern Art* (Amsterdam, 1956). See also Wingler, 15 and 343.

53. Illustrated in Banham, 233.

54. Illustrated in Hans-Joachim Mrusek, *Magdeburg* (Leipzig, n.d.), 127, which provides, in very brief compass, the only recent treatment of Magdeburg's architectural development in the twenties. Taut himself described the first year of his work in "Mein erstes Jahr 'Stadtbaurat,'" *Frühlicht* (Berlin, 1963), 215–221. See also n. 14 above.

55. Taut had already used bright paint on the exteriors of many of the houses in the Falkenberg Siedlung. In "Beobachtung über Farbenwirkung aus meiner Praxis," *Die Bauwelt*, X (1919), 12–13, Taut urged that bright color

patterns be used on both interiors and exteriors of buildings "in order to make a festival of everyday life." The combination of light and color thus produced was, Taut said, ideally provided by glass, but color must act as a stopgap, since glass was too expensive. The article was printed in connection with Hugo Zehder's "Aufruf zum farbigen Bauen!", *ibid.*, 11, which Taut reprinted in Magdeburg newspapers in July of 1921 and in *Frühlicht* (Berlin, 1963), 97. In his interest in the effects of abstract color patterns on both surface and space, Taut was far ahead of the De Stijl movement.

56. In *Mein Lebenswerk als Architekt* ([East] Berlin, 1957), 5, Haesler says that he got the idea from Taut and that the color design of the Siedlung Italienischer Garten was done by Karl Völker, who had redecorated the Magdeburg Rathaus under Taut's direction.

57. *Die neue Wohnung; Die Frau als Schöpferin* (Leipzig, Jan. 1924). It went through a second edition of 11,000 copies in 1924, and a fifth of 26,000 in 1928. Page references are to the second edition.

58. Speech of May 24, 1922, reported in *Das Volk* (Jena), June 2, 1922.

59. "Die Mitarbeit des Künstlers in Wirtschaft und Technik," given in Chemnitz, Feb. 15, 1923, and reported in the *Allgemeine Zeitung für Chemnitz und das Erzgebirge*, Feb. 22, 1923. The same speech, or a very similar one, was given in Weimar, Berlin, Stuttgart, Magdeburg, and Cologne between February and May of 1923, though on some occasions he called it "Die Einheit von Kunst, Technik und Wirtschaft."

60. "Idee und Aufbau des staatlichen Bauhauses Weimar," in *Staatliches Bauhaus in Weimar*, 15. The essay was also published separately by the Bauhaus Verlag, Munich, and appeared in several newspapers, including the *Frankfurter Zeitung*, April 14, 1923. I have used Gropius' own translation in Bayer, 27.

61. "Mitarbeit," *Allgemeine Zeitung für Chemnitz*.

62. *Das Volk*, June 2, 1922; and "Mitarbeit" as reported in the *Schwäbische Chronik*, April 21, 1923.

63. *Das Volk*, June 2, 1922.

Chapter III / The Controversy over the Bauhaus

1. Which ignored the fact that negotiations with Gropius toward the founding of the Bauhaus had been begun in the prerevolutionary period, by the Grand Duke himself. See Hans-Maria Wingler, *Das Bauhaus — 1919–1933 — Weimar, Dessau, Berlin* (Bramsche, 1962), 27–34.

2. Their refusal is reported in the pamphlet *Streit um das Bauhaus* (Weimar, Spring 1920), published by the Bauhaus. See "Anmerkung 1."

3. According to a letter from Lyonel Feininger to his wife on June 27, 1919, reporting on a speech Gropius gave at the Bauhaus, "Gropius declared he would always intercede for the most extreme in art, as a manifestation of the times we live in." See Wingler, 43.

4. Gropius collected all types of clippings from newspapers and periodicals from December 1919 on. He used the favorable ones in his public defenses of the Bauhaus and he published answers to nearly every charge made by the unfavorable ones. The best sources in his archive for the disputes of 1919–1920 are two pamphets: *Streit um das Bauhaus* (n. 2, above), a rather full description of the events of December, January, and February; and "Ergebnisse der das Staatliche Bauhaus in Weimar betreffenden Untersuchung. Vom Kultusministerium in Weimar überreicht," May 1, 1920, a typewritten report issued by the Ministry of Culture of the government of Saxe-Weimar on its investigations into the complaints of the school's opponents. (Excerpts of the two pamphlets are printed in Wingler, 48–52.) I have supplemented these with the clippings and other materials contained in the files labelled "Zeitungsarchive" in the Gropius Archive, which pertain exclusively

to the Bauhaus and offer a nearly complete record of its history from 1919–1924. Unless otherwise noted, all references in this chapter are to materials in the "Zeitungsarchive."

5. The meeting, held on the twelfth, was intended to include a discussion of candidates in the by-elections and a few other civic questions, but the first item on the agenda was the issue of "modern art in Weimar," and discussion of the Bauhaus dominated the meeting. For the agenda, see the *Thüringer Landeszeitung "Deutschland"* (henceforth cited as *Deutschland*), Dec. 10, 1919, and for a description of the meeting, the *Thüringer Tageszeitung*, Dec. 13. (When no year is given, the year of the preceding citation within the same footnote is understood.)

6. Kreubel was referring to Hanz Prinzhorn's important discussions of the way in which the abstract and subjective character of the paintings of the insane could be used as a key to understanding mental illness. Kreubel's comparison came to be such a favorite with the opponents of modern art that Prinzhorn felt obliged to reply to it in the second edition of his *Bildnerei der Geisteskranken* (Berlin, 1923), 346.

7. See, in addition to the *Thüringer Tageszeitung*, Dec. 13, 1919; Leonhard Schrickel, "Die neue Kunst in Weimar," *Deutschland*, Dec. 14.

8. Quoted in *Deutschland*, Dec. 22, 1919. A slightly different version in "Ergebnisse," Wingler, 50.

9. According to "Ergebnisse" (original, n. 4, above), Gross denied to the investigating commission that he had intended to attack the Bauhaus, and the report concluded that his motives had been merely exhibitionist. But the speech gave rise to a sharp disagreement among the students, when a number of the new arrivals criticized him for his supposed attack. Their criticisms were unofficial, but Gross resigned from the school, claming falsely that he had been censured by the student council and that Gropius had withdrawn his scholarship. Thirteen other former academy students followed him. The treatment of the case in *Streit um das Bauhaus* suggests that although the school's leadership did not officially censure Gross, and whether or not his speech represented a direct attack on the school, appeals to "German art" were not in general well received at the Bauhaus: "Germanness in art cannot be cultivated. There has been no real German art for several hundred years. First let there be a true spiritual community in the nation [ein wahrhaft geistiges Volkstum], and then it will express itself in art" (5).

10. On Freytag-Loringhoven's attitude in the City Council, see "Weimarer Gemeinderat," *Deutschland*, Dec. 19, 1919.

11. Schrickel, "Was geht vor?" *Deutschland*, Dec. 18, 1919.

12. The latter was the pamphlet, *An alle Künstler* (Berlin, Spring 1919), sent free to all art schools by the Berlin government. The essays and speeches it contained were revolutionary in tone, and discussed the role of the arts in the socialist state. See Chapter II, n. 10.

13. Schrickel, "Um was gehts?" *Deutschland*, Jan. 5, 1920; "Der Weimarische Kunststreit," *Leipziger Neueste Nachrichten*, Jan. 14; and "Manifeste," *Deutschland*, Jan. 21. Freytag-Loringhoven, "Was ist neue Kunst?" *Deutschland*, Jan. 1, 1920, and Jan. 28. For *Deutschland*'s editorial comment, see especially the issue of Jan. 11.

14. Statement of Leitung and Meisterrat of the Bauhaus in "Das 'Staatliche Bauhaus' in Weimar und das öffentliche Diskussion," *Deutschland*, Dec. 23, 1919; and *Streit um das Bauhaus*. Schrickel's views were on one occasion buttressed by an anti-Semitic argument. The anonymous pamphlet, *Vom Weimarer Bauhaus* (Weimar, Dec. 31), written as a reply to the Bauhaus statement in *Deutschland*, argued that "Germanness" was not a matter of citizenship but of race, and that the statistics offered by the school's leadership on the national origins of its students were therefore meaningless (3). In general, anti-Semitism played a very minor role in the Weimar controversy, but that it was present at all was prophetic.

15. Two petitions were reported in the press, but the texts were identical. See the *Thüringer Tageszeitung* of Jan. 1, 1920, which quotes a petition of Dec. 19, 1919, and *Deutschland*, Jan. 1, 1920, which quotes a petition of Dec. 30, 1919. "Ergebnisse" reports the latter date (1), *Streit um das Bauhaus*, the former (5). The signers are listed in a typewritten copy from the *Thüringer Tageszeitung* in "Zeitungsarchiv 1."

16. The *Thüringer Tageszeitung*, Jan. 9, 1920, reports the beginning of the investigation; the results are contained in "Ergebnisse."

17. In addition to the articles already cited, see *Volkszeitung* (Jena), Dec. 30, 1919; *Thüringer Tageszeitung*, Jan. 9, 1920; and *Thüringer Allgemeine Zeitung* (Erfurt), Jan. 13, 1920.

18. According to "Die Weimar Kunstkampf," *Vossische Zeitung* (Berlin), Jan. 23, 1920.

19. A full description of the meeting is given in "Eine imposante Kundge- bung für Weimars Kunstschule," *Deutschland*, Jan. 23, 1920. In the pamphlet which summed up the resolutions of the meeting, Herfurth says there were two citizens' committees, one of lay citizens and one of artists. See Emil Her- furth, *Weimar und das Staatliche Bauhaus* (Weimar, Feb. 1920), 4. Hans Kyfer, in "Der Kampf um das 'Staatliche Bauhaus,'" *Vossische Zeitung*, Dec. 27, 1919, claims that opposition to the school among local artists was led by Professor Fleischer, who had resigned his post after discovering that Gropius would not give him tenure. A picture of the sheet which advertised the meet- ing is printed in Herbert Bayer, Ise Gropius, and Walter Gropius, eds., *Bauhaus 1919–1928* (Boston, 1952), 9.

20. The resolutions are quoted in *Deutschland*, Jan. 23; and in Herfurth, 6–15. Excerpts in Wingler, 47.

21. "Offene Erklärung des Künstlerschaft Weimars," *Deutschland*, Jan. 29, 1920. The declaration began with the statement that "our motives are not nationalistic ... or anti-Semitic," and was in part an effort to dignify the po- sition of the academicians in response to the accusations of the school's sup- porters. The Werkbund, for example, had published a statement accusing the opposition of "comfortable philistinism, legalistic pedantry, and political motives" (*Berliner Tageblatt*, Jan. 20). Similar charges were made by the "Offener Brief an die Staatsregierung Sachsen-Weimar-Eisenach" of, among others, Reichskunstwart Redslob and Hans Poelzig (*Deutschland*, Jan. 24); and a number of radical artists' organizations published attacks on "anti- Semitic witch-hunting," and "odious political reaction" in Weimar (see *Deutschland*, Jan. 22; Bielefeld *Volkswacht*, Jan. 19; and the untitled clipping containing the statement of the Darmstädter Künstlerkolonie, dated Jan. 21, in "Zeitungsarchiv 1"). Thus, although in his public statements Gropius took great care to write in a strictly factual and unemotional manner and the other local supporters of the school like Paul Klopfer and Johannes Schlaf followed his example, the friends of the school outside Weimar did much to inflame the debate. Their accusations prompted Schrickel to ask "How much longer are we going to be sneered at?" ("Offener Brief an die alten Weimar- aner," *Deutschland*, July 7), and drew indignant denials from Herfurth and the "Citizens' Committees" (Herfurth, 3–4).

22. Professors Max Thedy and Otto Fröhlich, neither of whom had signed the earlier petition or petitions. Thedy was a well-known teacher of painting, had taught at the academy since 1883, and had been a candidate for the direc- torship of the academy in 1917, when its previous director, Fritz Mackensen, resigned.

23. *Deutschland*, Jan. 29, 1920, reported that Minister President Paulssen had very recently given an informal promise to this effect.

24. Gropius and Herfurth carried on a debate in *Deutschland* during February on the question of whether the Grand Duke had intended in 1917 to establish an institution like the Bauhaus, but the paper's editors maintained a neutral position. Gropius, "Die Antwort des Weimarer Staatlichen Bau-

hauses auf die Angriffe," Jan. 29, 1920; Herfurth, "Audiatur et altera pars," Feb. 8; "Walter Gropius gegen Herfurth," Feb. 15. On the same issue, see C. Rothe (former Marshal at the Ducal Court), "Eine Aufklärung in der Weimarer Bauhausfrage," *Deutschland*, Feb. 21; and the pamphlet by Freytag-Loringhoven, *Das Staatliche Bauhaus und die Kunstschule im Staatshaushaltsplan für 1920* (Weimar, c. March 1920).

25. "Weimarische Landtag," *Deutschland*, June 27, 1920.

26. The debate lasted from June 30 to July 17. Gropius spoke in defense of the school on the ninth. See "Weimarische Landtag," *Volkszeitung*, July 10, 1920; and Wingler, 52–53.

27. Deputies Neumann and Eichel-Streiber, *Volkszeitung*.

28. Deputy Leutert, *Volkszeitung*.

29. Deputy Benewitz, on July 1, "Weimarische Landtag," *Deutschland*, July 1, 1920.

30. Vote on July 17, reported in "Landtag von Sachsen-Weimar," *Thüringer Tageszeitung*, July 21, 1920, which says the academy was now to be known as the "Hochschule für Malerei." The opening of the school as a separate institution is reported in "Kunst und Wissenschaft," *Deutschland*, March 2, 1921. The new director was Rothe, former Marshal at the Ducal Court.

31. Gropius encountered some criticism in 1921 when he designed a monument for the SPD to commemorate those of its members who died in the Kapp putsch. The party's monument Commission chose a site in the main graveyard of Weimar, and a few members of the City Council, led by Freytag-Loringhoven, sought to prevent its construction there on the basis that the abstract forms of the monument would dominate the entire graveyard. This dispute had, however, little relation to the Bauhaus itself, and was in any case rapidly settled in favor of the Commission. See "Weimarer Gemeinderat," *Deutschland*, April 12, 1921, and "Öffentliche Sitzung des Weimarer Gemeinderat vom 8. April 1921," *Das Volk*, April 13, 1921. The SPD held its May day celebration at the monument in 1922.

32. The *Stuttgarter Neues Tageblatt*, for example, praised the "exceptional formal elegance" of the buildings (April 19, 1923), and the *Berliner Börsenzeitung* saw in them "the right way to an architecture which is truly appropriate to our time" (Aug. 24, 1923). Even the arch-conservative *Neue Preussische Kreuz-Zeitung* waxed enthusiastic over the "new spirit of progress which is being combined with the great past traditions of Weimar" (Berlin, Aug. 31, 1923). Similar reports fill two entire folders of "Zeitungsarchive" in the Gropius Archive.

33. Klopfer, "Bauhaus Ausstellung," *Deutschland*, May 3, 1922, and July 5; Adler, "Architektur-Ausstellung im Staatlichen Bauhaus," *Das Volk* (Jena), July 12, 1923, and "Bauhaus-Ausstellung," October 2.

34. Freytag-Loringhoven, "Die neuesten Weimarer Kunstausstellungen und meine Ansicht," *Deutschland*, May 12, 1922, and "Die Ausstellung des Staatlichen Bauhauses in Weimar," *Deutschland*, Aug. 30, 1923.

35. "Viel Lärm um Nichts," *Jenaische Zeitung*, Aug. 16, 1923. This accusation referred to the display of "international architecture" included in the exhibition and to the fact that local firms carried out the actual construction of the model house.

36. "Viel Lärm um Nichts." With heavy humor, the anonymous author described it as follows: "It has a desperate resemblance to those little houses in the public squares of large cities, with a sign which says 'ladies' on one side and 'gents' on the other." See also Egbert Delpy, "Die Weimarer Bauhaus-Ausstellung," *Leipziger Neueste Nachrichten*, Aug. 22, 1923.

37. Arthur Buschmann, "Die Bauhaus-Siedlung von Gropius," *Jenaische Zeitung*, July 27, 1922. Buschmann may have derived the general idea of his racial interpretation of housing from Spengler's second volume which had just been published (Oswald Spengler, *Die Untergang des Abendlandes: Welthistorische Perspektiven*, Munich, 1922; especially 422–424), although his

belief in the cultural vitality of neoclassicism diverged, of course, from Spengler's views.

38. Franz Kaibel, "Bauhausarbeit," *Deutschland*, Aug. 24, 1923.

39. On the sensationalist treatment given to Spengler's works in the popular press at this time, see H. Stuart Hughes, *Oswald Spengler: A Critical Estimate* (New York, 1952). That it was very fashionable to be familiar with Spengler's ideas is shown by the fact that Kaibel "quotes" him, but refers to him as "Oskar Spengler," and had therefore probably not read the book himself.

40. Sitting of March 16, as reported in "Thüringer Landtag," *Deutschland*, March 16, 1923, and March 17.

41. "Thüringer Landtag." Herfurth had made a similar attack on the school on June 30, 1922, but his remarks gave rise to no general debate at that time. See "Die heutige Landtags-Sitzung," *Das Volk*, June 30, 1922.

42. "Das staatliche Bauhaus vor dem Landtag," *Das Volk*, March 20, 1923.

43. Deputy Brill, "Das staatliche Bauhaus vor dem Landtag."

44. Information about internal Thuringian history is scarce. In addition to the standard reference works such as the *Politischer Almanach*, I have used the newspaper reports in the Gropius Archive, which are necessarily selective on purely political matters; H. J. Gordon, *The Reichswehr and the German Republic: 1919–1926* (Princeton, 1957), which employs material from General Hasse's diary; and the documents relating to Nazi and "völkische" groups in the Fritz Sauckel file, microfilms of German war documents prepared by the American Historical Association Committee for the study of war documents, series T–81, frames 136429–137002. F. Sauckel, *Kampf und Sieg in Thüringen* (Weimar, 1934) provides a useful chronology; Georg Witzmann's memoirs, *Thüringen von 1918–1933; Erinnerungen eines Politikers* (Meisenheim am Glan, 1958) are very brief for this period.

45. The results of the elections were as follows: KPD, 13; SPD, 17; Democrats, 4; Ordnungsbund, 35; Nationalsozialistische Freiheitspartei (NSFP), a proto-Nazi group led by Willi Marschler, which joined the NSDAP later in the twenties, 6; "NSDAP," 1 (Artur Dinter). See *Politischer Almanach* (Berlin, 1925). According to a "Declaration" of the NSFP on Dec. 12, 1924 (microfilms of Fritz Sauckel file, frame 136479), Dinter was not yet a member of Hitler's party although he gave himself the title of Deputy for the NSDAP. The eight Landbund members of the Ordnungsbund tended to vote with the NSFP and with Dinter. On Dinter's later career, see George L. Mosse, *The Crisis of German Ideology* (New York, 1964), 306, n. 36.

46. "Thüringer Personalwirtschaft," *Weimarische Zeitung*, Dec. 21, 1923. See also "Allerlei politische Nachdenklichkeiten," Jan. 1, 1924.

47. Julius Elbau, "Die Weimarer Tagung," *Vossische Zeitung*, April 7, 1924, describes the investigation, but does not identify the authors of the charges. *Das Volk* later claimed that Herfurth was behind the attack ("Das Ende des Bauhauses in Weimar, IV," Dec. 13), but Herfurth was always careful to avoid making explicit charges of political activity against the school. It appears more likely that the complaints came from miscellaneous private citizens, responding to the type of hearsay evidence which gave rise to similar attacks in 1919 and 1920 (see "Ergebnisse").

48. Walter Gropius, "Beschwerdebrief vom 24. November 1923 an Generalleutnant Hasse, Militärbefehlshaber in Thüringen," Gropius Archive, excerpts in Wingler, 89.

49. Letter from Arno Müller, printed in *Deutschland*, Sept. 3, 1923. Gropius answered in *Deutschland*, Oct. 6. The bulk of Müller's campaign against the school took place in the following spring, and at that time a statement published by the Bauhaus accused him of acting from purely "political" motives. Müller was, according to various newspaper reports, "Obermeister der Schlosserinnung, Weimar," "Vorsitzender des Gewerbevereins Weimar," "1. Vorsitzender des Thüringer Handwerkerbundes," "Vorstandsmitglied des Haus-

besitzervereins zu Weimar," and "Führer der Handwerkerbewegung." Despite the impressive titles, he apparently did not hold a position in the only state organization empowered to license craftsmen, the Handwerkskammer.

50. *Deutschland*, Feb. 6, 1924.

51. In February and March, rumors of the dissolution of the school or the discharge of its staff were reported by both left-wing and right-wing papers. See Leonhard Schrickel, "Bauhaus Abbau?" *Weimarische Zeitung*, Feb. 19, 1924, and "Weitere Opfer der Ordnungswut in Thüringen," *Das Volk*, March 22. These reports were proved to be merely rumors in "Falschmeldungen zum Beamtenabbau," *Deutschland*, March 27.

52. Richard Leutheusser was a judge in the Thuringian Oberverwaltungsgericht and head of the Thuringian branch of the DVP.

53. The "Kulturrat" included professors Richard Engelmann and Walter Klemm, who had resigned from the Bauhaus in November of 1920 because of "growing radicalism" there and who subsequently taught at the academy, and Professor Fleischer, a leading opponent of the Bauhaus in 1919 and 1920. On the formation of the organization see "Ein Weimar Kulturrat," *Deutsche Allgemeine Zeitung* (Berlin), March 31, 1924; on membership, "Eine Mahnung des Weimarer Kulturrates," *Berliner Tageblatt*, April 23. Schrickel accused the Bauhaus again of "perpetrating injustices upon our indigenous artists," in the *Weimarische Zeitung* in February (Feb. 19), but after that date took up the arguments of the extremists outlined below. The sole mention of the academy in the newspaper debate of 1924 after Schrickel's article was a statement of the so-called "Kammer der bildenden Künstler in Thüringen, Sitz Weimar" ("Eine Erklärung . . . ," *Eisenacher Tagespost*, May 21), which complained that "Gropius denies all value to the tradition of the Weimar art academy." The academy still functioned separately, but it had lost much of its student body since 1921.

54. *Das staatliche Bauhaus Weimar und sein Leiter* (Weimar: Arno Müller, n.d.). The principal author was Hans Beyer, who had obtained the post of business manager of the Bauhaus on false credentials and was fired without severance pay in 1922 after a state investigation. Beyer had then filed suit against Gropius, and the case was being tried in the Thuringian courts at the time of the publication of the Brochure. That Beyer was the author was made known to the public by newspaper statements issued by Gropius and the staff during the ensuing month. Hans-Maria Wingler suggests that Louis Häusser, a wandering preacher of a kind of Nietzschean religion, also had a hand in preparing the Brochure. Other contributors were Joseph Zachmann and Karl Schlemmer, former teachers in the crafts workshops of the school.

55. See, for example, Schrickel, "Kunst und Wissenschaft," *Mitteldeutsche Zeitung* (Erfurt), April 2, 1924, and the same column on May 2. The latter article was reprinted in the *Eisenacher Zeitung*, May 2, and *Rheinisch-Westfälische Zeitung* (Essen), May 7.

56. "Um das Bauhaus in Weimar," *Weimarische Zeitung*, June 13, 1924. See also, "Sonntagsbrief," June 24, 1924; and "Bauhaus und Kunstschule," Nov. 9.

57. Nonn's original article, "Das Staatliche Bauhaus in Weimar," *Zentralblatt der Bauverwaltung*, Feb. 6, 1924, 42–44, was republished in *Deutschland* as "Nachklänge zur Bauhaus-Ausstellung," April 2. Klopfer answered in a letter to *Deutschland* on April 9; Nonn replied in the article "Um das Weimarer Staatliche Bauhaus," April 14. Among Nonn's subsequent articles were "Das staatliche Bauhaus in Weimar," *Kölnische Zeitung*, April 23; "Zur Propaganda für das Bauhaus in Weimar," *Deutsche Bauhütte*, April 21, 114; "Staatliche Müllzufuhr: Das staatliche Bauhaus in Weimar," *Deutsche Zeitung* (Berlin), April 24, 1924 (excerpts in Wingler, 90–91); and "Das staatliche Bauhaus in Weimar," *Die Hilfe*, June 1, 182–183. The answers of the Bauhaus and its supporters included: Adolf Behne, "Nonn-sens, eine Erwiderung . . . ," *Kölnische Zeitung*, June 13; and the letter of Klee, Feininger,

Hartwig and Muche, in "Noch einmal das Staatliche Bauhaus," *Die Hilfe*, August 1. Brief answers by Nonn followed each of the latter articles.

58. *Kölnische Zeitung*, April 23, 1924. Nonn was here confusing the program of 1919 with a prospectus for the 1923 exhibition written by Schlemmer and retrieved from circulation by Gropius, who feared the effect of the reference to "socialism" on public opinion, after only a few copies had been distributed. See Oskar Schlemmer, *Die erste Bauhaus-Ausstellung in Weimar* (Weimar, c. Feb. 1923). The correct text read: "Das Staatliches Bauhaus, gegründet nach der Katastrophe des Kriegs, im Chaos der Revolution und zur Zeit der Hochblüte einer gefühlgeladenen explosiven Kunst, wird zunächst zum Sammelpunkt derer, die zukunftsgläubig-himmelstürmend die Kathedrale des Sozialismus bauen wollen" (excerpts in Wingler, 79–80).

59. *Deutschland*, April 4, 1924; *Jenaische Zeitung*, May 26; *Weimarische Zeitung*, July 23.

60. Dr. med. Kahle ("auf Veranlassung der Vereinigung zur Pflege deutschen Kultur in Thüringen"), "Das staatliche Bauhaus in Weimar als Kulturinstitut," *Weimarische Zeitung*, May 28, 1924. See also Professor Sigismund, "Thüringische Kulturpflege," *Neue Tägliche Rundschau* (Berlin), Feb. 27, 1925.

61. "Kundgebung gegen das Bauhaus," *Weimarische Zeitung*, July 6, 1924.

62. Deputy Wünsche, NSFP, introduced the interpellation and the resolution on the fifteenth according to "Thüringer Landtag," *Deutschland*, April 16, 1924. See also "Staatliches Bauhaus und Rechtspolitik," *Vossische Zeitung*, April 17; and Walter Gropius, "Staatliches Bauhaus und Thüringer Landtag," *Deutschland*, April 24, which gives the date of the first interpellation as April 12. Wünsche probably spoke for Deputy Dinter as well as for his own party.

63. According to "Der Kampf um das staatliche Bauhaus – Gegen den Ordnungsbarbaren Herfurth," *Das Volk*, April 22, 1924.

64. Leutheusser's answer to the interpellation is quoted in "Staatliches Material über das Staatliche Bauhaus," *Deutschland*, June 5, 1924. For the DVP's attitude to the Yellow Brochure, see "Das Ende des Bauhauses in Weimar, III," *Das Volk*, Dec. 12.

65. "Thüringer Landtag," *Weimarische Zeitung*, June 21 and 24, 1924, on sittings of June 19 and 20. On Dinter, see n. 45, above.

66. "Thüringer Regierung und Verwaltung," *Deutschland*, Sept. 24, 1924.

67. It also paid a visit to the school. See "Politisches aus Thüringen," *Weimarische Zeitung*, Oct. 26, 1924.

68. The best description of the whole debate is the long article "Das Ende des Bauhauses in Weimar," *Das Volk*, published in four sections on Dec. 10, 11, 12, and 13, 1924. See also "Das Schicksal des Staatlichen Bauhauses," *Thüringer Allgemeine Zeitung*, Nov. 16; "Politisches aus Thüringen," *Deutschland,* Nov. 8; "Haushaltsausschuss des Landtags," *Weimarische Zeitung*, Nov. 18 and 19; and Wingler 103–105.

69. From 120,000M to 50,000M (*Das Volk*, Dec. 13, 1924).

70. But, in a statement of Jan. 18, 1925 ("Walter Gropius gegen Leutheusser," *Das Volk*), Gropius accused Leutheusser of requesting the resignation of Kandinsky solely because the latter was Russian.

71. In December Gropius and his staff formally announced the dissolution of the Weimar Bauhaus and accused the government of seeking the destruction of the school out of political motives ("Erklärung der Auflösung des Instituts," open letter to several newspapers, Dec. 26, 1924, Wingler, 106. See also "Das Ende des Weimarer Bauhauses," *Das Volk*, Dec. 27, 1924). The government denied the accusation in a public announcement on the thirty-first, claming that it did not intend to close the school and aimed only at "economies" ("Der Streit um das Weimarer Bauhaus: Eine Erklärung der Thüringer Regierung," *Leipziger Tageblatt*, Dec. 31, 1924). On the Bauhaus in Dessau, see Chapter IV.

72. See Chapter II. Most of Bartning's commissions had come from the Protestant Church, a particularly good recommendation in Thuringia. On his appointment see "Das Weimarer Bauhaus und Weimar," *Dresdner Anzeiger*, April 23, 1925, and the *Deutsche Allgemeine Zeitung*, May 17, 1925.

73. *Vorwärts*, April 12, 1924.

74. *Berliner Lokal-Anzeiger*, June 24, 1924. Complete text contained in typewritten copy entitled "Abschrift, BDA, Schreibe an den Landtag und Regierung der Thüringer Freistaaten Weimar," May 25, 1924, "Zeitungsarchiv 4."

75. "Kundgebungen für das Bauhaus," *Deutschland*, Oct. 19, 1924, lists thirty-five petitions and statements. Their signers also included Reichskunstwart Redslob; leading citizens of Hannover, Erfurt, and Jena; Eugen Diederichs, the important neoconservative publisher; and the following organizations: "Schutzverband Deutscher Schriftsteller, Verband Deutscher Kunstkritiker, Bundesvorstand des Allgemeinen Gewerkschaftsbundes, Afa-Bund, Deutscher Baugewerkenbund, Verband sozialer Baubetriebe." The last four were trade union organizations.

76. Werner Scholz, "Zur politischen Polemik um das Weimarer Bauhaus," *Königsberger Hartungsche Zeitung*, Oct. 18, 1924. The same point of view is illustrated in the following partial list of articles from leading moderate and liberal newspapers: Walter Curt Behrendt, "Das Schicksal des Bauhauses," *Deutsche Allgemeine Zeitung*, April 5; Alexander Dorner, "Das Weimarer Bauhaus," *Hannoverscher Courier*, April 14; Fritz Wichert, "Das Staatliche Bauhaus in Weimar," *Frankfurter Zeitung*, April 23; E. Preetorius, "Das Bauhaus in Weimar," *Münchner Allgemeine Zeitung*, May 11; Werner Krug, "Heute in Weimar," *Hamburger Anzeiger*, May 14; "Um das stattliche Bauhaus in Weimar. Eine Frage der Kunst oder der Politik?" *Berliner Tageblatt*, May 20; Max Osborn, "Der Kampf um das Bauhaus," *Vossische Zeitung*, May 26; "Walter Gropius und das Bauhaus," *Germania* (Berlin: Center Party), Oct. 14.

77. Unidentified clipping of June 1924, "Zeitungsarchiv 4."

78. "Die Reaktion in Thüringen," *Vorwärts*, April 9, 1924.

79. "Abbau des Weimarer Bauhauses," *Die Rote Fahne*, April 5, 1924.

80. "Abbau der Novembergrossen," *Berliner Lokal-Anzeiger*, March 22, 1924.

Chapter IV / The New Architecture in the Service of Society

1. For descriptions of the housing shortage and its causes see Hermann Mattutat, "Die Krisis im Wohnungsbau," *Sozialistische Monatshefte*, XXX (1924), 441–445; Peter Tremmel, "Die Wohnungsfrage," in Georg Schrieber, ed., *Politisches Jahrbuch 1927/28* (Gladbach, 1928), 491–494; and Albert Gut, *Der Wohnungsbau in Deutschland nach dem Weltkriege* (Munich, 1928). Statistics given here and in the following pages represent sums or averages of figures taken from successive years of the *Statistisches Jahrbuch deutscher Städte* (Leipzig, 1890–).

2. The best descriptions of federal housing policy are given by Rolf Spörhase, *Wohnungsunternehmen im Wandel der Zeit* (Hamburg, 1947) and W. Luetge, *Wohnungswirtschaft* (Munich, 1948).

3. These gave priority to small, single-family dwellings in a suburban setting.

4. The government devised a series of interim measures including a system of direct subventions to make up the difference between prewar and postwar prices in building materials to aid building societies and municipalities in new construction, but with little effect.

5. The tax was known as the Hauszinssteuer. Its framers made provision for a progressive decrease in the tax rate and the eventual abolition of the

tax itself in the expectation that the entrance of private capital into building construction would soon make federal housing loans superfluous. As it worked out, the tax was reduced but not abolished: private capital was not induced to enter into the construction of small dwellings on a large scale, and the tax itself provided too valuable a source of revenue (a portion of the revenue was always used for purposes other than housing). The tax fell on landlords; and since rent controls were maintained, they were not able to compensate for the loss by a rent increase. The SPD, which was among the sponsors of the tax, justified its punitive effects by the claim that the landlord class had profited from the housing shortage. The DNVP was to describe the effect of the Hauszinssteuer as "expropriation without legal recourse" (Walther Rademacher, "Die 'kalte Sozialisierung,'" Flugschriften der DNVP [Berlin, 1828], nr. 251, 8).

6. On the building society movement in general see 30. Jahre Wohnungs-reform 1898–1928 (Berlin, 1928).

7. The DNVP opposed, not public participation in housing construction, but the extent it reached during Weimar, and the emphasis on urban housing rather than rural resettlement. See Flugschriften der Deutschnationalen Volks-partei (Berlin), nrs. 177 (1924), 194 (1924), 266 (1926), 273 (1926), 279 (1927), which reprint the Reichstag speeches of party members on the housing issue; and the speeches in Deutschnationale Mittelstandstagung in Berlin (Berlin, 1928) and Reichsausschuss für den Mittelstand der DNVP.

8. Most municipalities also built housing directly, with their own funds and occasionally with Hauszinssteuer loans.

9. On Haesler's work see Otto Haesler, Mein Lebenswerk als Architekt ([East] Berlin, 1957).

10. This plan had already been used in urban housing in 1919 by Theodor Fischer in his "Siedlung Alte Heide" in Munich, conservative in style but very progressive in all aspects of planning. The finger plan, by giving the buildings more land or by seeming to do so, introduced a suburban feeling into urban housing and in this respect carried out the aims of the prewar garden city movement.

11. 40. Jahre Aktienbaugesellschaft für kleine Wohnungen (Frankfurt am Main, 1930), 5–20, and Emil Klar, "Die Entwicklung der Wohnungswesens von 1870–1914," in Das Wohnungswesen der Stadt Frankfurt am Main (Frank-furt am Main, 1930), 55–92.

12. Wolfgang Bangert, Baupolitik und Stadtgestaltung in Frankfurt am Main (Würzburg, 1937), 57–75.

13. Hans Drüner, Im Schatten des Weltkrieges. Zehn Jahre Frankfurter Geschichte vom 1914–1924 (Frankfurt am Main, 1934), 303.

14. Ludwig Landmann, "Zum Geleit," Das neue Frankfurt. Monatsschrift für die Probleme moderner Gestaltung, I (1926), 1–2.

15. Bangert, 87–90.

16. The Aktienbaugesellschalt für kleine Wohnungen, of which Landmann was chairman from 1923–1927. May became assistant chairman in 1925 and succeeded Landmann in 1927.

17. "Der neue Frankfurter Städtebauer," Frankfurter Zeitung, June 6, 1925, in May's private archive, which contains letters and newspaper clippings re-lated to all aspects of his work in Frankfurt.

18. These models employed a typography derived from the publications of the Bauhaus.

19. "Der neue Frankfurter Städtebauer."

20. May's earlier work, consisting of bare-surfaced, semidetached housing with sloped roofs, is illustrated in the Werkbund's periodical Die Form, I (1926), 160.

21. Ernst May, "Das neue Frankfurt," Das neue Frankfurt, I (1926), 4.

22. Ibid.

23. Illustrated in Gut, Wohnungsbau, 69.

24. Because of the great demand for small dwellings, the apartments contained few rooms, but in addition, the floor area per resident was unusually small.

25. See Chapter V.

26. The entire housing program is described in *Das Wohnungswesen der Stadt Frankfurt am Main* (Frankfurt am Main, 1930).

27. For enthusiastic accounts of May's work see "Das neue Frankfurter Bauwesen," *Frankfurter General-Anzeiger*, Oct. 28, 1926; "Die künstlerische Formgebung des Hochbauamtes," *Frankfurter General-Anzeiger*, March 5, 1927; *Volkstimme*, August 26, 1927; "Das weisse Haus," *Frankfurter Nachrichten*, Oct. 27, 1928; May Archive. Cartoons on the new housing and humorous "reports" that the residents had to keep their furniture on the roof, hold their Christmas dinner in the garden, and play the piano out the window, appeared often in the *Nachrichten,* the *Frankfurter Rundschau* and the *General-Anzeiger*. But only the *Frankfurter Fackel* and the *Frankfurter Post* consistently, through infreqently, opposed May's work; see for example, "Was sagen die Mieter der 'May-Wohnungen,'" *Post*, July 22, 1928, and "Offene Anfrage betr. Stadtrat May," *Fackel*, n.d.

28. "Unter dem flachen Dach, Was die Mieter sagen," unidentified clipping of mid–1928, May Archive; "Die Römerstadt im Fackelglanz," *Volksstimme*, Aug. 19, 1929; "Objektivität, keine Interessenpolitik!" unidentified clipping of late 1929.

29. The *Sachsenhäuser Anzeiger*, with a large circulation among conservative members of the building trades, criticized May's construction methods constantly; but the magazine *Stein-Holz-Eisen*, published in Frankfurt, was more favorable to the new architecture than any other trades journal in Germany.

30. Two unidentified clippings in May's Archive from later 1929, "Diktatur auf dem Friedhof," and "Das Recht auf die Grabstätte," summarize local opinion on the latter question. The new, streamlined Frankfurt eagle was much criticized in the City Assembly (see "Die Vermayerung Frankfurts," *Frankfurter Post*, Nov. 8, 1927), which, however, eventually adopted it.

31. Campaign pamphlets of the DVP, DNVP, and NSDAP for the city elections of 1929, May Archive. In an SPD leaflet of the same date, also among May's papers, the party claimed credit for May's housing. The Nazi pamphlet saw May as part of the "Jewish domination" of Frankfurt but made no comment on his work. According to "Die Läuternde Flamme," unidentified clipping of November 8, 1929, a Nazi member of the City Assembly threatened to burn down May's "ape cages" when Hitler came to power; the clipping pointed out that he would thus be burning down the dwellings of several of his Nazi colleagues.

32. This figure represents, of course, a much smaller proportion of total new housing than in Frankfurt. Some 150,000 new buildings were built in Berlin between 1926 and 1932, of which about ninety per cent were constructed with the help of public funds.

33. The best illustrations of modern buildings in Berlin are published in E.M. Hajos and L. Jahn, *Berliner Architektur der Nachkriegszeit* (Berlin, 1928); and Heinz Johannes, *Neues Bauen in Berlin* (Berlin, 1930).

34. On the Berlin building societies in general, see *Geschichte der gemeinnützigen Wohnungswirtschaft in Berlin* (Berlin, 1957).

35. Wagner's earliest writings included works on city planning and economical building construction: *Städtische Freiflächenpolitik* (Berlin, 1915), and *Neue Bauwirtschaft* (Berlin, 1918). In 1924 he founded the magazine *Wohnungswirtschaft*, which was devoted largely to the problems of housing construction, although in the later twenties it included articles on aesthetic theory. Wagner was probably more interested in the practical side of building construction than any other leading radical architect; in fact, in *Wohnungs-*

wirtschaft, Dec. 1, 1924, 170–171, Taut accused him of being "just an engineer."

36. The fourth story which was usually provided was empty and was used for storage or for drying clothes.

37. Much of the landscaping was done by Leberecht Migge, a noted landscape architect and prominent advocate of the garden city.

38. The majority of dwellings in both the Gehag and the Frankfurt projects contained two to two and a half rooms, but the Gehag's were a few square feet larger.

39. Four standard plans were followed at Britz, three at Zehlendorf.

40. Otto Rudolf Salvisberg and Bruno Ahrends.

41. Johannes, *Neues Bauen,* 31, 61, 70, 75, 89.

42. On one of his suburban plans see Walter Koeppner, "Generalbebauungsplan Gatow-Cladow," *Das neue Berlin,* I (1929), 114–116.

43. *Das neue Berlin* (Berlin, 1929), contained articles on photography, literature, painting, and the theater as well as architecture.

44. For enthusiastic press reactions to Wagner's work see the reports on the housing exhibitions he arranged and participated in in 1931 and 1932 in *Vorwärts,* June 7, 1931; *Vossische Zeitung,* May 14, 1932; and *Acht Uhr Abendblatt,* August 6, 1932. Reporting on Wagner's proposed exhibit of prefabricated housing, *Der Tag,* Dec. 9, 1931, warned that "the red Stadtbaurat" was attempting to crush independent craftsmen; but on May 14, 1932, the same paper gave the exhibition warm praise. It is impossible to obtain enough complete runs of Berlin newspapers to do a valid survey of press opinion on Wagner's work; and since Wagner's own collection of press clippings was discarded after his death, I have relied on the rather scant selection of clippings on this subject in the Gropius Archive, together with the verbal information of Mrs. Gertrud Wagner and Senatsrat Felix Unglaube, a former assistant of Wagner's.

45. Martin Wagner, "Verkehr und Tradition," *Das neue Berlin,* I (1929), 129–135, which contains a very interesting sampling of quotes from government officials and art critics.

46. *Gehag, 1924–1957* and Unglaube.

47. See Chapter V.

48. Opposition to the school in Dessau was brief and ineffectual before 1932. In 1925 the right-wing parties (DNVP and DVP) in the City Council voted against the adoption of the school on financial grounds but were decisively overruled by the Democratic party and the SPD ("Das Bauhaus kommt nach Dessau," *Anhaltische Rundschau,* March 24, 1925, Gropius Archive). In the same year Georg Büchlein, a local tradesman, organized a "citizens' committee" against the school and revived the charges made by the Yellow Brochure in a public meeting, but this sort of criticism was cut short at the start by the successful libel suit lodged against Büchlein by Mayor Hesse ("Die ewigen Angriffe auf Professor Gropius," *Magdeburgische Zeitung,* July 1, 1925). Right-wing political opposition to the school revived in 1929 and 1930, during the directorship of Hannes Meyer, when the activities of a group of vocal Communist sympathizers among the students again helped to identify the school and its work with radical politics. But this opposition died down again as soon as Hesse replaced Meyer with Mies van der Rohe and forced the expulsion of the group of students. It was not until January 1932, when the Nazis gained a plurality in the City Council, that the Bauhus experienced significant political opposition (see Chapter VII). The press of Dessau and Anhalt was, on the whole, favorably disposed toward Gropius' buildings.

49. The loose leaf binder labeled "Presse 1930 I" in the Gropius Archive is largely devoted to newspaper and magazine clippings on Törten.

50. Mies's introductory speech, quoted in the *Staats-Anzeiger für Württemberg,* July 23, 1927.

51. The exhibition included, among other displays, pictures of the Frankfurter Küche and May's building methods. (*Staats-Anzeiger für Württemberg,* August 4, 1927). A model kitchen was also erected in which cooking classes were held (*Staats-Anzeiger für Württemberg,* August 3).

52. *Staats-Anzeiger für Württemberg,* Oct. 11 and July 23.

53. A collection of quotes from press notices on the Weissenhof Siedlung is included in "Bericht über die Siedlung am Weissenhof," *Sonderhefte der Reichsforschungsgesellschaft* (Berlin, 1929), nr. 6.

54. On the origins, purposes, administration, and budget of the RFG, see E. Weber, "Die Reichsforschungsgesellschaft für Wirtschaftlichkeit im Bau- und Wohnungswesen e. V. Ihr Werden und Wollen," *Schlesisches Heim,* VIII (1927), 425–434.

55. "Bericht über die Versuchssiedlung in Frankfurt am Main-Praunheim"; "Bericht über die Siedlung in Stuttgart am Weissenhof"; "Bericht über die Versuchssiedlung in Dessau"; *Sonderhefte der Reichsforschungsgesellschaft* ... (Berlin, 1929), nrs. 4, 6 and 7. See also "Berichte und Vorträge," *RFG Technische Tagung in Berlin* (Berlin, 1929).

56. See the illustrations in Gut, *Wohnungsbau,* 393–395, 402–403, 406–407; and in Bruno Taut, *Modern Architecture* (London, 1929), 121–122.

57. In Breslau, Siedlung Zimpel, 1929, and another set of exhibition houses constructed by the Werkbund in 1929, designed in part by Scharoun and Rading. In Hamburg, Karl Schneider's buildings (Taut, 102), and Erich Schmurje's work in 1931. In Düsseldorf, Konrad Rühl's housing (Taut, 120). The influential Siedlung Dammerstock was constructed in Karlsruhe in 1927–1928, designed by Haesler, Riphahn, Roeckle, and Gropius. Stuttgart constructed the large Siedlung Wallmer in 1930, Leipzig the Wohnstadt Neu-Gohlis at the same time. Even in Munich, where nearly all public housing continued to be designed in conservative styles, Baurat E. Herbert built a few projects in the new style from 1930 on. The housing of Dresden, Hannover, and Nürnberg remained conservative in appearance.

58. Bruno Taut, "Mein erstes Jahr 'Stadtbaurat,'" *Frühlicht* (Berlin, 1963), 215–222; letter of Feb. 2, 1960 from Konrad Rühl, who held a subsidiary post in Magdeburg's building administration from 1922 to 1927; letter of Jan. 7, 1960 from Johannes Göderitz and verbal information from Mr. Göderitz.

59. Letter of Jan. 15, 1960 from Otto Haesler; letter of Feb. 9, 1960 from Rühl, who from 1928 to 1933 directed a branch of the state building administration in Düsseldorf; letter of Jan. 28, 1960 from Hans Mehrtens, Stadtbaurat in Cologne from 1925 to 1935. There were, of course, isolated instances of opposition to the new style on aesthetic grounds, particularly from the various "Heimatschutz" organizations, which had their origins in a prewar movement to protect the landscape and historic shrines from shoddy industrial building. When, for example, Haesler attempted to erect a modern youth hostel in the countryside near Celle, the local Heimatschutz organization opposed him vigorously, claiming that the flat roof was not suited to a rural landscape (Wilhelm Lotz, "Neue Form und Heimatschutz," *Die Form,* VI [1930] 46–47). A protest against the "dwelling machines" of the Weissenhof Siedlung was published by Württemberg's Bund für Heimatschutz, one of the most influential in the country ("Schwäbischer Heimatschutz," *Deutsche Bauhütte,* Nov. 15, 1927, 316). In those cities where the new style never became popular in housing, local officials often rejected the flat roof for aesthetic reasons. See, for example, Walter Riezler, "Der Kampf gegen das flache Dach," *Die Form,* III (1927), 26–27, on the Munich building code department's ruling against a flat-roofed house in 1927; and "Wieder einmal das flache Dach," *Die Form,* V (1929), 272, on a similar ruling in Nürnberg in 1929.

Chapter V / The Debate over the New Architecture

1. Walter Gropius, *Internationale Architektur* (Munich, 1925), and *Bau-*

hausbauten Dessau (Munich, 1930); ed., with Laszlo Moholy-Nagy, *Bauhaus Bücher* (Dessau, 1926–1931). Bruno Taut, *Bauen: Der neue Wohnbau* (Leipzig, 1927), and *Neues Bauen in Europa und Amerika* (Leipzig, 1929). Taut also wrote an English version: *Modern Architecture* (London, 1929).

2. Martin Wagner, ed., *Wohnungswirtschaft* (Berlin, 1924–1933); and *Das neue Berlin* (Berlin, 1929). Ernst May and Fritz Wichert, eds., *Das neue Frankfurt — Monatsschrift für die Probleme moderner Gestaltung* (Frankfurt am Main, 1926–1931), continued 1931–1933 as *Die neue Stadt,* ed. Joseph Gantner. Adolf Behne, *Der moderne Zweckbau* (Munich, 1926); *Neues Wohnen, neues Bauen* (Leipzig, 1927); and *Eine Stunde Architektur* (Stuttgart, 1928). Ludwig Hilberseimer, *Groszstadt Architektur* (Stuttgart, 1927); and *Internationale neue Baukunst* (Stuttgart, 1928).

3. Walter Riezler, ed., *Die Form* (Berlin, 1925–1935). The Werkbund exhibitions included the permanent housing developments at Stuttgart ("Weissenhof," 1927) and Breslau (1929), the group of permanent buildings erected in Cologne in 1928 (which included Bartning's steel church), the German Pavilion by Mies van der Rohe at the International Exhibition in Barcelona in 1929, the international exhibition held in Paris in 1930 directed by Gropius, and a number of minor exhibits, such as the display of church furnishings held in Berlin in 1930 under the title "Kult und Form."

4. On the membership and formation of Der Ring, see *Die Form*, II (1926), 225. The members claimed that "Ring" symbolized "a form closed within itself, without a head," thus a perfectly cooperative organization and a pure geometric form. On one of the group's exhibitions, see Ludwig Hilberseimer, "Die neue Küche," *Zentralblatt der Bauverwaltung*, IL (1929), 28–29. The Ring published a section in *Bauwelt* from 1926 and also published Taut's *Bauen: Der neue Wohnbau*, which consisted in part of comparisons of modern buildings with historicist ones, to the detriment of the latter. On the BDA elections see *Hannoverscher Courier,* Sept. 13, 1927, File "Presse 1925/1927," Gropius Archive.

5. On the formation of CIAM, see *Die Form*, V (1929), 124.

6. Gustav Adolf Platz, *Die Baukunst der neuesten Zeit* (Berlin: Propyläen-Verlag, 1927). Walter Müller-Wulckow, *Deutsche Baukunst der Gegenwart* (Leipzig: Langewiesche Verlag, 1929): vol. I, *Bauten der Arbeit und des Verkehrs;* vol. II, *Wohnbauten und Siedlungen;* vol. III, *Bauten der Gemeinschaft.*

7. See, for example, Siegfried Giedion, "Zur Situation deutscher Architektur," *Der Cicerone*, XVIII (1926), 216–224; Theodor Heuss, "Das Werden der neuen Baukunst," *Die Hilfe*, XXXV (1929), 397–398; and A. Ewald, "Baustil und Staatsform," *Die Hilfe*, XXXV (1929), 353–354.

8. See, for example, "Das neuzeitliche Heim," *Haus, Hof, Garten: Illustrierte Wochenschrift des Berliner Tageblatts,* n.d., File "Presse 1930 III," Gropius Archive; and "Grundbegriffe der neue Wohnlichkeit," *Frauenmode,* June 1929, File "Presse 1930 I." The interest of the women's magazines in "the new dwelling" dated from the publication of Taut's book of that name; see "Wohnkultur," *Frau und Gegenwart,* June 1925, "Zeitungsarchiv 6." On the Weissenhof Siedlung, see the quotes from newspaper clippings in *Bau und Wohnung: Die Bauten der Weissenhofsiedlung* (Stuttgart, 1927).

9. See, for example, the report of speeches at Magdeburg's Colloquium on City Planning in the *Magdeburger Generalanzeiger*, Oct. 16, 1927, File "Presse 1925/1927," Gropius Archive; and reports on Gropius' speeches in Munich, Hagen, Leipzig, Frankfurt, and Dortmund during 1927 in the same file. The radio forum took place from January 19–25, 1930; May, Haesler, Riphahn, and Gropius were among the participants. See "Neues Bauen, neues Wohnen," *Mitteilungen des deutschen Werkbundes,* Jan. 15, 1930.

10. "200 Worte Deutsch," *Uhu*, 1930, 67; and "Nur 10 Jahre—eine andere Welt," *Münchner Illustrierte Presse*, Nov. 4, 1928, File "Presse 1930 I," Gropius Archive.

11. Jacques Mortane, ed., *Das neue Deutschland* (Leipzig, 1928), especially 205. The book, which contained an introduction by Aristide Briand, was published simultaneously in Paris as *La nouvelle Allemagne.*

12. *Deutschland-Führer,* with English text (Reichsbahnzentrale für den deutschen Reiseverkehr, n.d.), File "Presse 1930 I," Gropius Archive. See also the reports on the Werkbund exhibition in Paris in the *Neue Leipziger Zeitung,* June 13, 1930; *Berliner Tageblatt,* May 31, 1930; and *Stuttgarter Neues Tageblatt,* May 23, 1930, same file.

13. Walter Gropius, "Systematische Vorarbeit für rationellen Wohnungsbau," *Bauhaus,* II (1927), 1.

14. See, in addition to "Systematische Vorarbeit...," "Wie wollen wir in Zukunft bauen," *Wohnungswirtschaft,* I (1924), 152–154, on the use of machine-made materials and parts in housing; "Wohnungsbau der Zukunft," *Wohnungswirtschaft,* II (1925), 11–12; "Das kreisrunde Zukunftshaus," speech on prefabrication reported in the *Neue Leipziger Zeitung,* April 20, 1926 and repeated on several other occasions; and the frequently repeated talk "Flach-, Mittel- oder Hochbau," reprinted in *Moderne Bauformen,* XXX (1931), 321–340.

15. "Das kreisrunde Zukunftshaus."

16. Wagner thought that economical building methods were necessary as the means to building large-scale suburban communities so that "the German people may live and work in the pure air of the garden city" ("Englische Gartenstädte," *Wohnungswirtschaft,* II, 1925, 145). He believed, in addition, that the use of machines in construction helped to provide year-round work for the building trades and thus formed the necessary foundation for the establishment of permanent profit-sharing cooperatives like the soziale Bauhütten ("Probleme der Baukosten-Verbilligung," *Soziale Bauwirtschaft,* IV [1924] 131–132). He thought of these cooperatives in turn as microcosms of "economic democracy," which he likened to English guild socialism ("Neue Wege zum Kleinwohnungsbau: Ein Programm der Selbsthilfe," *Soziale Bauwirtschaft,* IV [1924] 22–23; and "Der Gildenstaat," *Soziale Bauwirtschaft,* V [1925], 252–256). See also "Der rationelle Wohnungsbau," *Wohnungswirtschaft,* I (1924), 157–163; "Jedem Deutschen eine gesunde Wohnung," *Wohnungswirtschaft,* II (1925), 169–171; and "Rationalisierter Wohnungsbau," *Soziale Bauwirtschaft,* V (1925), 269–270.

17. Ernst May, "Rationalisierung des Bauwesens," *Frankfurter Zeitung,* April 14, 1926.

18. For Taut's views on economical building methods, see "Ersparnis im Wohnungsbau durch rationelle Einrichtung," *Wohnungswirtschaft,* I (1924), 2–25; and "Die industrielle Herstellung von Wohnungen," *Wohnungswirtschaft,* 157–158. The statement on the "scientific" work of the architect is from *Modern Architecture,* 134.

19. "Fünf Jahre Wohnungsbau in Frankfurt am Main," *Das neue Frankfurt,* V (1930), nrs. 2–4.

20. See the reports on Gropius' speech "Die funktionelle Stadt," in the File "Presse 1931 III"; Hilberseimer, *Groszstadt Architektur,* 3–21; Wagner, "Verkehr und Tradition," *Das neue Berlin,* I (1929), 129–135; and May, "Rationalisierung des Bauwesens."

21. Gropius, "Idee und Arbeit des Bauhauses," *Berliner Börsen-Zeitung,* March 6, 1926; and "Die Wurzeln der neuen Baukunst," *Aachener Anzeiger,* Nov. 9, 1927, File "Presse 1925/1927," Gropius Archive. As Gilbert Herbert has pointed out in *The Synthetic Vision of Walter Gropius* (Johannesburg, 1959), Gropius has continued to maintain these beliefs to the present day. In both *Bauen: Der neue Wohnbau* (16) and *Modern Architecture* (9), Taut argued again that it was the purpose of the new architecture to transform utilitarian objects through art, thus giving them intellectual and spiritual content. See also Mies van der Rohe's speech "Die neue Zeit," given at the joint meeting of the Austrian and the German Werkbund in Vienna in 1930, reprinted in *Die Form,* VI (1930), 406.

22. Quoted in *Welt am Montag*, July 12, 1926, File "Presse 1925/1927," Gropius Archive.

23. W.C. Behrendt, "Geleitwort," *Die Form*, I (1925), 1. Together with Behrendt's opening words (which immediately precede the quote) these sentences present a very clear statement of the belief that lay behind most of the radical architects' writings, that "form" in the arts is intimately related to, and thus "reflects," form or structure in society and culture. Behrendt began: "Alle gestaltende Arbeit findet ihr Ende und ihren sichtbaren Ausdruck in der Form. Form ist Ordnung. Die neue Welt der Arbeit aber, die um uns erstanden ist, hat für sich bisher noch keine Ordnung gefunden." On the basis of these ideas, the Werkbund planned a grandiose exhibition for 1932 which was to be called "The New Era" and which was to illustrate the new "form" in every aspect of modern life, from architecture to sport to politics and the League of Nations. This extraordinary project was conceived by Ernst Jäckh and is described by him in "Idee und Realisierung der internationalen Werkbund-Ausstellung 'Die neue Zeit' Köln 1932," *Die Form*, V (1929), 401–421.

24. Emil Utitz, "Zweckmässigkeit und Sachlichkeit," *Dekorative Kunst*, XXVI (1923), 194. A good study of the origins of the term "Die neue Sachlichkeit" is Fritz Schmalenbach's article in the *Art Bulletin*, XXII (1940), 161–165, which traces its first use to an exhibition of postexpressionist painting planned by Gustav Hartlaub, Director of the Mannheim art gallery, in mid-1923. But Schmalenbach does not recognize that the words were being applied to architecture at the same time that Hartlaub used them to describe painting.

25. Ernst von Niebelschütz, "Moderne Baukunst," *Magdeburgische Zeitung*, Jan. 25, 1924, "Zeitungsarchiv 5," Gropius Archive; Paul Westheim, "Architektur-Entwicklung," *Die Glocke*, X (1924), 181–185. For another similar view see Fritz Stahl, "Der gebrochene Bann," *Berliner Tageblatt*, Feb. 10, 1923, "Zeitungsarchiv 3."

26. Behne, *Zweckbau*, 33, 59, 72.

27. *Ibid.*, 45.

28. *Ibid.*, 40.

29. Platz, *Die Baukunst der neuesten Zeit*, 112, 78, 91.

30. Gustav Hartlaub, "Ethos der neuen Baukunst," *Die Form*, V (1929), 101–106. See also the letter from Hartlaub to Alfred Barr, July 8, 1929, quoted in Schmalenbach, 162.

31. Recent historians of painting and literature have used the term to signify the end of expressionism and the disillusionment with expressionism's utopian hopes. See, for example, Bernard Myers, *The German Expressionists: A Generation in Revolt* (New York, 1956) and Walter Sokel, *The Writer in Extremis: Expressionism in Twentieth-Century German Literature* (Stanford, 1959).

32. Max Osborn, "Walter Gropius," *Vossische Zeitung*, April 9, 1930, File "Presse 1930 I," Gropius Archive; Alexander Dorner, "Walter Gropius," *Bauwelt*, April 10, 1930, same file; and Osborn, "Gropius und die Seinen," *Vossische Zeitung*, May 22, 1930, same file.

33. Müller-Wulckow, *Bauten der Arbeit*, 10, referring to buildings by Mendelsohn and Luckhardt & Anker.

34. Henry-Russell Hitchcock's *Painting toward Architecture* (New York, 1948), which pointed out that many of the formal qualities of the new style derived from modern painting, marked a turning point in architectural historiography; and other historians, such as Giedion and Joedicke, have recently begun to emphasize the formal development of modern architecture.

35. *Bauten Schultze-Naumburgs* (Weimar, 1940) and Chapter I. The essays were his *Kulturarbeiten* (Munich, 1907–1910), 6 vols.

36. Paul Schultze-Naumburg, *ABC des Bauens*, 2nd ed. (Stuttgart, 1927), 24.

37. Kurt Hager, "Das flache Dach," *Deutsche Bauzeitung*, LX (1926), 151; Gropius, "Das flache Dach: Eine Entgegnung," 188–192; Schultze-Naumburg,

"Zur Frage des schrägen und des flachen Daches bei unserem Wohnhausbau,"
761–766; 777–780.

38. Konrad Nonn, "Zusammenfassendes über das Bauhaus," *Zentralblatt der Bauverwaltung,* XXXXVII (1927), 105. The *Zentralblatt* also published letters of congratulation from Schultze-Naumburg and Emil Högg to Nonn (137, 138), and a letter from the Ring answering his charges (762).

39. See, for example, "Kurzlebige Moden für Wohnhausbauten?" *Deutsche Bauhütte,* XXXII (1928), 66; and "Kritisches zur RFG," 156-157.

40. H. A. Waldner, "Über Herstellung von Wohnhäusern in Industriebetrieb," *Deutsche Bauhütte,* XXVIII (1924), 217–218.

41. *Reform-Bauweisen für Siedlungs-Verbilligung* (Hannover, 1930); *Bausünden und Baugeld-Vergeudung* (Hannover, c. 1930).

42. Letter from the Innungs-Verband deutscher Baugewerksmeister, Berlin, March 25, 1927, *Zentralblatt,* XXXXVII (1927), 153; letter from the Reichsverband der deutschen Dachdeckers, n.d., 152, which says that Nonn has "freed the German building trades from a threat which has long been a great burden to them." "Baugewerksmeister" may refer to "building contractors" rather than to "building foremen."

43. See the letters from Gropius to Paulsen, editor of *Bauwelt,* Oct. 11 and 27, 1926, File "Flache Dach," Gropius Archive, which refer to several articles published by *Deutsches Dachdecker-Handwerk* during 1926. See also "Das deutsche Dach," *Deutsches Dachdecker-Handwerk,* 1926, nr. 52, same file.

44. *Dachdecker Zeitung,* XXXVII (1930), nr. 13 (March 30), May Archive.

45. In the Gropius Archive see "Zum Abtritt Walter Gropius," *Der deutsche Zimmermeister,* July 19, 1928; "Gegen die Haesler-Bauten in Kassel," *Ziegel und Zement,* June 6, 1930; "Reform Bauweisen," *Deutsche Ziegelzeitung,* June 14, 1930; "Neues sachliches Bauen: Weitere Misserfolge des Flachdaches!" *Ziegelwelt,* July 9, 1931; "Kritik an der RFG," *Der deutsche Steinbildhauer,* May 15, 1932.

46. Emil Högg, "Wege und Ziele deutscher Baukunst," reprinted in *Deutsche Bauzeitung,* LX (1926), 653–56, 658–64. The National Congress was not the BDA, but a rival organization.

47. According to Gropius' letter to Paulsen, Oct. 27, 1926 (n. 43 above), Högg's speech was reprinted in *Deutsches Dachdecker-Handwerk* late in 1926. J. Wienkoop's "Wandlungen der Baukunst im Lichte der deutschen Kultur," *Deutsche Bauzeitung,* LX (1926), 701–704, 718–720, followed Högg's arguments very closely. Bettina Feistel-Rohmeder, *Im Terror des Kunstbolschewismus* (Karlsruhe, 1938), Folge 11/12, August/September 1928, refers to other repetitions and reprints of Högg's speech. Martin Elsaesser, May's assistant in Frankfurt, attempted to answer Högg's and Wienkoop's arguments in *Deutsche Bauzeitung,* LX (1926), 721.

48. Hans F. K. Günther, *Rasse und Stil* (Munich, 1926). Schultze-Naumburg, "Zur Frage ... des flachen Daches," 780; Albrecht Haupt, "Rasse und Baukunst," *Deutsche Bauhütte,* XXX (1926), 135. See also the debate between Gropius and Schultze-Naumburg in the April issue of *Uhu:* "Wer hat Recht? Traditionelle Baukunst oder Bauen in neuen Formen," *Uhu,* VII (1926), 30–40; and Hugo Häring, "Die Tradition, Schultze-Naumburg und wir," *Die Form,* II (1926), 180.

49. Schultze-Naumburg, *Kunst und Rasse* (Munich, 1928); *Das Gesicht des deutschen Hauses* (Munich, 1929).

50. Schultze-Naumburg, *Kunst und Rasse,* 127.

51. *Ibid.,* 106–108.

52. *Ibid.,* 106–107.

53. *Ibid.,* 133.

54. *Ibid.,* 135, 119.

55. *Ibid.,* 120, 132.

56. Schultze-Naumburg, *Das Gesicht des deutschen Hauses,* 90.

57. *Ibid.,* 9.

58. *Ibid.*, 10.

59. Paul Schmitthenner, "Vom neuen Bauen," *Schwäbischer Merkur*, Feb. 28, 1930; "Neues Bauen und Tradition," *Schwäbischer Merkur*, April 2, 1931; *Das deutsche Wohnhaus* (Stuttgart, 1931). Schmitthenner's writings were not, however, explicitly racist.

60. Schultze-Naumburg, *Kunst und Rasse*, 128.

61. For a description of Senger's historicist architecture see Paul Renner, *Kulturbolschewismus?* (Munich and Leipzig, 1932), 24. Renner was a leader of the Munich Werkbund; his book presented an incisive defense of the new style.

62. *Krisis der Architektur* (Zürich, 1928); *Die Brandfackel Moskaus* (Zurzach-Schweitz, 1931). Senger's terminology probably inspired Konrad Nonn to change his own: late in the twenties Nonn also began to call the new style "communist" and "bolshevist" ("Die bolschewistische Architektur," *Deutsche Zeitung*, April 21, 1929; and "Homunkulus Architektur," *Deutsche Bauhütte*, XXXIV [1930], 142).

63. Renner, 24–25.

64. In several German newspapers, according to Renner. I have used the version in the *Völkischer Beobachter*, Oct. 22, Nov. 5, 7, 21, 1930, entitled "Bolschewismus im Bauwesen." Senger did not become a Nazi until 1932 or 1933; on the attitude of the *VB* toward him, see Chapter VI.

65. *VB*, Oct. 22, 1930. See also, *Krisis*, 46.

66. It has been necessary to do considerable violence to the chronology and sequence of Senger's exposition in order to compress his argument and render it readable.

67. *Brandfackel,* 47. Senger could not, of course, offer any proof that prefabrication had deprived the building trades of work, for radical architects' various projects for factory-produced building units were never put into production during the interwar period. Senger fell back on the claim that the use of concrete (he called it "cement") in the RFG Siedlungen had caused "the bankruptcy of numerous brick factories" (69) and that the use of new, factory-produced insulating materials had harmed masons and carpenters (31), presumably because they now had to construct thinner walls.

68. *Ibid.*, 47.

69. *Ibid.*, 50.

70. *Ibid.*, 74.

71. *Ibid.*, 38.

72. *Krisis*, 18; *VB*, Oct. 22, 1930.

73. *VB*, Oct. 22, 1930.

74. *Ibid.*

75. *Ibid.*

76. *Brandfackel*, 35.

77. *Ibid.*, 37.

78. "Kulturbolschewisten," *Der Ring*, II (1929), 611; Egon Trümpener, "Bolschewisierung in der Architektur," *Neue Preussische Kreuz-Zeitung*, Oct. 1, 1929. On the political complexion of *Der Ring*, see Fritz Stern, *The Politics of Cultural Despair* (Berkeley, 1961), 264–265.

79. Rosa Kurzweil-König, "Deutsches Heim und moderne Baukunst," *Ludendorffs Volkswarte,* Feb. 16, 1930.

80. Hugo Hübsch, "Berliner Kunstchronik," *Deutsche Tageszeitung*, April 16, 1930; Gustav Steinlein, "Das wahre Gesicht der neuen Baukunst," *Münchner Zeitung*, Dec. 31, 1930; and "Politik, Wirtschaft, Baukunst," *Münchner Zeitung*, Jan. 21, 1931.

81. Hasso Becker, "Vom neuen Bauen," *Der Jungdeutsche*, July 21, 1932, File "Presse 1932/1934," Gropius Archive; "eine eingestürzte 'Kathedrale,' " *Berliner Lokal-Anzeiger*, Aug. 24, 1932, same file; Reinhold Goering, "Käfige oder Gemeinschaftsraum," *Der Tag*, Sept. 30, 1932. Goering said that housing in the new style, with its small rooms, consisted of "stalls for animals," which

caused both physical and mental illness, thus weakening the race.

82. According to Bettina Feistel-Rohmeder, *Im Terror des Kunstbolsche-wismus*, Introduction, the column was paid for in part by the Dresden Deutsche Kunstgesellschaft, an organization of local artists and minor public officials, and in part by the above-named groups, which also published it in their newspapers. On the Deutschbund, anti-Semitic heir of Julius Langbehn's "Germanic irrationalism," see Stern, *The Politics of Cultural Despair*, 167–168. The ideals of the Bartelsbund are outlined in the writings of its founder, Adolf Bartels; see his *Der völkische Gedanke* (Weimar, 1923). The Deutschvölkische Schutz- und Trutzbund was a semipolitical national organization. In Thuringia, it joined Marschler's NSFP.

83. *Im Terror des Kunstbolschewismus*, Folge 25, June 1930.

84. *Ibid.*, Folge 11/12, Aug./Sept., 1928.

85. *Ibid.*, Folge 49, July, 1931; Folge 40/41, Oct./Nov., 1930; Folge 22/23, July/Aug., 1929.

86. *Ibid.*, Folge 49, July 1931.

87. Hermann Schluckebier, "Unsere Stellung zum Wohnungsbau (Rede auf der Tagung des kommunalistischen Reichsausschusses der DNVP, Jan. 29, 1928)," *Flugschriften der DNVP* (Berlin, 1928), nr. 316. The early part of the speech contained a particularly virulent attack on Wagner and the "Marxist" Gehag and soziale Bauhütten (16–21).

88. *Volk erwache! Was will die Deutschnationale Volks-Partei? Die Rede Dr. Hugenbergs im Berliner Sportspalast am 14. August, 1930* (Berlin, August 18, 1930).

Chapter VI / The New Architecture and National Socialism

1. Adolf Hitler, *Mein Kampf*, English translation, John Chamberlain *et al.*, eds. (New York, 1940), I, 352. The principal treatment of cultural decline in *Mein Kampf* is Chapter X, Volume I, on the causes of the military collapse; but Hitler elaborates on these ideas in Chapter XI, on nation and race, and Chapter II, Volume II, discusses the relationship among culture, art, race, and the state.

2. "Some fundamental demands of the Party," Sept. 18, 1922, and "The paradise of the Jew," April 27, 1923, in N.H. Baynes, ed., *The Speeches of Adolf Hitler* (London, 1942), I, 66, 108.

3. Speech at the Hofbräuhaus on Aug. 13, 1920 (photostatic copy of text in the Archive of the Institut für Zeitgeschichte, Munich, Gruppe I, Stück 62), 5. *Mein Kampf*, I, 360–64. Speech of April 4, 1929, quoted in Otto Dietrich, "Adolf Hitler als künstlerischer Mensch," *Nationalsozialistische Monatshefte*, III (1933), 473.

4. Bettina Feistel-Rohmeder, *Im Terror des Kunstbolschewismus*, Folge 11/12, Aug./Sept., 1928, reported a meeting of the Kampfbund in Munich early in 1928. Eugen Haug (leader successively of the Reichshammerbund, the Deutschvölkische Schutz- und Trutzbund, and the Nazi party in Stuttgart) describes the founding of a chapter of the Kampfbund in Stuttgart in 1928 in "Aufzeichnungen zur Vorgeschichte der Entstehung der NSDAP in Stuttgart" (manuscript in the Archive of the Institut für Zeitgeschichte, Munich, Gruppe VI, Stück 166), 9.

Hildegard Brenner, in *Die Kunstpolitik des Nationalsozialismus* (Hamburg, 1963), provides a fuller discussion of the origins of the Kampfbund and treats in detail many of the other tendencies in Nazi artistic policy touched upon in this and the next two chapters. Since my account differs from Brenner's in a great many points of fact and in most of its interpretations, I have not thought it necessary to provide in the notes many cross-references to her discussion.

5. "Die Kulturkrise der Gegenwart," *VB*, Feb. 27, 1929, describes the meeting of the previous day as the "first" meeting of the Kampfbund.

6. *Ibid.* Clearly Rosenberg was already developing the central idea of his *Mythus des 20. Jahrhunderts*, published the following year. See also *VB*, April 27.

7. "Deutsche aller Berufe und Stände," *Kampfbund für deutsche Kultur*, Flugblatt Nr. I, n. d. Internal evidence suggests a publication date early in 1929.

8. *Ibid.*, and *Ein Kampfbund für deutsche Kultur* (Munich, n.d.). Internal evidence demonstrates a publication date in the summer of 1930.

9. "Deutsche aller Berufe und Stände."

10. The last named was headed by Eugen Hönig, professor of architectural history at Munich's art academy and later President of the Reichskammer der bildenden Künste. See Feistel-Rohmeder, Introduction, and Chapter VII, below.

11. The Kampfbund attempted at first to give the appearance of a nonpartisan organization. Thus, none of the above-named men was obliged explicitly to support the NSDAP, but when they spoke to Kampfbund gatherings they were introduced by Nazi dignitaries.

12. Winifred Wagner; Eva Chamberlain; Freiherr von Wolzogen, editor of the *Bayreuther Blätter*; and Ludwig Schemann, translator of Gobineau and professor at Göttingen (*Kampfbund für deutsche Kultur*, 3–4).

13. Among Mielke's many writings the best known were his works on the village architecture of the later middle ages.

14. The academic members included Friedrich Wilhelm, Freiherr von Bissing, professor of Egyptology, Munich; Carl Cornelius, art history, Munich; Arthur Prüfen, musicology, Leipzig; Andreas Heusler, Germanic philology, Basel; Adalbert Wahl, history, Tübingen (*Kampfbund für deutsche Kultur*, *ibid.*).

Feistel-Rohmeder, Introduction, describes the union in 1930 of seventeen cultural organizations, including the Kampfbund, in a "Führerrat der Vereinigten Deutschen Kunst- und Kulturverbände," under the leadership of her own Deutsche Kunstgesellschaft. In Folge 43, Jan. 1931, she says that the Kampfbund has taken over the "Führerrat." Some of the groups were Adler und Falken, Bund völkischer Lehrer Deutschlands, Deutscher Frauenkampfbund, Bayreuther Bund Deutscher Jugend, and the Nordischer Ring. See also the statement of Stuttgart's Deutscher Befreiungs-Bund (June 16, 1930, Eugen Haug, "Aufzeichnungen zur Vorgeschichte," 42–43) on the occasion of its absorption into the Kampfbund, giving its reasons for joining.

15. The Kampfbund had chapters in Munich, Stuttgart, Dresden, Weimar, Frankfurt, and Augsburg by the end of 1930 ("Kampfbund für deutsche Kultur," *VB*, Nov. 12, 1930, and other scattered references in the same paper 1929–1930); in Karlsruhe, Wiesbaden, Darmstadt, and Kaiserslautern in 1931 ("Kampfbund für deutsche Kultur," *Nationalsozialistische Monatshefte*, I [1931], 64–65, and *VB*, 1931, *passim*); and during the course of 1932, chapters and subchapters were founded in Berlin, Essen, Mannheim, Jena, Cologne, and eighteen other cities ("Übersicht der Organisationsleiter, Obleute und Sachreferenten des KfdK-Gross-Berlin," *Deutsche Kultur-Wacht*, II, 1933, H. 5, 18). The political leader of the Berlin Ortsgruppe was Hans Hinkel, another frustrated artist turned party propagandist, who after 1933 held a series of influential posts in the Propaganda Ministry. The architectural directors of the Berlin group included Schultze-Naumburg and Nonn.

16. "Ein Vortrag des Kampfbundes für deutsche Kultur," *VB*, March 3, 1929, reports talks given by Heuss in Weimar and Munich. See also *VB*, March 9, 1929.

17. "Der ewige Kampf zwischen Chaos und Gestalt. Eine Rede Alfred Rosenbergs über den Schicksalskampf der deutschen Kultur," *VB*, April 27, 1929, reports on Rosenberg's speeches in Munich, Berlin, and Dresden.

18. See, for example, the report of the speech on "cultural bolshevism" given by Dr. Werner Kulz in Kaiserslautern, in "Kulturumsturz in Deutschland," *VB*, June 25, 1931.

19. "Der Kampfbund für deutsche Kultur zum sächsischen Staatsliteraturpreis," *VB*, August 1, 1929. The state government accepted the money but refused to award the prizes to the Kampfbund's nominees.

20. "Kampfbund für deutsche Kultur," *VB*, Oct. 30, 1929, describes several of these occasions. See also "Ein Rückblick auf die Pfingsttagung des Kampfbunds zum Schutze der deutschen Kultur," *VB*, June 17, 1930.

21. "Die Kampfbund-Bühne München steht!" *VB*, Oct. 23/24, 1932.

22. The *Völkischer Beobachter* was of course edited by Rosenberg, but since Hitler always took an interest in the paper, and since from 1928 Goebbels was in charge of all party propaganda activities, Rosenberg was not solely responsible for its editorial policy.

23. See, for example, "Neue Verhöhnung der deutschen Frontsoldaten auf der Bühne," March 3, 1928; Hans von Wolzogen, "Vergangenheit und Zukunft: Eine Betrachtung der Gegenwart," Nov. 3, 1928; and the lead article on Reinhardt in the issue of April 16, 1929.

24. Gottfried Feder, "Gegen die Negerkultur," *VB*, Jan. 31, 1930.

25. "Gegen den Kulturbolschewismus," Jan. 16, 1929, a very inclusive article, which attacks most of the men and works which the Kampfbund attacked and uses Rosenberg's characteristic terminology.

26. "Der Dessauer Bauhausfilm; wie bauen wir gesund und wirtschaftlich?" *VB*, June 16/17, 1927; and "Neues Bauen–Neues Wohnen," Sept. 24, 1927.

27. "Neues Bauen...."

28. "Das technische Gesicht der neuen Münchner Ausstellung," *VB*, May 4, 1928. See also "Eröffnung der Ausstellung 'Heim und Technik,'" May 27, 1928; "Ausstellung Heim und Technik München," July 4, 1928; "Die moderne Technik des Haushalts," Oct. 5, 1928.

29. "Die Groszstadt ohne Strasse. Ein phantastisches Zukunftsbild," *VB*, June 20, 1929. See also "Die Groszstadt der Zukunft," Dec. 19/20, 1926; "Berlins Stadtplan bestimmend für den Stadtsorganismus," Sept. 23, 1927; "Wovon leben die deutschen Groszstädte," Sept. 26, 1928.

30. No adequate study of Darré's career and influence exists, but the following provide brief discussions: A. Bullock, *Hitler, a Study in Tyranny*, rev. ed. (New York, 1962); K. Heiden, *Der Führer* (Boston, 1944); K. D. Bracher et al., *Die nationalsozialistische Machtergreifung* (Cologne and Opladen, 1960); the section by Heinz Haushofer on Darré in *Neue Deutsche Biographie*, vol. III (Berlin, 1957); and the section on Darré in *Wer Ist's* (Berlin, 1953). There is considerable disagreement among these writers about the facts of Darré's life between 1926 and 1933 and particularly about the date of his enrollment in the party. All agree, however, in rejecting Darré's own contention (in his defense before the International Military Tribunal at Nürnberg) that he joined the party only in April of 1930 and had no contact with it before that date.

31. *Wer Ist's*, 1935, and Heiden, 336–337. Haushofer, in *Neue Deutsche Biographie*, III, 517, has 1928. Darré was apparently dismissed from this position because of his aggressive geopolitics and his associations with Karl Haushofer's Deutsche Akademie in Munich.

32. Bullock, 155.

33. *Wer Ist's*, 1935. On the RUSHA, see Gerald Reitlinger, *The SS, Alibi of a Nation* (London, 1956).

34. *Das Bauerntum als Lebensquell der Nordischen Rasse* (Munich, 1929). Page references are to the seventh edition of 1938. According to the foreword to the first edition, Darré completed the manuscript in the fall of 1928. He frequently emphasized his intellectual debt to Mielke's *Die Siedlungskunde des Deutschen Volkes* (Munich, 1927) and to Günther's works.

35. *Bauerntum*, 289–292.

36. *Ibid.*, 227–299.

37. *Ibid.*, 77–80; 367.

38. "Aus der Asphaltkultur der Groszstadt," *VB*, July 13, 1928.

39. "Berlin, die unfruchtbarste Stadt der Welt," *VB*, April 30, 1929.

40. "Unsere Stellung zu Damaschkes Bodenreform: Kulturpolitisches Irrtum," *VB*, June 23, 1931; part of a series on land reform, which endorses *Neuadel aus Blut und Boden* as representative of the Nazi program.

41. "Ein Rückblick auf die Pfingsttagung des 'Kampfbunds zum Schutze der deutschen Kultur,' " *VB*, June 17, 1930.

42. The sequence of events is not entirely clear. It is certain that Darré and Schultze-Naumburg became close friends at some point during the spring of 1930, since *Neuadel aus Blut und Boden*, finished in the spring, was written at Schultze-Naumburg's home in Saaleck (foreword to the first edition, Munich, 1930), and contains many expressions of gratitude and admiration. But there is no evidence to indicate that this friendship preceded Frick's interest in Schultze-Naumburg.

43. Fritz Sauckel, *Kampf und Sieg in Thüringen* (Weimar, 1934), 21.

44. Sauckel, "Zeittafel" at end of book, and *General-Anzeiger* (Dortmund), April 14, 1930, File "Presse 1930 I," Gropius Archive.

45. Justus Bier, "Zur Auflösung der Staatlichen Bauhochschule in Weimar," *Die Form*, VI (1930), 269–274; "Wider die Negerkultur," *VB*, April 15, 1930; F. Sauckel, "Die Rettung Thüringens," *VB*, April 20/21/22, 1930; "Die Weimarer Hochschule für Baukunst," *VB*, April 11, 1930.

46. K.D. Bracher, *Die Auflösung der Weimarer Republik* (Villingen/ Schwarzwald, 1960), 360, n. 100; Georg Witzmann, *Thüringen von 1918–1933*; *Erinnerungen eines Politikers* (Meisenheim am Glan, 1958), 153 ff.; "Jüdische Hetze gegen Schultze-Naumburg," *VB*, Aug. 23, 1930; "Schultze-Naumburg und die zünftige Kritik," *VB*, March 13, 1931; "DVP sabotiert den Kulturaufbau," *VB*, March 21, 1931; "Was geht in Weimar vor?" *VB*, Oct. 3, 1931; *Jahrbuch der Deutschen Sozialdemokratie für das Jahr 1931* (Berlin: Vorwärts, 1931), 230–232; "Thüringer Kulturabbau Professor Schultze-Naumburgs," *VB*, Jan. 16, 1932.

47. "Ostische Bilder," *Hannoverscher Kurier*, Nov. 29, 1930, File "Presse 1930 I," Gropius Archive.

48. "Das Bauhaus in Weimar," *Der Nationalsozialist* (Weimar), March 2, 1930, File "Presse 1930 I," Gropius Archive; "Das Bauhaus in Weimar," *VB*, March 14, 1930; Paul Schultze-Naumburg, "Die Weimarer Kunsthochschule," *Niederdeutscher Beobachter* (Schwerin), Jan. 27, 1931, File "Presse 1931 II," Gropius Archive. According to "Neues Bauen und Tradition," *VB*, Feb. 13, 1931, many of the new teachers whom Schultze-Naumburg hired had been students of Paul Schmitthenner at Stuttgart.

49. Except for a brief review of *Kunst und Rasse* (April 4, 1928), which dealt only with the sections on painting, and a brief preview of *Das Gesicht des Deutschen Hauses* (June 19, 1929).

50. "Was geht in Weimar vor," Oct. 3, 1931; "Jüdische Hetze gegen Schultze-Naumburg," Aug. 23, 1930; H. F. Schmidt, "Moderne Baukunst," March 27, 1930.

51. See the leaflet *Deutsche Kunst und Rasse*, reprinted in *Kampfbund für Deutsche Kultur*, c. mid-1930. It is anonymous, but quotes directly from *Kunst und Rasse* and also corresponds very closely in wording to a speech which Schultze-Naumburg gave before the "Kulturpolitische Tagung" of the DNVP's Thuringian branch in April, 1930 ("Idioten und Dirnen," *Welt am Montag*, April 14, 1930, File "Presse 1930 I," Gropius Archive).

52. "Kultur und Macht; Machtentwicklung als Voraussetzung echter Volkskultur; Alfred Rosenberg auf der Tagung des KfdK in Weimar," *VB*, June 13, 1930; "Ein Rückblick auf die Pfingsttagung des Kampfbunds zum Schutze der deutschen Kultur," *VB*, June 17, 1930; "Ansprache des Staatsministers Dr. Frick auf dem Kongress des Kampfbundes für deutsche Kultur, Pfingsten 1930," in *Kampfbund für deutsche Kultur*, c. mid-1930, 19.

53. Felix Schmidt, "Der Kampfbund der Deutschen Architekten und Ingenieure im Kampfbund für Deutsche Kultur," *Deutsche Technik*, I (1933),

47–49. *Deutsche Kultur-Wacht*, II (1933), H. 5, 18, describes the founding of the organization in Berlin during February 1932 and its subsequent history.

54. Gottfried Feder, ed., *Deutsche Technik* (Berlin, 1933 ff.). The meetings, which are described in more detail in Chapter VII, took place on June 24–25 in Weimar and on December 15 in Berlin. See "Führertagung der deutschen Architekten und Ingenieure," *Deutsche Kultur-Wacht*, II (1933), H. 13, 8–9; and "Wider den Kulturbolschewismus! Machtvolle Kundgebung des Kampfbund der deutschen Architekten und Ingenieure," *VB*, Dec. 16, 1933.

55. *Kampf um die Kunst* (Munich: Eher, 1932), 5.

56. *Ibid.*, 68.

57. Dresden and Munich: "Schultze-Naumburg in München im 'Kampfbund für deutsche Kultur,' " *VB*, Feb. 10, 1931; "Schultze-Naumburg und die zünftige Kritik," *VB*, March 13, 1931; "Wo bleibt die gute, moderne Kunst?! ... Schultze-Naumburg, Panizza, Grassmann, und was Herr Esswein dazu zu sagen hat," *VB*, April 10, 1931. Paul Renner in his *Kulturbolschewismus?* (Munich, 1932), 8–10, gives a vivid description of the second Munich lecture, where the storm troopers bludgeoned the painter Wolf Panizza for calling out "Where is the *good* modern art?" while Schultze-Naumburg was showing his slides. See also "Der Kampf um die Kunst," *VB*, Feb. 13, 1931; "Schultze-Naumburg spricht in Wiesbaden," *VB*, March 17, 1931; and "Schultze-Naumburg in Darmstadt und Frankfurt," *VB*, March 24, 1931.

58. K. J. Fischer, "Kampf um Schultze-Naumburg," *VB*, March 5, 1931; "Schultze-Naumburg und die zünftige Kritik."

59. From the speech "Neues Bauen und Tradition," which Schmitthenner gave first in Weimar in February, 1931 ("Neues Bauen und Tradition," *VB*, Feb. 11, 1931), and repeated frequently thereafter. Quoted from the verbatim transcription in K.W. Straub, "Bekenntnisse eines deutschen Baumeisters," *VB*, March 30, 1932, which describes a repeat performance in Berlin. For other versions, see: "Neues Bauen und Tradition," *Schwäbischer Merkur*, April 2, 1931; "Kampfbund Kundgebung in Württemberg," *Deutsche Kultur-Wacht*, II (1933), H. 9, 13–14; "Tradition und neue Kunst," *Bauwelt*, XXIV (1933), 789; "Tradition und neue Kunst," *VB*, July 16/17, 1933.

60. "Sachlichkeit in alter und neuer Bauweise; ein Vortragsabend des Kampfbund für deutsche Kultur," *VB*, March 3, 1932.

61. "Architektur und Revolution," *VB*, Feb. 2, 1933. Brenner is mistaken in her belief that Senger was one of the earliest Kampfbund lecturers (Hildegard Brenner, *Die Kunstpolitik des Nationalsozialismus* [Hamburg, 1963], 11–13). As late as 1931 he refused to write or speak under the auspices of the organization (Renner, *Kulturbolschewismus?* 59–60).

62. The subchapter meetings are described in "Kampfbund der deutschen Architekten und Ingenieure," *Deutsche Kultur-Wacht*, II (1933), H. 5, 18. For other major speeches which Schultze-Naumburg gave before KDAI meetings, see: "Architekten und Ingenieure vor die Front! Zur Reichstagung des KDAI," *VB*, Nov. 6/7, 1932; and "Führertagung der deutschen Architekten und Ingenieure," *Deutsche Kultur-Wacht*, II (1933), H. 13, 8–9.

63. "Kampfbund der deutschen Architekten und Ingenieure," *VB*, March 3, 1932.

64. Winfried Wendland, "Moderne Baukunst–Junge Baukunst," *Bauwelt*, XXIII (1932), 740–741.

65. "Führertagung des Kampfbundes deutscher Architekten und Ingenieure," *VB*, June 29, 1933; and "Wider den Kulturbolschewismus! Machtvolle Kundgebung des Kampfbundes der deutschen Architekten und Ingenieure," Dec. 16, 1933.

66. "Rosenberg spricht über Kunst," *Deutsche Allgemeine Zeitung*, May 8, 1934; Rosenberg, "Kampf um die Kunst," speech of Sept. 26, 1934, Berlin, reprinted in the *Nationalsozialistische Monatshefte*, IV (1934), 1095–1099; and "Gesinnung und Kunst," speech of June 7, 1935, Düsseldorf, reprinted, V (1935), 607. Rosenberg also expressed a view of technology similar to Schultze-

Naumburg's and Feder's in "Kultur und Technik," speech of June 6, 1935, reprinted in *Gestaltung der Idee* (Munich, 1939), 319–328.

67. Attacks upon the new architecture began to appear in the VB in the summer of 1929, but the editors still published articles representing the contrary view during this period. Among the former the columns by Friedrich Imholz are notable: "Die Orientalisierung der deutschen Baukunst," Aug. 22, 1929; "Die Gefahren der Orientalisierung unserer Baukunst," Nov. 19, 1929; "Kirchenbau und 'moderner' Baustil," Jan. 15, 1930. In February the VB published an elaborate refutation of Imholz: Karl J. Fischer, "Neuer Baustil als Ausdruck neuer Zeit," Feb. 14, 1930; and in March a refutation of Fischer: H. F. Schmidt, "Moderne Baukunst," March 27, 1930. In June the editors were still undecided about their attitude to the new style—see the favorable report on Gropius' part in the Werkbund exhibition at Paris, "Die Wohnung für das Existenzminimum," June 28, 1930. But on July 2 another review of the same exhibition accused Gropius of working toward "proletarian dictatorship in art" ("Der deutsche Werkbund in Paris"); from this date forward every reference to the work of the Ring architects was uniformly unfavorable.

68. There are many examples of this identification of the new architecture with modern art. See especially "Bolschewismus oder Deutschland," March 2, 1933; "Jetzt wird der Schlussstrich gezogen!" election appeal of March 5/6, 1933; and a similar article in *Der Angriff*: "Vierzehn Jahre Marxistischer Baukunst," March 1, 1933. The article "Irrung und Entwirrung. Bildende Kunst gestern, heute und morgen," VB, Sept. 28, 1932, promises that "the new German art will express itself first in architecture...."

69. "Eine Abrechnung mit dem System May, Gropius, Taut und Konsorten!" July 12/13, 1931. See also Paul Schmitthenner, "Gestalteter Zeitgeist. Baukunst und Stil im Jahrhundert der Technik," VB, Jan. 27, 1933.

70. For a particularly clear statement of this equation between the new architecture and "cultural bolshevism," see "Entscheidungskämpfe um die deutsche Kultur," Feb. 11, 1932.

71. "Berliner Bauausstellung und Wohnungsnot," June 6, 1930; "Der deutsche Werkbund in Paris," July 2, 1930; "Auch Schweden lehnt sich gegen das 'Neue Bauen' auf," Nov. 5, 1930; "Was die Berliner Bauausstellung zeigt!" July 8, 1931; "Nachwort zur Berliner Bauausstellung," Aug. 7, 1931; "Leuchtende Wände—Lichtgaswände," March 2, 1932; "Sonne, Luft und Haus für alle: Berliner Sommerschau 1932," June 8, 1932.

72. See, for example, "Wider den Bolschewismus in der Baukunst," Dec. 3, 1930; "Flachdachkrach!..." July 3, 1931; and "Kampf um Gropius," Jan. 28, 1932.

73. "Bolschewismus in Bauwesen," Oct. 22, Nov. 5, Nov. 7.

74. "Das Ziel unseres kulturpolitischen Kampfes," Nov. 4, 1932. Under this page heading are three articles; the passage quoted is from the second: "Schrankenloses Bekenntnis zu einer deutschen Kunst," "Die 'Kathedrale des Marxismus' — und ihre 'Gläubigen,'" "Kulturelle Erneuerung aus Volks- und Rassebewusstsein."

75. "Bauelend und Kulturverödung im heutigen Staate," Aug. 19, 1930. See also "Die neue Architektur und ihre Gefahren," July 12, 1930.

76. "Bauelend...." See also "Zum Thema; Wohin unsere Steuergelder kommen?" July 4, 1931; and "Wo unsere Steuergelderhinkommen: Die 'R.F.G.' oder wie mit öffentlichen Mitteln eine Überorganisation genährt wurde," Sept. 4, 1931.

77. "Eine Abrechnung...," July 12/13, 1931. See also all the articles cited in n. 71.

78. "Schultze-Naumburg und die zünftige Kritik," March 13, 1931.

79. "Bauelend...," Aug. 19, 1930.

80. "Jetzt wird der Schlussstrich gezogen!" election appeal, March 5/6, 1933.

81. "Vom deutschen Kunstreich jüdischer Nation," Feb. 2, 1933.

82. "Eine Abrechnung . . . ," July 12/13, 1931.

83. "Das Ziel unseres kulturpolitischen Kampfes . . . ," Nov. 4, 1932.

Chapter VII / The Evolution of Architectural Control under the Nazi Regime

1. See Chapter IV, n. 48, and Hans-Maria Wingler, *Das Bauhaus—1919–1933—Weimar, Dessau, Berlin* (Bramsche, 1962), 173–186.

2. Hofmann, "Was wird aus dem Bauhaus," *Anhalter Tageszeitung*, July 10, 1932, File "Presse, Bauhaus," Gropius Archive.

3. *Ibid.* See also "Kampf um Gropius," *VB*, Jan. 28, 1932; and Minutes of the Dessau Gemeinderat, 1929–1933, Stadtarchiv Dessau, nr. 1284, selections in Wingler, *Bauhaus*, 181–182.

4. "Das Bauhaus bekommt ein Holzdach," *Frankfurter Zeitung*, Jan. 21, 1932. According to P. A. Otte, "Vier Monate Hitler-Regime," *Berliner Tageblatt*, July 29, 1932, the closing of the Bauhaus was virtually the only accomplishment of the Nazi regime in Anhalt during its first four months in power. Thus, as in Thuringia in 1930 and as was often the case after 1933, its cultural policy served the party as a substitute for other types of political and social action.

5. "Haussuchung im Bauhaus Steglitz," *Berliner Lokal-Anzeiger*, April 12, 1933; "Razzia im 'Bauhaus,'" *VB*, April 12, 1933.

6. Geheimes Staatspolizeiamt, Berlin, letter of July 21, 1933, to Ludwig Mies van der Rohe (photostatic copy at the Busch-Reisinger Museum, Harvard University).

7. Ludwig Mies van der Rohe, letter of July 20, 1933, to Winfried Wendland, Preussische Ministerium für Wissenschaft, Kunst und Volksbildung, Berlin (photostatic copy at the Busch-Reisinger Museum, Harvard University); and "Gedächtnisprotokoll einer aus Anlass der Schliessung des Bauhauses mit Alfred Rosenberg am 12. April 1933 geführten Unterredung," Berlin, April 13, 1933 (Mies van der Rohe Archive; copy lent by Mr. Wingler; brief extract in Wingler, *Bauhaus*, 194).

8. Ludwig Mies van der Rohe, "An die Studierenden des Bauhauses," Berlin, August 10, 1933, announcement to the students of the faculty's decision to close the school and its reasons for the decision (photostatic copy at the Busch-Reisinger Museum, Harvard University).

9. At the same time as a number of art critics and museum directors friendly to modern art and architecture, including Gustav Hartlaub, Curt Glaser, Walter Riezler, and Max Osborn. See "Beurlaubte Kunstwerke, beurlaubte Künstler, beurlaubte Kunsthistoriker," *Das Werk*, XX (1933), July, xxxviii.

10. "Neuorganisation an den preussischen Kunstanstalten," *Münchner Zeitung*, Dec. 27, 1933.

11. Schmitthenner was given the post at the urging of the Kampfbund, but soon resigned because of differences with Goebbels and Rust (verbal information from Mr. Schmitthenner and the correspondence in the Schmitthenner file, membership files of the Berlin division of the Reichskammer der bildenden Künste, U.S. Documents Center, Berlin). See also n. 10, above.

12. "Kleine Chronik," *National Zeitung* (Basle), Oct. 30, 1933; and "Kunstchronik," Oct. 30, 1934.

13. For example, Hans Mehrtens, Otto Ernst Schweitzer, Johannes Göderitz.

14. "Fünf Stadträte beurlaubt," *Vossische Zeitung*, March 14, 1933; "Wieder zahlreiche Beurlaubungen," March 19; "Weitere Beurlaubungen," March 23; "Stadtrat Czeminski beurlaubt," March 29; "Beurlaubungen," March 30.

15. After the Kampfbund had attacked him in *Deutsche Kultur-Wacht*, II (1933), H. 6, 11.

16. Johannes Göderitz, Taut's successor in Magdeburg, letter to the author of Jan. 7, 1960, and verbal information. Konrad Rühl, Göderitz's assistant from 1922–1927, and director of the building program of the district adminis-

tration (Provinzialverwaltung) in Düsseldorf, was discharged from the latter position in 1933 (letter to the author of Feb. 9, 1960).

17. "Wieder zahlreiche Beurlaubungen," *Vossische Zeitung*, March 19, 1933; and *Geschichte der gemeinnützigen Wohnungswirtschaft in Berlin* (Berlin, 1957), 129.

18. *Ibid.,* and *Gehag: Gemeinnützige Heimstätten-Aktiengesellschaft 1924–1957* (Berlin, 1957), 25.

19. See Chapter VIII.

20. "Neuer Vorstand des BDA," *Vossische Zeitung*, March 24, 1933.

21. *Bauwelt*, May 11, 1933, quoted in "Deutsche Zeitungsausschnitte," *Das Werk*, XX (1933), June, xlv–xlvi.

22. Copies of the questionnaires sent out to the members of the BDA by the new Executive Council are included in nearly all the membership files of the Berlin division of the RDBK, U.S. Documents Center, Berlin. "Deutsche Zeitungsausschnitte," *Das Werk*, XX, announces the distribution of the questionnaires.

23. "Deutsche Zeitungsausschnitte."

24. Report of a meeting of the Rhein-Ruhr division of the BDA, *Kölnische Zeitung*, May 7, 1933, quoted in "Deutsche Zeitungsausschnitte."

25. "30. Deutscher Architektentag," *Deutsche Journalpost* (Rudolstadt, Thuringia), XXXXI (1933), nr. 33; copy lent by Hans Eckstein.

26. "DWB Mitteilungen," *Die Form*, IX (1933), 126–127.

27. "Die neue Werkbundleitung," *Die Form*, IX (1933), 191. The members of the Council included Haesler, Hilberseimer, Jäckh, and Poelzig.

28. "Der neue Deutsche Werkbund," *Deutsche Kultur-Wacht*, II (1933), H. 18, 15.

29. *Die Form*, IX (1933), 126–127; "Der neue Deutsche Werkbund," *Deutsche Kultur-Wacht*; and Winfried Wendland, letter to Hans Hinkel, Aug. 21, 1935, Wendland file, membership files of the Berlin division of the RDBK, U.S. Documents Center, Berlin.

30. Winfried Wendland, "Der Deutsche Werkbund im neuen Reich," *Die Form*, IX (1933), 257–258. Later in the year Lörcher announced that the DWB should concentrate upon peasant housing. See "Tagung des deutschen Werkbundes in Würzburg," *Stuttgarter Neues Tageblatt*, Oct. 3, 1933.

31. "Die Arbeit der KDAI," *VB*, April 10, 1933; "Neuorganisation des deutschen Werkbundes," *Deutsche Kultur-Wacht*, II (1933), H. 22, 15; *Die Form*, IX (1933), 315-317; "Bund deutscher Architekten," *Deutsche Kultur-Wacht*, II (1933), H. 27, 16; Felix Schmidt, "Der Kampfbund der Deutschen Architekten und Ingenieure im Kampfbund für Deutsche Kultur," *Deutsche Technik*, I (1933), 47–49.

32. The Reichskulturkammer was established by the Reichskulturkammergesetz of Sept. 22, 1933, but did not begin to function until Nov. 15. Hellmut Lehmann-Haupt (*Art under a Dictatorship* [New York, 1954], 68) wrongly calls Hinkel the President of the RKK. Hinkel was Goebbels' deputy in charge of personnel in the Kulturkammer. See Hans Hinkel, *Handbuch der Reichskulturkammer* (Berlin, 1937), 28–32; and E. Wernert, *L'art dans le III*ᵉ *Reich* (Paris, 1936), 46–47.

33. Hinkel, *Handbuch*, 17; and Karl-Friedrich Schreiber, "Das geltende Reichskulturrecht," *Deutsches Kulturrecht* (Hamburg, 1936), 18.

34. Hinkel, *Handbuch*, 28–32; Wernert, 46. The legal structure of authority in the RKK was very intricate indeed and is treated in great detail by Wernert and Lehmann-Haupt and by Schreiber, *Das Recht der Reichskulturkammer* (Berlin, 1935–1937), 5 vols. The subject does not appear to this writer to be of particular importance in understanding the policy of the RKK, since Goebbels appointed his subordinates, and since he made or reviewed most of the important decisions. For example, every decision to exclude a member, or to refuse an application for membership, was referred to Goebbels (Schreiber, vol. I, "Reichskammer der bildende Künste," section II, part 1).

35. Schreiber, "Das geltende Reichskulturrecht," 18.

36. "Jeder wirklichen Künstler wird das Feld freigemacht . . . ," VB, April 12, 1933; and Goebbels, "Die deutsche Revolution," Nationalsozialistische Monatshefte, III (1933), 247.

37. "Die deutsche Kultur vor neuen Anfang," VB, Nov. 16, 1933. Reprinted in Signale der neuen Zeit (Munich, 1934), 323–336.

38. "Wir halten der Kunst unsere Hand hin!" VB, May 10, 1933.

39. "Die bildende Kunst im Dritten Reich," National-Zeitung (Basle), March 28, 1934. See also, "Nationalsozialismus und Kunst in Deutschland," Neue Zürcher Zeitung, August 28, 1933; and "Deutsche Jugend kämpft für die lebendige Kunst," Das Werk, XX (1933), July, xxxiv–xxxvii.

40. In his speech at the opening of the RKK (n. 37 above), Gobbels emphasized that the new state should "lead, not legislate" Germany's artistic activity and explained that a principal task of Nazism must be to convince the foreign observer that the new regime is not "barbarian."

41. Wassili Luckhardt, "Vom preussischen Stil zur neuen Baukunst," Deutsche Allgemeine Zeitung, March 26, 1933.

42. Although he replaced Max Osborn, an even more enthusiastic supporter of the radical architects: see Vossische Zeitung, March 17, 1933. Werner's article, "Die Kunst im dritten Reich," Deutsche Allgemeine Zeitung, March 29, 1933, was also addressed to Hinkel and Rust. Hans Hinkel at this point had a position in Rust's ministry, but had been an associate of Goebbels for many years. His entry into Rust's ministry was therefore thought to represent a liberalizing of its policies.

43. Max Cetto, "Briefe eines jungen deutschen Architekten an dem Herrn Reichsminister für Propaganda und Volksaufklärung Dr. Goebbels," Die neue Stadt, VII (1933), 27–28. Die neue Stadt was the successor magazine to Das neue Frankfurt.

44. Robert Scholz, "Krisis der Kunstanschauung," June 20, 1933.

45. "Führertagung der KDAI," VB, June 29, 1933.

46. Otto-Andreas Schreiber, "Bekenntnis der Jugend zur deutschen Kunst," Deutsche Allgemeine Zeitung, July 12, 1933. Shortly after the University exhibition was announced, Alois Schardt, the new director of the Berlin National Gallery, gave a speech in defense of the leading expressionist artists, describing their works as true "German" art; and the title of the speech, "What is German art?", became one of the slogans of the controversy thereafter. See n. 39 above and Scholz, "Ist das die deutsche Kunst?" VB, July 13, 1933, in answer to Schardt. On Schardt, Schreiber, and the official response to their views, see also "Brief aus Deutschland," Das Werk, XX (1933), July, xxxvii–xxxviii; and "Nationale Kunstpolitik im Dritten Reich," October, xxxvii–xxxviii. According to "Deutsche Jugend . . ." (n. 39, above), Schreiber also sent his letter to Goebbels and Rust. Hildegard Brenner, Die Kunstpolitik des Nationalsozialismus (Hamburg, 1963), discusses the later activities of Schardt, Schreiber, and Weidemann.

47. Rosenberg, "Revolution in der bildenden Kunst," VB, July 7, 1933.

48. Rosenberg, "Revolutionäre an sich!", VB, July 14, 1933.

49. Commenting later on Goebbels' success in winning Hitler's favor in cultural affairs, Rosenberg returned to this theme. Goebbels, he wrote, was always a revolutionary and "would have been a Communist . . . if he hadn't loved Germany a little" (E. Posselt, ed. and trans., Memoirs of Alfred Rosenberg [Chicago, 1949], 165 ff.).

50. Schmitthenner's speech is quoted in full in Sigurd Rabe, "Tradition und neue Kunst," VB, July 16/17, 1933. See also Schmitthenner, "Tradition und neues Bauen," Deutsche Kultur-Wacht, II (1933), H. 17 (July), 11–12, which ends with a plea to the Führer to cleanse Germany of the "spirit of 1918." The parable of the "unknown stonemason" was reprinted in Schmitthenner, Die Baukunst im neuen Reich (Munich, 1934), 17–18.

51. Rabe, "Tradition und neue Kunst."

52. "Hitler's Kulturrede...," *VB*, Sept. 3/4, 1933.

53. Robert Scholz, author of the refutation of Werner, in "Aufbruch der Kunst," *VB*, Sept. 7, 1933. The same interpretation appears in "Was ist deutsche Kunst?" *VB*, Jan. 5, 1934.

54. See, for example, "Die bildende Kunst im Dritten Reich," *National Zeitung* (Basle), March 28, 1934.

55. Speech at the cornerstone ceremony of the "House of German Art," Munich, Oct. 15, 1933: "Das junge Deutschland baut seiner Kunst ein eigen Haus," *VB*, Oct. 16, 1933.

56. For example, "Neue Kunstbücher," *Deutsche Allgemeine Zeitung*, Sept. 29, 1933, on the influence of the radical architects on Finnish architecture; "Stylo Tedesco," Jan. 10, 1934, on the influence of Gropius and Mies on recent Italian architecture; I. Johannes, "Im gläsernen Irrgarten," May 3, 1934, on the beauty of industrial materials. See also Werner's last attempt to defend the radical architects: "Wir brauchen jeden Mann! Kunst als Auslandspropaganda," *Deutsche Rundschau*, Oct. 1933, 41–43, reprinted in "Deutsche Rundschau," *Vossische Zeitung*, Oct. 14, 1933.

57. Gropius to Hönig, President of the Reichskammer der bildende Künste, March 27, 1934. See also Gropius to Lörcher, Chairman of the BDA within the Reichskammer der bildende Künste, Feb. 20, 1934. Both in File "Eigner Kampf mit Nazis," Gropius Archive.

58. Wagner to Lörcher, June 8, 1934, same file, Gropius Archive.

59. Hugo Häring, "Für Widererweckung einer deutschen Baukultur," manuscript, Jan. 1934, sent on Gropius' advice to Hönig, Lörcher, Wendland, and Hans Weidemann, who was at this point Vice President of the Reichskammer der bildende Künste, same file, Gropius Archive.

60. See, for example, Lörcher to Gropius, Feb. 28, 1934, same file, Gropius Archive.

61. "Wider den Kulturbolschewismus," *VB*, Dec. 16, 1933.

62. "Staatskommisar Hinkel über die Arbeit des KfDK," *VB*, Dec. 17/18, 1933. By February of 1934, the Deutsche Arbeitsfront had been made a corporate member of the Reichskulturkammer, and Goebbels and Ley had agreed that members of the latter need not be members of the former. This meant that the KDK lost its ideological control over "cultural producers" who had to join the Kulturkammer and thus did not participate either in the Labor Front or in its suborganization, Kraft durch Freude. See "Der deutschen Kunst. Dr. Goebbels über den Ausbau der Kulturberufe," *VB*, Feb. 9, 1934.

63. "Die neue Lebensgefühl in der Kunst. Alfred Rosenberg vor der Westdeutschen Künstlerschaft," *VB*, May 8, 1934; "Auf dem Wege zur echten Volkskultur," Sept. 27, 1934; n. 66, above. See also "Kunst aus Blut und Boden. Professor Schultze-Naumburg in Nürnberg," *VB*, June 3, 1934; and A. von Senger, "Der Baubolschewisums und seine Verkoppelungen mit Wirtschaft und Politik," *Nationalsozialistische Monatshefte*, IV (1934), 497–507.

64. The NSK was formed on June 14, 1934, as a result of the union of the KDK with the NS Bund Deutsche Bühne ("Die NS-Kulturgemeinde gegründet," *VB*, June 15, 1934). Its new head was Walter Stang, a dramatic critic previously active in the KDK. Most references in the *Völkischer Beobachter* to the activities of the NSK from 1934 to 1935 have to do with the theater productions it arranged for the members of Kraft durch Freude. At the same time as the transformation of the KDK into the NSK, the KDAI lost its architectural membership and was itself transformed ino the NS Bund Deutscher Technik under the leadership of Fritz Todt, the supervisor of Autobahn construction (*Deutsche Technik*, II, 1934, 585).

65. See, for example, Konrad Nonn, letters in the Peter Behrens file, membership files of the Berlin division of the RDBK, U.S. Documents Center, Berlin; and Winfried Wendland, letter to Eugen Hönig of Jan. 29, 1936, entitled "Kritische Anmerkungen zur Reichskammer der bildenden Künste," Wendland file.

66. Helmut Heiber, *Joseph Goebbels* (Berlin, 1962), 213, says that the emergence of Ribbentrop in foreign affairs infuriated Rosenberg and turned his attention back to cultural affairs.

67. "Dr. Goebbels verkündet die erste Verleihung des Nationalpreises für Kunst und Wissenschaft," *VB*, Sept. 8, 1937.

68. "Neuregelung des Architektenberufes," *VB*, Oct. 12, 1934; and *Deutsche Technik*, II (1934), 585. There is some evidence that the exclusion of Jews insisted upon by the BDA in 1933 did not begin to operate at first and that Goebbels' policy in this matter continued to be rather flexible. In his speech to German theater directors in May of 1933 (*VB*, May 10, 1933), Goebbels had said that no legal discrimination against Jews was necessary in cultural affairs. At the beginning of 1934 (*VB*, Feb. 9, 1934), he noted that the RKK did not exclude Jews from its membership but that it probably should. By 1935 the membership applications in the Berlin division of the RDBK had begun to include questions about the applicant's ancestry, and on this basis many Jews were excluded (see n. 73 below). But investigation of the same files suggests that some members were allowed to remain in the organization despite mixed parentage.

69. "Die Heimstatt der Kunst," *VB*, June 5, 1934 (description of the national convention of the RDBK in Munich); and "Im Glauben an die deutsche Kunst. Reichskulturamtsleiter Moraller über die Arbeit der Reichskulturkammer," *VB*, Sept. 5, 1935. Hönig was succeeded by Adolf Ziegler in 1936 (Hinkel, *Handbuch*, 71).

70. *Ibid.*

71. This was the "Verordnung über Baugestaltung" of Nov. 10, 1936, adopted as part of the professional code of the RDBK according to Schreiber, *Das Recht der Reichskulturkammer*, vol. I, "Reichskammer der bildende Künste," section IV, part 20 (37–50).

72. For this reason the German courts today deny that the law was ever intended as a means toward erecting a "dictatorship of taste." For a thorough study of the operation of the law and the court cases in which it has been invoked, see M. Büge, *Der Rechtsschutz gegen Verunstaltung* (Düsseldorf, 1952).

73. It has been possible to consult only the membership files of the Berlin division of the RDBK, which are preserved at the U.S. Documents Center in Berlin. These contain a list of some 300 architects excluded from membership in the RDBK on racial grounds ("Liste der seit 1933 aus den Reichskammer der bildende Künste ausgeschlossenen Juden, jüdischen Mischlingen und mit Juden verheiratet, an den Reichsminister für Volksaufklärung und Propaganda," June 8, 1938) but provide no evidence of exclusion on any other basis. Mies van der Rohe was a member until he emigrated, despite his work and his affiliation with the Bauhaus. So was Paul Bonatz, even though he had belonged to the SPD for a short time. Some files contain political denunciations of the members which they concern, but the denunciations seem to have had no effect upon continuation of membership. Among twenty architects whom I interviewed in Berlin, Munich, Frankfurt, Hamburg, Tübingen, and Braunschweig, none had ever heard of anyone being excluded from the RDBK on other than racial grounds. (See also n. 68 above.) Thus the legal requirement that every architect belong to the RDBK in order to practice his profession unquestionably provided a basis for the control of architectural style, but Lehmann-Haupt and Wernert are almost certainly wrong in believing that it was ever used in this way. I suspect that a thorough investigation of the membership files of the other "chambers" of the RKK would suggest the same conclusion.

74. Verbal information from Ernst May and Max Taut. Taut entered the country illegally in 1934 on his way to Japan and Istanbul, where he died in 1938.

75. Letter from Ursula Elsaesser, Stuttgart, Jan. 14, 1960.

76. Letter from Otto Haesler, Potsdam, Jan. 15, 1960.

77. Letters from Johannes Göderitz, Braunschweig, Jan. 7, 1960; Richard Döcker, Stuttgart, Jan. 4, 1960; and Wassili Luckhardt, Jan. 9, 1960.

78. For example, Hans Mehrtens, who taught at the Technische Hochschule in Aachen, and Otto Ernst Schweitzer, who taught at Karlsruhe.

79. Including Werner Hebebrand, formerly a member of May's staff in Frankfurt and now director of municipal construction in Hamburg, and Gustav Hassenpflug, now Professor at the Munich Technische Hochschule.

Chapter VIII / Nazi Architecture

1. "Rede auf der Kulturtagung," *Reden des Führers am Parteitag der Ehre 1936* (Munich, 1936), 33, 31.

2. *Ibid.*, 31, 34.

3. *Ibid.*, 33, and Richard Mönnig, ed. and trans., *Adolf Hitler from Speeches 1933–1938* (Berlin: Terramare Office, 1938), 81. Hitler of course liked to think of himself as both the chief artist and the chief politician of the Nazi state: hence the many references to him in Nazi literature as a "political artist" or as "the master builder of the Third Reich." See, for example, Otto Dietrich, "Adolf Hitler als künstlerischer Mensch," *Nationalsozialistische Monatshefte*, III (1933), 473; Hermann Giesler's dedication of one of his buildings to "Dem genialen Baumeister des dritten Reiches Adolf Hitler," *Die Kunst im deutschen Reich: Die Baukunst*, III (1939), 202; and Schmitt-henner's parable of the "unknown stonemason," Chapter VII, n. 50 above. Goebbels exploited Hitler's liking for this form of address in many speeches; see especially "Hier gilt's der Kunst: Im Geiste des Baumeisters des Dritten Reiches," *VB*, June 5, 1934; and "Die grosse Kundgebung der deutschen Künstler am Samstag," *VB*, July 19, 1937, when Goebbels described Hitler as "that great masterbuilder . . . whose state is a structure of truly classical proportions."

4. "Rede auf der Kulturtagung," *Reden des Führers am Parteitag der Arbeit 1937* (Munich, 1937), 47.

5. Speech at opening of Exhibition of Architecture, Munich, Haus der Kunst, Jan. 22, 1938, N. H. Baynes, ed. and trans., *The Speeches of Adolf Hitler*, I, 601.

6. "Rede auf der Kulturtagung," *Reden des Führers am Parteitag der Arbeit 1937*, 48.

7. Mönnig, 83.

8. "Rede auf der Kulturtagung," *Reden des Führers am Parteitag der Arbeit 1937*, 39–40.

9. Speech at the opening of the Haus der Kunst on July 18, 1937, Baynes, I, 590. See also the speech at the first exhibition of architecture and applied arts on Jan. 22, 1938: "This exhibition stands at the beginning of a new era" (Max Domarus, ed., *Hitler: Reden und Proklamationen 1932–1945* [Würzburg, 1962], I, 778); and the references to the "beginning of a new era" in "Die Führerrede auf der Kulturtagung der NSDAP," *VB*, Sept. 6, 1934.

10. Speech at the second exhibit of architecture and applied arts on Dec. 10, 1938, published in full in "Der Führer über die Baukunst des Dritten Reichs: Wir Bauen für die Zukunft," *VB*, Dec. 12, 1938.

11. "Address on Culture" at the 1935 Party Congress, quoted in Mönnig, 87–88; and Adolf Hitler, *Liberty, Art, Nationhood,* (Berlin, 1935), 51.

12. "Deutsche Kunst als stolzeste Verteidigung des deutschen Volkes," *VB*, Sept. 3/4, 1933; and *Liberty, Art, Nationhood*, 51.

13. "Deutsche Kunst als stolzeste Verteidigung. . . ."

14. *Ibid.*

15. *Ibid.*, and *Liberty, Art, Nationhood*, 47–50.

16. "Hitler's Kulturrede: Deutsch sein heisst klar sein," *VB*, Sept. 6, 1934;

"Adolf Hitler weiht das Haus der deutschen Kunst," *VB,* July 19, 1937; and Domarus, I, 706.

17. Domarus, I, 569: speech of Jan. 25, 1936, to the NSD-Studentenbund in the Zirkus Krone, Munich.

18. *Liberty, Art, Nationhood,* 51.

19. "Rede des Führers zur Eröffnung der 'Zweiten deutschen Architektur- und Kunsthandwerk-Ausstellung,' " *Die Kunst im dritten Reich: Die Baukunst,* III (1939), 9. See also n. 10, above.

20. These paper projects are discussed in detail in Dr. Armand Dehlinger's "Architektur der Superlative," a manuscript written under the auspices of the Institut für Zeitgeschichte in Munich. I wish to thank the Institut for permission to examine the book.

21. Speech at the cornerstone ceremony of the new military division of the Berlin Technische Hochschule, Nov. 27, 1938, during which Hitler announced his plans for the "reconstruction" (Neugestaltung) of Berlin (Domarus, I, 765). See also Hitler's enthusiastic references to the prospect of bringing "infinite numbers of people" into Berlin, speech at the cornerstone cermony of the "House of German Tourism," June 14, 1938 (Domarus, I, 873–874).

22. As Reichssiedlungskommissar: see below.

23. Otto Weichen, "Grundsätzliches über die Gestaltung des Bauernhofes," *Architektur-Wettbewerbe: Bauernhöfe* (Stuttgart, n.d.), 5. The article lays down rules for entrants in a design competition for farm buildings sponsored by Darré's Ministry of Food and Agriculture.

24. "Baustil für die Jugend," *Frankfurter Zeitung,* March 6, 1936.

25. Wilhelm Lotz, *Schönheit der Arbeit in Deutschland* (Berlin, 1940), 49. "Amt Schönheit der Arbeit" was a subsidiary of the Labor Front which designed model "Kameradschaftshäuser" for the Labor Front's members and carried out a program, chiefly propagandistic in intent, of cleaning up and redecorating factory workshops. See also *Schönheit der Arbeit—Sozialismus der Tat* (Berlin, 1936); Herbert Steinwarz, *Wesen, Aufgaben, Ziele des Amtes Schönheit der Arbeit* (Berlin, 1937); and Anatol von Hübbenet, *Das Taschenbuch Schönheit der Arbeit* (Berlin, 1938). Despite the claim, reiterated in each of these publications, that the organization wished to create a "functional" workers' architecture, the Kameradschaftshäuser were often carried out in "folk" styles (see below).

26. The *VB* claimed that Hitler designed the building himself ("Adolf Hitlers Monumentalbaupläne für München," April 22/23, 1933), and in his speech at the opening of the museum, Hitler said he had begun to plan the building long before 1933 (July 13, 1937: "Adolf Hitler weiht das Haus der deutschen Kunst," *VB,* July 19, 1937).

27. After Troost's death, his Munich buildings were completed according to his plans by his widow, Gerdy Troost, and his former assistant, Leonhard Gall.

28. Illustrated in *Bauten in der Stadt der Reichsparteitage Nürnberg* (Nürnberg, 1942). Speer's other work for Hitler included the new Reichs Chancellery buildings in Berlin, the German pavilion at the Paris World's Fair of 1937, Hitler's retreat at Berchtesgaden, and many of the plans for the "reconstruction" of Berlin.

29. See, for example, the army headquarters in Kassel and the State Theater in Dessau (Gerdy Troost, *Das Bauen im neuen Reich* [Bayreuth, 1943], I, 75, 79).

30. "Nach Mitteilung der Gauleiter sind Gemeinschaftshäuser bereits erbaut in . . . ," manuscript report of Nov. 20, 1940, in "Files of Reichsorganisationsleiter der NSDAP," U.S. Documents Center, Berlin, Box 342, Folder 965.

31. The training program at the Ordensburgen, offered to selected graduates of the Hitler Youth, included sports, eugenics, and German history. See "Die drei Ordensburgen der NSDAP," *Nationalsozialistische Monatshefte,* VI (1936), 566–567.

32. Both organizations constructed a number of model structures which they ordered their local chapters to follow "in general outline," and the Hitler Jugend also held a general competition for youth hostels and youth homes in which participants were required to follow regional traditions. See Erhard Brünninghaus, *Heime der Hitler-Jugend* (Stuttgart, 1940); and Herbert Steinwarz, *Das Kameradschaftshaus im Betrieb* (Berlin, 1939).

33. The firm of Herbert Rimpl, which employed men who had formerly worked for May.

34. Werner Rittich, *Architektur und Bauplastik der Gegenwart* (Berlin, 1938), 45. Rittich was the editor, together with Speer, of the party-sponsored periodical *Die Kunst im deutschen Reich*.

35. The Gesetz über Beaufsichtigung und Anerkennung gemeinnütziger Wohnungsunternehmungen of March 26, 1934. The older state and municipal Wohnungsfürsorgegesellschaften and the municipal planning staffs remained after the reorganizations of 1933, but after 1934 they acted primarily as local instruments of national policy. For a more detailed discussion of the workings of the Nazi housing policy, see Rolf Spörhase, *Wohnungsunternehmen im Wandel der Zeit* (Hamburg, 1947), 124–127; and *Geschichte der gemeinnützigen Wohnungswirtschaft in Berlin* (Berlin, 1957), 125–131.

36. Feder was appointed to this position by Hitler on March 20, 1934, and retained it for a little more than a year. During his term of office he directed the housing policy of the Reichsheimstättenamt, a new form of the old organization of the same name which had supervised the granting of federal loans for rural housing during the Weimar period (Gottfried Feder, "Das deutsche Siedlungswerk," *Siedlung und Wirtschaft*, XVI [1934], 184). After 1935 the Heimstättenamt had control of the entire housing program of the regime with the exception of new Siedlungen for farmers, which were planned and financed by Darré's Ministry (*Die deutsche Heimstätten-Siedlung*, Berlin: DAF, 1935). On the basis of the "Gesetz zur Neubildung des deutschen Bauerntums" of July 14, 1933, Darré projected a vast program of new agricultural settlements, but those actually constructed were too few in number to be considered here. See Fritz Wenzel, *Der Sieg von Blut und Boden* (Berlin, 1934); Wilhelm Grebe, *Gegenwarts- und Zukunftsaufgaben im ländlichen Bauwesen* (Berlin: Reichsnährstand, c. 1936); and Kurt Kremmer, "Das ländliche Bauwesen im Dienst der Landfluchtbekämpfung und der Neubildung des deutschen Bauerntums," *Nationalsozialistische Monatshefte*, IX (1939), 133.

37. Feder, "Das deutsche Siedlungswerk," 183–185.

38. *Ibid.*, 186.

39. These are the titles of the two sections of *Die deutsche Heimstätten-Siedlung* (Berlin: DAF, 1935).

40. "Das nationalsozialistische Siedlungswerk," *Wege zur neuen Sozialpolitik* (Berlin: DAF, 1936), 215. The same ideas appeared in all the publications of the Heimstättenamt. See, for example, *Ein Beispiel aus der Siedlungsplanung* (Berlin: DAF, 1934); *Städtebild und Landschaft* (Berlin: DAF, 1939); and *Die Siedlung* (Berlin: DAF, 1938).

41. Spörhase, *Wohnungsunternehmen*, 122.

42. *Die Neuordnung der Kleinsiedlung* (Berlin, 1938).

43. "Vorstädtische Kleinsiedlungen," *Statistisches Jahrbuch deutscher Städte* (Leipzig), XXXIV–XXXIX (1933–1938).

44. *Die deutsche Heimstätten-Siedlung*, 22–23.

45. "Deutsche Wohnkultur der Zukunft. Presse besichtigt Muster-Siedlung Ramersdorf," *VB*, March 10, 1934; "Die Siedlungsausstellung München 1934," June 8, 1934; and Guido Harbers, "Sinn und Aufbau der Ausstellung," June 9, 1934 (special issue devoted to the exhibition).

46. Wilhelm Ludovici, "Nationalsozialismus und Siedlung," *VB*, June 9, 1934.

47. Düsseldorf, 1937, containing two large permanent developments, and Frankfurt, 1938. See "Siedlung Schlageterstadt," *Baukunst und Städtebau*,

1937, 210–212, 233–240, 353–355; "Wilhelm-Gustloff-Siedlung," 213–214; and "Dr. Ley eröffnete die Deutsche Bau- und Siedlungsausstellung Frankfurt am Main," *VB*, Sept. 5, 1938.

48. The most important architectural publications of the party and government were: *Bauen im nationalsozialistischen Deutschlands* (Munich: NSDAP, 1940); Albert Speer, *Neue deutsche Baukunst* (Prague, 1943); Gerdy Troost, *Das Bauen im neuen Reich* (Bayreuth, 1943), 2 vols.; Werner Rittich, *Architektur und Bauplastik der Gegenwart* (Berlin, 1938); and Speer and Rittich, eds., *Die Kunst im deutschen Reich* (Munich, 1937 ff.), the official art and architectural periodical, published in two editions, of which "Ausgabe B" dealt with architecture and had the title *Die Kunst im deutschen Reich – Die Baukunst*. In addition to these publications, a long series of more specialized periodicals were published by the various offices and agencies involved in the building program; nearly every type of building project had several books devoted to it; and most of the Gaue issued books or pamphlets on their building programs.

49. "Ein Werk des Führers. Die Münchener Bauschöpfungen im Werden," *VB*, Oct. 29, 1934. See also "Tempel der neuen deutschen Kunst," *VB*, July 19, 1933, and n. 26, above.

50. Described in a series of articles under the heading "München wieder Hauptstadt der deutschen Kunst," *VB* (Süddeutsche Ausgabe), Oct. 16, 1933. See also *Grundsteinlegung des Hauses der deutschen Kunst* (Munich, n.d.), a pamphlet which contains illustrations of models of the building and reprints the speeches given at the ceremony.

51. " 'Tag der deutschen Kunst' in München," *Das Werk*, XX (Nov. 1933), xxxviii. The high point of the day was a parade designed to illustrate "2000 years of German art," which included a float carrying a plaster reproduction of the Bamberg Rider, thus reflecting Schultze-Naumburg's definition of "German" art.

52. See, for example, the eulogies to Troost and the description of his elaborate funeral in the *VB*, Jan. 23–27, 1934; "Vom Haus der deutschen Kunst," April 9, 1934; "Haus der deutschen Kunst: Ein Meisterwerk der Gründungstechnik," Sept. 30, 1934; "Das Haus der Deutschen Kunst ein Werk der ganzen Nation!" June 26, 1935; and "Das Haus der deutschen Kunst. Der jetzige Baustand und die künftige Ausgestaltung," June 28, 1935.

53. Described in a series of articles in the *VB*, July 19 and July 20, 1937. See especially "Adolf Hitler weiht das Haus der deutschen Kunst," July 19. The opening of the museum was also the occasion for the opening of the notorious exhibition of "decadent art" organized by the RDBK. Set up in a building nearby the House of German Art, this latter exhibition contained many of the works of Germany's most modern artists, badly hung and often accompanied by derisive captions. It is discussed in detail in P. O. Rave, *Entartete Kunst* (Hamburg, 1949); and Hildegard Brenner, *Die Kunstpolitik des Nationalsozialismus* (Hamburg, 1963). The exhibition contained no reference to the works of the radical architects; in fact when Nonn urged the inclusion of pictures representing the new architecture in the exhibition, Ziegler explicitly refused (see Nonn letters in the Behrens file, membership files of the Berlin division of the RDBK, U.S. Documents Center, Berlin).

54. See, for example, Hitler's speeches of Sept. 11, 1935 (Domarus, I, 527) and Sept. 9, 1937 (Domarus, I, 720).

55. "Der Reichspressechef begrüsst im Auftrag des Führers die Weltpresse," *VB*, Sept. 9, 1936.

56. "Der Führer über die Baukunst des dritten Reiches: Wir Bauen für die Zukunft," *VB*, Dec. 12, 1937. On the first exhibition, held in January 1938, see Baynes, I, 601–602, and Domarus, I, 778–779. On the third exhibition, held in July 1939, see Baynes, I, 606–608.

57. See n. 48, above.

58. See especially Troost, *Das Bauen im neuen Reich,* and Rittich, *Architek tur und Bauplastik der Gegenwart.*

59. See, for example, "Ein Kraftpostneubau in Würzburg," *VB,* April 3, 1935; and "Penzburg's grosser Tag. Ein Weihung des H. J. Heime, der Hans-Dauser-Siedlung und des Sparkassengebäudes," Sept. 1, 1936.

60. And when Nonn's office in the Prussian Finance Ministry published the collection of illustrations entitled *Bauten der Bewegung* (Berlin: Zentralblatt der Bauverwaltung, 1938), Speer attempted to prevent its distribution because it "places too much emphasis on the work of Schultze-Naumburg" (Speer, letter to Gerdy Troost of Dec. 30, 1938, Troost papers, file no. 674, Library of Congress, Manuscript Division).

61. Bruno Zevi, *Towards an Organic Architecture* (London, 1950).

Index

Page references to illustrations are italicized.